thoreau's animals

I would at least know what these things
unavoidably are—make a chart of our life,
know how its shores trend, that butterflies
reappear and when—know why just this
circle of creatures completes the world.

thoreau's animals

HENRY DAVID THOREAU

Edited by Geoff Wisner

Illustrated by Debby Cotter Kaspari

Yale
UNIVERSITY PRESS

New Haven and London

Yale University Press books may be purchased in quantity for educational, business, or promotional use. For information, please e-mail sales.press@yale.edu (U.S. office) or sales@yaleup.co.uk (U.K. office).

Designed by Sonia L. Shannon.
Set in Adobe Garamond type by
Tseng Information Systems, Inc.
Printed in the United States of America.

Library of Congress Control Number: 2016941945
ISBN 978-0-300-22376-7 (hardcover : alk. paper)

A catalogue record for this book is available from the British Library.

This paper meets the requirements of ANSI/NISO z39.48-1992 (Permanence of Paper).

10 9 8 7 6 5 4 3 2 1

ONCE AGAIN, IN MEMORY OF

Professor Joel Porte

CONTENTS

Preface   ix

Acknowledgments   xi

Introduction   xiii

A Note on the Text   xxi

thoreau's animals   1

Notes   235

Map of Concord and Key to Place-Names   238

Bibliography   241

Index   245

PREFACE

THE TWO MILLION WORDS of Thoreau's Journal contain a treasury of thoughts and stories about animals. *Thoreau's Animals* collects many of the best of these, including Thoreau's capture of a screech owl and a flying squirrel in his handkerchief (not at the same time), his discovery of a new species of fish in the waters of Walden Pond, and the adventurous day he spent tracking and capturing his family's runaway pig. The reader feels the mystery of the elusive "night warbler" and is cheered by the bright spring promise of the bluebird, which "carries the sky on its back."

Like its companion volume, *Thoreau's Wildflowers,* and for similar reasons, *Thoreau's Animals* is arranged not by different kinds of animal or in simple chronological order but by the days of the year. Like the blooming of cowslips in the spring or asters in the fall, the arrival and departure of animals followed the seasons and gave them meaning. Even the home of the humble muskrat or musquash was an important element in the turning year. "So surely as the sun appears to be in Libra or Scorpio," Thoreau wrote in 1859, "I see the conical winter lodges of the musquash rising above the withered pontederia and flags."

To showcase the significance of animals in the world of Concord—"the most estimable place in all the world," as Thoreau believed—I have presented only Thoreau's thoughts and observations about the creatures of Concord and neighboring communities, omitting animals seen in zoos and most of those killed by hunters and trappers. His opinions on the edibility of clams and the sportsmanship of moose hunters can be found in *Cape Cod* and *The Maine Woods*.

Along with some of the sketches with which Thoreau illustrated his Journal, this book is enriched by the drawings of Debby Cotter Kaspari, many of them made in the field on visits to Massachusetts from her home in Oklahoma. They combine deep familiarity with the ways of animals and a spontaneous response to the moment that echoes Thoreau's own descriptions in words.

I hope that *Thoreau's Animals* will prove interesting and enjoyable to hikers, campers, bird-watchers, naturalists, and anyone who enjoys watching a woodchuck sun itself on a log. It also offers rewards for those seeking insight into the life and personality of one of America's greatest writers.

ACKNOWLEDGMENTS

FOR THEIR HELP AND SUPPORT, I would like to thank Jeff Cramer, Jack Shoemaker, and my old friends Bill Schwartz and Chris Carduff. I was pleased to have another opportunity to work with Jean Thomson Black and Samantha Ostrowski at Yale University Press, and to have the benefit of Dan Heaton's meticulous editing.

For identifications of birds, I have relied on *Thoreau on Birds*, edited by Francis H. Allen, first published in 1910, and reissued by Beacon Press in 1993. For identification of insects, I am indebted to David Spooner, author of *Thoreau's Vision of Insects*. Concord author and naturalist Peter Alden reviewed all common and scientific names used for animals in this book, and provided additional observations that appear in the notes.

Special thanks to Debby Cotter Kaspari, whose drawings capture the field-note quality of Thoreau's own observations. Although Debby is based in Oklahoma, many of these images were drawn in the field on past visits to New England. Others were created especially for this book.

Once again, many thanks to my wife, Jenn, for her love and patience.

INTRODUCTION

THOREAU'S JOURNAL is famous for its precise and beautiful descriptions of the natural world and for its insights into the problems of human life. It is also a treasury of pungent and memorable stories. In his biography of Thoreau, Robert D. Richardson noted that around 1852 Thoreau became more interested in stories of country life. "An entire volume of such stories could easily be extracted from Thoreau's journals, and many of the best would be about animals, or encounters between people and animals."

According to Richardson, many of Thoreau's neighbors noticed his intimacy with the creatures of Concord, and believed he had some version of the legendary ring of King Solomon, which gives the wearer the ability to talk with animals. In one of the most remarkable passages in his Journal, Thoreau corners a woodchuck in a field, teases and turns it over with a stick, and gazes at it until both he and the woodchuck feel "mesmeric influences." He speaks "forest lingo" to it, feeds it checkerberry leaves, and even touches it briefly with his hand before standing up and going on his way.

When we think of Thoreau at Walden Pond, we are likely to think of his life among animals: playing his flute to the perch at night, chasing a loon across the surface of the pond, observing a battle between red ants and black ants, or trying to protect his bean field from hungry woodchucks. Each of these stories related in the pages of *Walden* had its origin in the Journal, and many of the most moving, surprising, or funny stories of Thoreau's life with animals were recorded nowhere else.

But Thoreau was more than just an amateur naturalist and storyteller. His Journal shows familiarity with the works of zoological authorities: the entomologists William Kirby (1759–1850) and William Spence (1783–1860), the ornithologists Alexander Wilson (1766–1813), Thomas Nuttall (1786–1859), and Thomas Mayo Brewer (1814–1880), the zoologist James Ellsworth DeKay (1792–1851), and the ichthyologist and herpetologist David Humphreys Storer (1804–1891). Dr. Storer knew of Thoreau as well, and in January 1847 his son Horatio, a student at Harvard, wrote to ask Thoreau for help in adding to Horatio's collection of birds' eggs.

Thoreau gave several excuses for his unwillingness to comply, saying he was "not so attentive an observer of birds as I was once" and that Horatio might find more nests in the open terrain of Cambridge than Thoreau would in the forests of Concord. "Moreover," he noted, "I confess to a little squeamishness on the score of robbing their nests, though I could easily go to the length of abstracting an egg or two gently, now and then, and if the advancement of science obviously demanded it might be carried even to the extreme of deliberate murder."

By May of that year, however, Thoreau had overcome his compunction about collecting and supplied a surprising number of specimens to Professor Louis Agassiz of Harvard, then considered the world's leading zoologist, if not its greatest scientist. A letter from James Elliot Cabot, Agassiz's assistant, thanked Thoreau for specimens of pout, bream, painted turtles, spotted turtles, and snapping turtles. Later in the month Agassiz expressed appreciation for the gift of a live fox, and noted that one or two fish sent by Thoreau belonged to new species.

With time, Thoreau's enthusiasm for collecting diminished, and in 1854 he appeared to reach a turning point. "I have just been through the process of killing the cistudo [Blanding's turtle] for the sake of science," he wrote in his Journal, "but I cannot excuse myself for this murder, and see that such actions are inconsistent with the poetic perception, however they may serve science, and will affect the quality of my observations." He went on, "I have a murderer's experience in a degree."

Thoreau's attitude to Agassiz soured as well, and after a while nearly every reference to the great man was a notation of an apparent blunder. "Agassiz tells his class that the intestinal worms in the mouse are not developed except in the stomach of the cat." "Agassiz says he has discovered that the haddock, a *deep-sea* fish, is viviparous." After a visit to his neighbor Ralph Waldo Emerson, Thoreau writes, "R.W.E. says that Agassiz tells him he has had turtles six or seven years which grew so little compared with others of the same size killed at first, that he thinks they may live four or five hundred years."

As his own ideas developed, Thoreau had less and less use for science as it was typically practiced. In 1853 he received a questionnaire from the Association for the Advancement of Science, an organization Agassiz had helped found five years before. Thoreau responded in his Journal: "I felt that it would be to make myself the laughing-stock of the scientific community to describe to them that branch of science which specially interests me, inasmuch as they do not believe in a science which deals with the higher law. So I was obliged to speak to their condition and describe to them that poor part of me which alone they can understand. The fact is I am a mystic, a transcendentalist, and a natural philosopher to boot."

For Thoreau, these three titles—mystic, transcendentalist, and natural philosopher—overlapped and reinforced one another. As a mystic, Thoreau was open to the deeper spiritual meaning of his life and the lives of others. As a transcendentalist, he sought a direct relationship to the spirit of the universe, holding himself apart from the chilly Unitarians of Massachusetts and the fiery evangelicals of his day. And as a natural philosopher, he looked for clues to the nature of the universe in the fields and forests and wetlands of Concord.

Each harsh New England winter was a challenge to faith, and to the very survival of man and animal. The turn of the seasons was of deep concern to Thoreau, as it has been to pagan and Christian. Through the winter he looked for clues that spring was on its way, or hidden somewhere deep beneath the snow. In a gesture more transcendental than Christian, he tried from time to time to bring frozen creatures back to life: snow fleas, pickerel, or frogs. Sometimes he was even successful, as with the woolly bear caterpillar he carried home in his hat one January. When spring arrived at last, Thoreau was careful to note when each bird appeared for the first time, and when each flower first bloomed—data used in the twenty-first century by Professor Richard B. Primack and others to study the effects of climate change.

For Thoreau, the dividing line between wild and domestic creatures was not hard and fast. Watching one of the usually well-behaved cattle of Concord break out of its pasture, wade through the watery meadows, then swim several hundred feet across the Concord River, he wrote, "I love to see the domestic animals reassert their native rights—any evidence that they have not lost their original wild habits and vigor." Thoreau regarded the dog as a somewhat more civilized fox, and in the long and funny journal entry of August 8, 1856, he described how much havoc could be caused by one runaway pig.

Similarly, Thoreau saw much that was human in the behavior and emotions of animals, an insight that sometimes expressed itself in what may seem an old-fashioned sort of anthropomorphism. "I had always instinctively regarded the horse as a free people somewhere—living wild," he wrote. Seeing a muskrat emerge from a hole in the ice, he thought, "He is a man wilder than Ray or Melvin," two local hunters and trappers. A newly hatched snapping turtle "impresses me as the rudiment of a man worthy to inhabit the earth." Thoreau records that, after a cow is killed by lightning, the other cattle gather around and bellow. More whimsically, he has a red squirrel call out impudently, "Look here! just get a snug-fitting fur coat and a pair of fur gloves like mine and you may laugh at a northeast storm."

Unlike many who make anthropomorphic comparisons, Thoreau made zoomorphic comparisons as well, seeing animal qualities in human beings. "I see men like frogs," he observed, "their peeping I partially understand." Observing the earthiness of old people, he wrote, "They remind me of earthworms and mole crickets."

He saw these qualities in himself as well. He expressed the wish to "lurk in crystalline thought like the trout under verdurous banks—where stray mankind should only see my bubbles come to the surface." Watching two ospreys flying through a turbulent sky, he thought, "Where is my mate—beating against the storm with me?" Feeling hard-pressed on a cold, dark November afternoon, he wrote, "You are as dry as a farrow cow." Deer had long been hunted out of Concord, but they survived in his imagination. Skating along the Concord River, he felt, "A man feels like a new creature, a deer perhaps, moving at this rate."

This close identification with animals underlined his sensitivity to the sometimes casual cruelty to animals he saw around him. Spotting a star-nosed mole by the railroad, he notes, "Some inhuman fellow has cut off his tail." His description of a hunter at work is as stark as a crime-scene photo by Weegee. "I see a brute with a gun in his hand," he writes, "standing motionless over a musquash house which he has destroyed. I find that he has visited every one in the neighborhood of Fair Haven Pond above and below—and broken them all down laying open the interior to the water—and then stood watchful close by for the poor creature to show its head there for a breath of air. There lies the red carcass of one whose pelt he has taken on the spot, flat on the bloody ice."

Learning about animals was a lifelong process for Thoreau, and along the way he had mysteries to unravel. Though he saw the tracks of the otter, he never glimpsed one. He was fascinated by the "dreaming" song of an unknown frog, only to discover that it came from the humble toad. Several times he asked himself what bird sang *tull-a-lull, tull-a-lull* before he learned that it was the white-throated sparrow. He never identified the nocturnal singer that he called the night warbler.

Thoreau's search for these creatures was a spiritual quest, since each was a unique part of the divine creation. In 1856 he lamented the animals no longer found in Concord—cougar, wolf, bear, moose, deer, beaver, and wild turkey—as if by driving them out mankind had torn up the great book of life itself.

"I take infinite pains to know all the phenomena of the spring, for instance—thinking that I have here the entire poem—and then to my chagrin I hear that it is but an imperfect copy that I possess and have read, that my ancestors have torn out many of the first leaves and grandest passages—and mutilated it in many places.

"I should not like to think that some demigod had come before me and picked out some of the best of the stars. I wish to know an entire heaven and an entire earth."

Most of all, Thoreau turned to the animal world for insights into the nature of life in the wild, and clues to the hidden impulses of his own soul. Certain animals were especially significant. The cricket was the pulse of the earth, heard from deep underground in early spring and persisting until the coldest days of November. The wood thrush was a symbol of wildness at the fringes of civilization, its song rarely heard in the village. The long slow growth of the snapping turtle in its egg, buried beneath the sand all summer, was a lesson in patience and faith in the rhythms of nature. The muskrat that chewed its leg off to escape a trap was an inspiring example of courage, while the woodchuck's fat belly and love of warmth showed that life in the wild could be enjoyable.

Thoreau's sense of connection with his environment was so intense that he sometimes felt the world would not turn without him. "These regular phenomena of the seasons get at last to be (they were *at first* of course) simply and plainly phenomena or phases of my life. The seasons and all their changes are in me. I see not a dead eel or floating snake—or a gull—but it rounds my life, and is like a line or accent in its poem. Almost I believe the Concord would not rise and overflow its banks again were I not here."

Passages like these may sound as if Thoreau's ego has expanded to the point where he thinks of himself as a god—until we see that he attributes similar powers to other creatures. The call of the flicker, which he calls the pigeon woodpecker, "really *quickens* what was dead. It seems to put a life into withered grass and leaves and bare twigs—and henceforth the days shall not be as they have been." Seeing some hens strike out bravely from the barn on a mild day in February, Thoreau writes approvingly, "The hens ... strive to fetch the year about."

In September 1854, Thoreau considers the summerlong incubation of turtle eggs, alluding to the Native American tradition that the world rests on the back of a giant turtle.

I am affected by the thought that the earth nurses these eggs. They are planted in the earth, and the earth takes care of them—she is genial to them and does not kill them. It suggests a certain vitality and intelligence in the earth—which I had not realized. This mother is not merely inanimate and inorganic. Though the immediate mother turtle abandons her offspring, the earth and sun are kind to them. The old turtle on which the earth rests takes care of them while the other waddles off. Earth was not made poisonous and deadly to them. The earth has some virtue in it—when seeds are put into it, they germinate, when turtles' eggs they hatch in due time. Though the mother turtle remained and brooded them—it would still nevertheless be the universal world turtle which through her cared for them as now. Thus the earth is the mother of all creatures.

India, China, and North America all have traditions of a turtle that holds up the world. Thoreau takes this idea even farther. The correspondence he traces between wild and tame, human and animal, seasons and spirituality, culminates in a vision of the world as more than a home for people and animals—as a living creature in itself.

A NOTE ON THE TEXT

THE TEXT OF *Thoreau's Animals* is drawn from the fourteen-volume 1906 edition of *The Journal of Henry D. Thoreau*, edited by Bradford Torrey and Francis H. Allen. Each selection has been checked against the Princeton University Press edition of the Journal or (for selections not included in the Princeton edition) against the unedited transcript of the Journal, made available online by the library of the University of California, Santa Barbara.

Omitted text is indicated by ellipses without brackets. Penciled additions by Thoreau, rendered as footnotes in the 1906 edition, are identified in brackets. Words and phrases in italics were emphasized in the original.

As with *Thoreau's Wildflowers*, comparing the 1906 edition with the verbatim Princeton edition and transcripts has made it possible to delete many commas, often four or five in a single sentence, and a number of hyphens and exclamation points. I have replaced other commas and semicolons with the original dashes, and restored paragraph breaks and parentheses (against which Torrey and Allen seem to have had an irrational prejudice). Sentence fragments that Torrey and Allen linked with other text to form complete sentences (though sometimes ungainly ones) have been restored. The effect is a rapid, modern-seeming style that more closely reflects what Thoreau actually wrote in his Journal.

The strings of adjectives Thoreau sometimes deployed are much more effective without added commas: the "low soft rippling note" of the snow bunting (March 3, 1859), the "graceful limber undulating motion" of a great blue heron in flight (April 19, 1852), or the "green herbaceous graminivirous ideas" of a locust (September 6, 1857).

As noted in *Thoreau's Wildflowers*, Thoreau used the dash in lieu of a comma, semicolon, paragraph, or even a period. More important, he often used it to set off an insight from the observation that prompted it. "I only see the ripple that he makes—in proportion in this brook only one foot wide like that made by a steamer in a canal" (March 15, 1857). "We find that we had virtually forgotten the note of each bird—and when we hear it again it is remembered like a dream, reminding us of a previous state of existence" (March 18, 1858).

Though the 1906 editors created some long paragraphs by combining Thoreau's short ones, Thoreau committed some very long paragraphs himself. In a few cases, I have broken these up for ease of reading: March 10, 1854 (skunk); April 16, 1852 (woodchuck); May 22, 1853 (cat); August 8, 1856 (pig); and September 30, 1852 (honeybees).

Thoreau commonly used labor-saving fractions in the Journal. When these are used in the context of everyday language, as in "about ½ their size" (September 27, 1860), I have followed Torrey and Allen in spelling them out. Where fractions are used in actual measurements, I have restored the original (for instance, "It is $1\frac{1}{20}$ of an inch long in the upper shell") rather than use the Torrey and Allen version ("It is an inch and one twentieth long in the upper shell"). In a few cases where Thoreau did painstakingly write out a fraction, as in "one tenth of an inch in diameter" (August 24, 1852), I have left the passage as he wrote it.

Thoreau wrote the important word "Nature" sometimes with a capital letter and sometimes without. "Nature" sometimes meant simply the natural world, but at other times it meant a spirit or deity. I have refrained from standardizing the capitalization so as not to erase clues that may be useful to readers and scholars.

In one or two cases I have changed dates to conform with those of the Princeton editors. I have accepted many alternate readings of doubtful passages from the Princeton edition and online transcripts, but in other cases I have retained the original, based on common sense and Thoreau's customary practices.

For instance, I find it more likely that Thoreau wrote about "a small fresh egg on the forest floor" than "a small ovish egg on the forest floor" (May 30, 1855), and that he described the eye of a mole as a dull blue-black bead rather than a blue-black head (June 6, 1856). Passages elsewhere in the Journal (as well as common sense) make it much more likely that he wrote, "I wonder that the very cows and the dogs in the street do not manifest a recognition of the bright tints about and above them," rather than "the very crows and the slugs in the street." The online transcripts refer in several places to the singing of the toad, but Thoreau's other references to the *ringing* note of the toad are so frequent and insistent that I have preferred "ringing" throughout.

Unlike many wildflowers, the animals Thoreau observed in and around Concord did not often present difficult problems of identification. As a result, he used fewer Latin names when writing about animals than he did about plants. I have indexed (and corrected or updated when necessary) the Latin names he did use, but have not attempted to supply Latin names for animals where he did not use them and have not updated or corrected Latin names in the text itself. I have included a number of passages about the "wild pigeon," which the villagers of Concord baited with pounded acorns and netted or shot by the dozen. This was the passenger pigeon, once the most common bird in America. Intensive hunting and trapping had caused a decline in population by Thoreau's day, and around 1900 the last wild passenger pigeon was killed.

This book begins in the month of March because, for Thoreau, that was when the year began. The seasons for him were more fluid than a calendar date could indicate, and he was continually searching for clues to the earth's changes as it turned on its axle. The year began for him with the melting of ice, the flowing of sap, and the return of birds from the south. Each day's dawn could recapitulate the dawn of the year. "It is chiefly the spring birds that I hear at this hour," he wrote on July 4, 1852, "and in each dawn the spring is thus revived."

Like the first shoots and blossoms of the birch and the skunk cabbage, animals played their part in ushering life back to a frozen world. As Thoreau wrote in the "Spring" chapter of *Walden,* "I am on the alert for the first signs of spring, to hear the chance note of some arriving bird, or the striped squirrel's chirp, for his stores must be now nearly exhausted, or see the woodchuck venture out of his winter quarters."

thoreau's animals

MARCH 2, 1855

Heard two hawks scream. There was something truly March-like in it—like a prolonged blast or whistling of the wind through a crevice in the sky, which like a cracked blue saucer overlaps the woods. Such are the first rude notes which prelude the summer's quire—learned of the whistling March wind.

MARCH 3, 1859

Going by the solidago oak at Clamshell Hill bank, I heard a faint rippling note and looking up saw about fifteen snow buntings sitting in the top of the oak all with their breasts toward me—sitting so still and quite white seen against the white cloudy sky. They did not look like birds—but the ghosts of birds—and their boldness, allowing me to come quite near, enhanced this impression. They were almost as white as snowballs, and from time to time I heard a low soft rippling note from them. I could see no features—but only the general outline of plump birds in white. It was a very spectral sight, and after I had watched them for several minutes I can hardly say that I was prepared to see them fly away like ordinary buntings when I advanced further. At first they were almost concealed by being almost the same color with the cloudy sky.

MARCH 4, 1854

What is that gray beetle [ribbed pine borer] of which I found many under the bark of a large dead white pine, ⅝ of an inch long, within an elliptical sort of log fort ⅞ of an inch or more in diameter piled around of fibers of the sap wood, perhaps ⅛ or ⅒ of an inch high—with some red bark chankings? Sometimes a curious chrysalis instead like a very narrow and long bandbox with flat and parallel top and bottom, but highest at one end like a coffin. Also some white grubs stretch themselves, and some earwig-shaped creatures under the bark.

What a perfectly New England sound is this voice of the crow! If you stand perfectly still anywhere in the outskirts of the town and listen—stilling the almost incessant hum of your own personal factory—this is perhaps the sound which you will be most sure to hear. Rising above all sounds of human industry and leading your thoughts to some far bay in the woods where the crow is venting his disgust.

This bird sees the white man come and the Indian withdraw—but it withdraws not. Its untamed voice is still heard above the tinkling of the forge. It sees a race pass away—but it passes not away. It remains to remind us of aboriginal nature.

Ch. [William Ellery Channing] talking with [George] Minott the other day about his health—said, "I suppose you'd like to die now." "No," said Minott, "I've toughed it through the winter and I want to stay and hear the bluebirds once more."

Going downtown this A.M. I heard a white-bellied [white-breasted] nuthatch on an elm within twenty feet uttering peculiar notes and more like a song than I remember to have heard from it. There was a [black-capped] chickadee close by to which it may have been addressed. It was *something* like *to-what what what what what* rapidly repeated, and not the normal *gnah gnah*. And this instant it occurs to me that this may be that earliest spring note which I hear—and have referred to a woodpecker! This is before *I* have chanced to see a bluebird, blackbird, or robin in *Concord* this year. It is the spring note of the nuthatch. It paused in its progress about the trunk or branch and uttered this lively but peculiarly inarticulate song—an awkward attempt to warble almost in the face of the chickadee, as if it were one of its kind. It was thus giving vent to the spring within

white-breasted nuthatch

it. If I am not mistaken, it is what I have heard in former springs or winters long ago—fabulously early in the spring season or when we had but just begun to anticipate (for it would seem that we in our anticipations and sympathies include in succession the moods and expressions of all creatures). When only the snow had begun to melt and no rill of song had broken loose. A note so dry and fettered still—so inarticulate and half thawed out—that you might (and would commonly) mistake for the tapping of a woodpecker. As if the young nuthatch in its hole had listened only to the tapping of woodpeckers and learned that music—and now when it would sing and give vent to its spring ecstasy it can modulate only some notes like that. That is its theme still. That is its ruling idea of song and music—only a little clangor and liquidity added to the tapping of the woodpecker. It was the handle by which my thoughts took firmly hold on spring.

MARCH 6, 1853
Two red squirrels made an ado about or above me near the North River, hastily running from tree to tree, leaping from the extremity of one bough to that of the nearest on the next tree—until they

red squirrel

gained and ascended a large white pine. I approached and stood under this, while they made a great fuss about me. One at length came partway down to reconnoiter me. It seemed that one did the barking—a faint short chippy bark, like that of a *toy* dog—its tail vibrating each time, while its neck was stretched over a bough as it peered at me. The other higher up kept up a sort of gurgling whistle, more like a bird than a beast. When I made a noise they would stop a moment.

MARCH 8, 1855
Stopping in a sunny and sheltered place on a hillock in the woods for it was raw in the wind, I heard the hasty, shuffling, as if frightened, note of a *robin* from a dense birch wood—a sort of *tche tche tche tche tche* and then *probably* it dashed through the birches—and so they fetch the year about.

MARCH 8, 1857
A partridge [ruffed grouse] goes off from amid the pitch pines. It lifts each wing so high above its back and flaps so low and withal so rapidly that they present the appearance of a broad wheel—almost a revolving sphere as it whirs off, like a cannonball shot from a gun.

MARCH 10, 1852
I am pretty sure that I heard the chuckle of a ground squirrel [eastern chipmunk] among the warm and bare rocks of the cliffs. The earth is perhaps two thirds bare today. The mosses are now very handsome—like young grass pushing up.

MARCH 10, 1852
Heard the phoebe note of the chickadee today for the first time.[1] I had at first heard their *day day day* ungratefully. Ah! you but carry my thoughts back to winter—but anon I found that they too had

become spring birds. They had changed their note. Even they feel the influence of spring.

MARCH 10, 1853
At Nut Meadow Brook crossing we rest awhile on the rail, gazing into the eddying stream. The ripple marks on the sandy bottom — where silver spangles shine in the river with black wrecks of caddis cases lodged under each shelving sand — the shadows of the invisible dimples reflecting prismatic colors on the bottom, the minnows already stemming the current with restless wiggling tails, ever and anon darting aside probably to secure some invisible mote in the water, whose shadows we do not at first detect on the sandy bottom — when detected so much more obvious as well as larger and more interesting than the substance — in which each fin is distinctly seen though scarcely to be detected in the substance. These are all very beautiful and exhilarating sights, a sort of diet drink to heal our winter discontent. Have the minnows played thus all winter?

MARCH 10, 1853
What was that sound that came on the softened air? It was the warble of the first bluebird from that scraggy apple orchard yonder. When this is heard then has spring arrived.

MARCH 10, 1854
Saw a skunk in the Corner Road — which I followed sixty rods or more. Out now about 4 P.M. — partly because it is a dark foul day. It is a slender black (and white) animal with its back remarkably arched — standing high behind and carrying its head low. Runs, even when undisturbed, with a singular teeter or undulation — like the walking of a Chinese lady. Very slow — I hardly have to run to keep up with it. It has a long tail which it regularly erects when I come too near and prepares to discharge its liquid. It is white at the end

of the tail—and the hind head—and a line on the front of the face. The rest black—except the flesh-colored nose (and I think feet). The back is more arched and the fore and hind feet nearer together than in my sketch.

It tried repeatedly to get into the wall—and did not show much cunning. Finally it steered, apparently, for an old skunk or wood-chuck hole under a wall four rods off, and got into it—or under the wall at least, for it was stopped up. And there I view at leisure close to. It has a remarkably long narrow pointed head and snout which enable it to make those deep narrow holes in the earth by which it probes for insects. Its eyes have an innocent childlike blu-ish black expression. It made a singular loud patting sound repeat-edly on the frozen ground under the wall—undoubtedly with its fore feet (I saw only the upper part of the animal) which reminded me of what I have heard about you stopping and stamping in order to stop the skunk. Probably it has to do with getting its food—patting the earth to get the insects or worms. Though why it did so then I know not.

Its track was small round showing the nails, a little less than an inch in diameter, alternate five or six inches by two or 2½, sometimes two feet together. There is something pathetic in such a sight—next to seeing one of the human aborigines of the country. I respect the skunk as a human being in a very humble sphere. I have no doubt they have begun to probe already where the ground permits—or as far as it does—but what have they to eat all winter?

MARCH 10, 1855
You are always surprised by the sight of the first spring bird or insect—they seem premature and there is no such evidence of spring as themselves, so that they literally *fetch* the year about. It is thus when I hear the first robin or bluebird—or looking along the brooks see the first water bugs [whirligig beetles] out circling. But you think—they have come, and Nature cannot recede.

9

MARCH 10, 1859

As we sit in this wonderful air, many sounds—that of woodchopping for one—come to our ears agreeably blunted or muffled even like the drumming of a partridge—not sharp and rending as in winter and recently. If a partridge should drum in winter, probably it would not reverberate so softly through the wood and sound indefinitely far.

Our voices even sound differently and betray the spring. We speak as in a house—in a warm apartment still—with relaxed muscles and softened voices. The voice—like a woodchuck in his burrow—is met and lapped in and encouraged by all genial and sunny influences. There may be heard now perhaps under south hillsides and the south sides of houses, a slight murmur of conversation, as of insects, out of doors.

MARCH 11, 1859

6 A.M.—By riverside I hear the song of many song sparrows. The most of a song of any yet. And on the swamp white oak top by the stone bridge, I see and hear a red-wing [red-winged blackbird]. It sings almost steadily on its perch there—sitting all alone, as if to attract companions (and I see two more also solitary on different treetops within a quarter of a mile) calling the river to life and tempting ice to melt and trickle like its own sprayey notes. Another flies over on high—with a *tchuck* and at length a clear whistle. The birds anticipate the spring—they come to melt the ice with their songs.

MARCH 12, 1854

I hear a [blue] jay loudly screaming *phe-phay phe-phay*—a loud, shrill chickadee's *phebe*. Now I see and hear the lark [eastern meadowlark] sitting with head erect—neck outstretched, in the middle of a pasture—and I hear another far off singing. Sing when they first come. All these birds do their warbling especially in the still sunny hour after sunrise—as rivers tinkle at their sources. Now is the time to be abroad and hear them—as you detect the slightest ripple in smooth water. As with tinkling sounds the sources of streams burst their icy fetters—so the rills of music begin to flow and swell the general quire of spring. Memorable is the warm light of the spring sun on russet fields in the morning.

MARCH 15, 1852
This afternoon I throw off my outside coat. A mild spring day. I must hie to the Great Meadows. The air is full of bluebirds. The ground almost entirely bare. The villagers are out in the sun—and every man is happy whose work takes him outdoors. I go by Sleepy Hollow toward the Great Fields. I lean over a rail to hear what is in the air, liquid with the bluebird's warble. My life partakes of infinity.

MARCH 15, 1853
There were fewer colder nights last winter than the last. The water in the flower-stand containing my pet tortoise froze solid, completely enveloping him though I had a fire in my chamber all the evening—also that in my pail pretty thick. But the tortoise having been thawed out on the stove was even more lively than ever. His efforts at first had been to get under his chip as if to go into the mud.

MARCH 15, 1857
The [brook] trout darts away in the *puny* brook there [Hubbard's Close] so swiftly in a zigzag course that commonly I only see the ripple that he makes—in proportion in this brook only one foot wide like that made by a steamer in a canal. Or if I catch a glimpse of him before he buries himself in the mud—it is only a dark film without distinct outline. By his zigzag course he bewilders the eye, and avoids capture perhaps.

northern flicker

Ah—there is the note of the first flicker, a prolonged monotonous
wick-wick-wick-wick-wick-wick, etc. or, if you please, *quick-quick*—
heard far over and through the dry leaves. But how that single
sound peoples and enriches all the woods and fields. They are no
longer the same woods and fields that they were. This note really
quickens what was dead. It seems to put a life into withered grass
and leaves and bare twigs—and henceforth the days shall not be
as they have been. It is as when a family, your neighbors, return to
an empty house—after a long absence—and you hear the cheerful hum of voices and the laugh of children, and see the smoke
from the kitchen fire. The doors are thrown open, and children go
screaming through the hall. So the flicker dashes through the aisles
of the grove, throws up a window here and cackles out it—and then
there—airing the house. It makes its voice ring upstairs and down-
stairs—and so as it were fits it for its habitation and ours and takes
possession. It is as good as a housewarming to all nature. Now I
hear and see him louder and nearer on the top of the long-armed
white oak—sitting very upright as is their wont—as it were calling
for some of his kind that may also have arrived.

MARCH 17, 1858
Sitting under the handsome scarlet oak beyond the hill, I hear a
faint note far in the wood which reminds me of the robin. Again I
hear it, it is he—an occasional peep. These notes of the earliest birds
seem to invite forth vegetation—no doubt, the plants concealed
in the earth hear them and rejoice. They wait for this assurance.

MARCH 17, 1859
As I float by the Rock, I hear rustling amid the oak leaves above
that new water line—and there being no wind I know it to be a
striped squirrel [eastern chipmunk] and soon see its long unseen

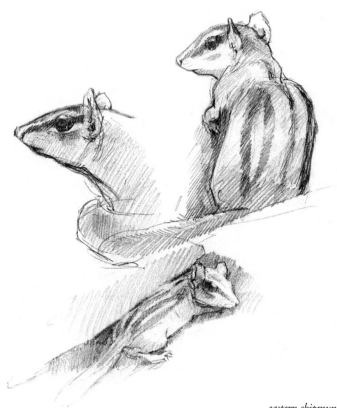

eastern chipmunk

striped sides flirting about the instep of an oak. Its lateral stripes, alternate black and yellowish, are a type which I have not seen for a long time, or rather a punctuation mark—where a new paragraph commences in the revolution of the seasons. Double lines.

MARCH 18, 1853
Everywhere also all over the town within an hour or two have come out little black two-winged gnats [crane flies] with plumed or fuzzy shoulders. When I catch one in my hands it looks like [a] bit of black silk raveling. They have suddenly come forth everywhere.

MARCH 18, 1855

I see with my glass as I go over the railroad bridge—sweeping the river—a great gull standing far away on the top of a muskrat cabin which rises just above the water opposite the Hubbard Bath. When I get round within sixty rods of him ten minutes later, he still stands on the same spot—constantly turning his head to every side looking out for foes. Like a wooden image of a bird he stands there, heavy to look at—head, breast, beneath, and rump pure white. Slate colored wings tipped with black and extending beyond the tail. The herring gull.

MARCH 18, 1858

Each new year is a surprise to us. We find that we had virtually forgotten the note of each bird—and when we hear it again it is remembered like a dream, reminding us of a previous state of existence. How happens it that the associations it awakens are always pleasing, never saddening—reminiscences of our sanest hours? The voice of nature is always encouraging. The blackbird—probably grackle this time—wings his way direct above the swamp northward with a regular *tchuck,* carrier haste, calling the summer months along, like a hen her chickens.

MARCH 19, 1842

I have been walking this afternoon over a pleasant field planted with winter rye—near the house. Where this strange people once had their dwelling place. Another species of mortal men but little less wild to me than the musquash [muskrat] they hunted. Strange spirits—daemons—whose eyes could never meet mine. With another nature—and another fate than mine. The crows flew over the edge of the woods, and wheeling over my head seemed to rebuke—as dark-winged spirits more akin to the Indian than I. Perhaps only the present disguise of the Indian. If the new has a meaning so has the old.

MARCH 19, 1858

It is a fine evening, as I stand on the bridge. The waters are quite *smooth*—very little ice to be seen. The red-wing and song sparrow are singing and a flock of tree sparrows is pleasantly warbling. A new era has come. The red-wing's *gurgle-ee* is heard when smooth waters begin—they come together. One or two boys are out trying their skiffs—even like the fuzzy gnats in the sun—and as often as one turns his boat round on the smooth surface the setting sun is reflected from its side.

MARCH 20, 1842

What is all nature and human life at this moment—what the scenery and vicinity of a human soul—but the song of an early sparrow from yonder fences, and the cackling hens in the barn. So for one while my destiny loiters within earshot of these sounds. The great busy dame nature is concerned to know how many eggs her hens lay.

The soul, the proprietor of the world, has an interest in the stacking of hay, the foddering of cattle, and the draining of peat meadows.... Was not Christ interested in the setting hens of Palestine?

MARCH 20, 1853

On the warm dry cliff looking south over Beaver Pond I was surprised to see a large [mourning cloak] butterfly, black with buff-edged wings.[2] So tender a creature to be out so early, and when alighted opening and shutting its wings. What does it do these frosty nights. Its chrysalis must have hung in some sunny nook of the rocks. Born to be food for some early bird.

MARCH 20, 1855

Trying the other day to imitate the honking of geese, I found myself flapping my sides with my elbows, as with wings—and uttering something like the syllables *mow-ack* with a nasal twang and twist

in my head—and I produced their note so perfectly in the opinion of the hearers that I thought I might possibly draw a flock down.

MARCH 20, 1857

Dine with Agassiz at R.W.E.'s [Ralph Waldo Emerson].

He thinks that the [white] suckers die of asphyxia—having very large air bladders and being in the habit of coming to the surface for air. But then, he is thinking of a different phenomenon from the one I speak of—which last is confined to the very earliest spring or winter. . . .

He had broken caterpillars and found the crystals of ice in them but had not thawed them. When I began to tell him of my experiment on a frozen fish, he said that Pallas had shown that fishes were frozen and thawed again—but I affirmed the contrary and then Agassiz agreed with me.

MARCH 20, 1858

The fishes are going up the brooks, as they open. They are dispersing themselves through the fields and woods—importing new life with them. They are taking their places under the shelving banks, and in the dark swamps. The water running down meets the fishes running up. They hear the latest news. Spring-aroused fishes are running up our veins too. Little fishes are seeking the sources of the brooks—seeking to disseminate their principles. Talk about a revival of religion! And business men's prayer meetings! With which all the country goes mad now. What if it were as true and wholesome a *revival* as the little fishes feel which come out of the sluggish waters and run up the brooks toward their sources! All nature *revives* at this season—with her it is really a *new life*—but with these churchgoers it is only a revival of religion or hypocrisy. They go downstream to still muddier waters. It cheers me more to behold the swarms of gnats which have revived in the spring sun. The fish lurks by the mouth of its native brook, watching its opportunity to dart up the stream by the cakes of ice.

Do the fishes stay to hold prayer meetings in Fair Haven Bay—while some monstrous pike gulps them down? Or is it not rather each one privately or with its kindred spirits as soon as possible stemming the current of its native brook—making its way to more ethereal waters? Burnishing his scaly armor by his speed—ofttimes running into osier creels and finding its salvation there even, as in the discharge of its duty.

No wonder we feel the spring influences—there is a motion in the very ground under our feet. Each rill is peopled with new life rushing up it. If a man do not revive with nature in the spring, how shall he revive when a white-collared priest prays for him?

MARCH 21, 1853

Ah then as I was rising this crowning road—just beyond the old lime-kiln there leaked into my open ear the faint peep of a hyla [spring peeper] from some far pool. One little hyla somewhere in the fens, aroused by the genial season, crawls up the bank or a bush, squats on a dry leaf and essays a note or two which scarcely rends the air—does no violence to the zephyr—but yet breaks through all obstacle, thick-planted maples and far over the downs to the ear of the listening naturalist, who will never see that piper in this world. As it were the first faint cry of the newborn year—notwithstanding the notes of birds. Where so long I have heard only the brattling and moaning of the wind, what means this tenser—far-piercing sound. All nature rejoices with one joy. If the hyla has revived again may not I? He is heard the first warm hazy evening.

MARCH 22, 1853

As soon as those spring mornings arrive in which the birds sing I am sure to be an early riser. I am waked by my genius. I wake to inaudible melodies and am surprised to find myself expecting the dawn—in so serene and joyful and expectant a mood. . . . To stay in the house all day such reviving spring days as the past have been—bending over a stove and gnawing one's heart—seems to me as absurd as for a woodchuck to linger in his burrow. We have not heard the news then! Sucking the claws of our philosophy when there is game to be had. The tapping of the woodpecker—*rat-tat-tat*—knocking at the door of some sluggish grub to tell him that the spring has arrived, and his fate. This is one of the season sounds, calling the roll of birds and insects—the reveille.

MARCH 22, 1855

Going [along] the steep side hill on the south of the pond about 4 P.M. on the edge of the little patch of wood which the choppers have not yet leveled—though they have felled many an acre around it this winter—I observed a rotten and hollow hemlock stump about two feet high and six inches in diameter, and instinctively approached with my right hand ready to cover it. I found a flying squirrel[3] in it which as my left hand had covered a small hole at the bottom ran directly into my right hand. It struggled and bit not a little, but my cotton gloves protected me and I felt its teeth only once or twice. It also uttered three or four dry shrieks at first— something like *cr-r-rack cr-r-r-ack cr-r-r-ack.* I rolled it up in my handkerchief and holding the ends tight, carried it home in my hand—some three miles. It struggled more or less all the way— especially when my feet made any unusual or louder noise going through leaves or bushes. I could count its claws as they appeared through the handkerchief, and once it got its head out a hole. It even bit through the handkerchief.

Color as I remember above a chestnut ash inclining to fawn or cream color (?) slightly browned—beneath white—the under edge of its wings (?) tinged yellow, the upper dark, perhaps black, making a dark stripe. Audubon and Bachman do not speak of any such stripe!

It was a very cunning little animal—reminding me of a mouse in the room. Its *very large and prominent* black eyes gave it an interesting innocent look. Its very neat flat fawn-colored distichous tail was a great ornament. Its "sails" were not very obvious when it was at rest—merely giving it a flat appearance beneath. It would leap off and upward into the air two or three feet from a table spreading its "sails" and fall to the floor in vain—perhaps strike the side of the room in its upward spring and endeavor to cling to it. It would run up the window by the sash—but evidently found the furniture and walls and floor too hard and smooth for it and after some falls became quiet. In a few moments it allowed me to stroke it though far from confident.

I put it in a barrel and covered it for the night. It was quite busy all the evening gnawing out—clinging for this purpose and gnaw-

southern flying squirrel

ing at the upper edge of a sound oak barrel, and then dropping to
rest from time to time. It had defaced the barrel considerably by
morning, and would probably have escaped if I had not placed a
piece of iron against the gnawed part. I had left in the barrel some
bread, apple, shagbarks, and cheese. It ate some of the apple and
one shagbark—cutting it quite in two transversely.

In the morning it was quiet and *squatted* somewhat curled up
amid the straw, with its tail passing under it and the end curled over
its head—very prettily—as if to shield it from the light and keep it
warm. I always found it in this position by day when I raised the lid.

MARCH 23, 1855
Carried my flying squirrel back to the woods in my handkerchief. I
placed it about 3:30 P.M. on the very stump I had taken it from. It

immediately ran about a rod over the leaves and up a slender maple sapling about ten feet, then after a moment's pause sprang off and skimmed downward toward a large maple nine feet distant whose trunk it struck three or four feet from the ground. This it rapidly ascended, on the opposite side from me, nearly thirty feet and there clung to the main stem with its head downward eying me. After two or three minutes' pause I saw that it was preparing for another spring—by raising its head and looking off—and away it went in admirable style more like a bird than any quadruped I had dreamed of—and far surpassing the impression I had received from naturalists' accounts. I marked the spot it started from and the place where it struck and measured the height and distance carefully. It sprang off from the maple at the height of 28½ feet, and struck the ground at the foot of a tree 50½ feet distant, measured horizontally. Its flight was not a *regular* descent—it varied from a direct line both horizontally and vertically. Indeed it skimmed much like a hawk and part of its flight was nearly horizontal—and it diverged from a right line eight or ten feet to the right, making a curve in that direction. There were six trees from six inches to a foot in diameter, one a hemlock, in a direct line between the two termini and these it skimmed partly round and passed through their thinner limbs— did not as I could perceive touch a twig—and skimmed its way like a hawk *between* and *around* the trees. Though it was a windy day, this was on a steep hillside *away from the wind* and covered with wood—so it was not aided by that. As the ground rose about two feet the distance was to the absolute height as 50½ to 26½—or it advanced about two feet for every one foot of descent. After its vain attempts in the house, I was not prepared for this exhibition. It did not fall heavily as in the house, but struck the ground gently enough—and I cannot believe that the mere extension of the skin enabled it to skim so far. It must be still further aided by its organization. Perhaps it fills itself with air first.

I spend a considerable portion of my time observing the habits of the wild animals, my brute neighbors. By their various movements and migrations they fetch the year about to me. Very significant are the flight of geese and the migration of suckers, etc. etc. But when I consider that the nobler animals have been exterminated here—the cougar, panther, lynx, wolverine, wolf, bear, moose, deer, the beaver, the turkey, etc., etc.—I cannot but feel as if I lived in a tamed and, as it were, emasculated country. Would not the motions of those larger and wilder animals have been more significant still. Is it not a maimed and imperfect nature that I am conversant with? As if I were to study a tribe of Indians that had lost all its warriors. Do not the forest and the meadow now lack expression—now that I never see nor think of the moose with a lesser forest on his head, in the one, nor of the beaver in the other? When I think what were the various sounds and notes—the migrations and works and changes of fur and plumage which ushered in the spring and marked the other seasons of the year—I am reminded that this my life in Nature, this particular round of natural phenomena which I call a year, is lamentably incomplete. I listen to a concert in which so many parts are wanting. The whole civilized country is to some extent turned into a city ...

I take infinite pains to know all the phenomena of the spring, for instance—thinking that I have here the entire poem—and then to my chagrin I hear that it is but an imperfect copy that I possess and have read, that my ancestors have torn out many of the first leaves and grandest passages—and mutilated it in many places.

I should not like to think that some demigod had come before me and picked out some of the best of the stars. I wish to know an entire heaven and an entire earth.

MARCH 23, 1859

We cross to Lee's shore and sit upon the bare rocky ridge overlooking the flood southwest and northeast.... Thus we sit on that
rock—hear the first wood frog's croak and dream of a russet ely-
sium. Enough for the season is the beauty thereof.... It is not the
rich black soil—but warm and sandy hills and plains which tempt
our steps. We love to sit on and walk over sandy tracts in the spring
like cicindelas [tiger beetles].

MARCH 23, 1859

The loud *peop* (?) of a pigeon woodpecker [northern flicker] is heard
in our sea—and anon the prolonged loud and shrill *cackle* calling
the thin-wooded hillsides and pastures to life. It is like the note of
an alarm clock set last fall so as to wake nature up at exactly this
date.

Up up up up up up up up up! What a rustling it seems to make
among the dry leaves.

MARCH 24, 1859

Southeast wind—begins to sprinkle—while I am sitting in Laurel
Glen, listening to hear the earliest wood frogs croaking. I think
they get under weigh a little earlier, i.e. you will hear many of them
sooner than you will hear many hylodes [spring peepers]. Now
when the leaves get to be dry and rustle under your feet—dried
by the March winds—the peculiar dry note, *wurrik wurrk wur ruk
wurk* of the wood frog is heard faintly by ears on the alert, borne
up from some unseen pool in a woodland hollow—which is open
to the influences of the sun. It is a singular sound for awakening
nature to make—associated with the first warmer days when you
sit in some sheltered place in the woods amid the dried leaves. How
moderate, on her first awakening—how little demonstrative! You
may sit half an hour before you will hear another. You doubt if the
season will be long enough for such Oriental and luxurious slow-

ness. But they get on nevertheless and by tomorrow—or in a day or two—they croak louder and more frequently. Can you ever be sure that you have heard the very first wood frog in the township croak? Ah! how weather-wise must he be! There is no guessing at the weather with him. He makes the weather in his degree—he encourages it to be mild. The weather, what is it but the temperament of the earth—and he is wholly of the earth, sensitive as its skin in which he lives, and of which he is a part. His life relaxes with the thawing ground. He pitches and tunes his voice and chord with the rustling leaves which the March wind has dried. Long before the frost is quite out—he feels the influence of the spring rains and the warmer days. His is the very voice of the weather. He rises and falls like quicksilver in the thermometer.

You do not perceive the spring so surely in the actions of men. Their lives are so artificial. They may make more fire or less in their parlors and their feelings accordingly are not good thermometers. The frog far away in the wood—that burns no coal nor wood—perceives more surely the general and universal changes.

MARCH 25, 1859

I thought the other day—How we enjoy a warm and pleasant day at this season. We dance like gnats in the sun.

MARCH 25, 1859

A score of my townsmen have been shooting and trapping musquash and mink of late. Some have got nothing else to do. If they should strike for higher wages now instead of going to the clam banks, as the Lynn shoemakers propose, they would go to shooting musquash. They are gone all day—early and late they scan the rising tide. Stealthily they set their traps in remote swamps, avoiding one another. Am not I a trapper too—early and late, scanning the rising flood, ranging by distant woodsides, setting my traps in solitude, and baiting them as well as I know how. That I may catch life and light—that my intellectual part may taste some venison and be invigorated, that my nakedness may be clad in some wild furry warmth.

MARCH 25, 1860
The boy's sled gets put away—in the barn or shed or garret, and there lies dormant all summer, like a woodchuck in the winter. It goes into its burrow just before woodchucks come out. So that you may say a woodchuck never sees a sled—nor a sled a woodchuck (unless it were a prematurely risen woodchuck—or a belated and unseasonable sled). Before the woodchuck comes out the sled goes in. They dwell at the antipodes of each other. Before sleds rise woodchucks have set. The ground squirrel too shares the privileges and misfortunes of the woodchuck. The sun now passes from the constellation of the sled into that of the woodchuck.

MARCH 26, 1846
A flock of geese have just got in late from the Canada line, now in the dark flying low over the pond. They came on, indulging at last like weary travelers in complaint and consolations, or like some creaking evening mail late lumbering in with regular anserine clangor. I stood at my door and could hear their wings when they suddenly spied my light and ceasing their noise wheeled to the east and apparently settled in the pond.

MARCH 26, 1853
Up the Assabet scared from his perch a stout hawk—the red-tailed undoubtedly for I saw very plainly the color red when he spread his wings from off his tail (and rump?). I rowed the boat three times within gunshot before he flew, twice within four rods. While he sat on an oak over the water. I think because I had two ladies with me which was as good as bushing the boat. Each time or twice at least he made a motion to fly before he started. The ends of his pri-

maries looked very ragged against the sky. This is the hen hawk of the farmer—the same probably which I have scared off from the Cliff so often. It was an interesting eagle-like object as he sat upright on his perch with his back to us, now and then looking over his shoulder—the broad-backed, flat-headed, curve-beaked bird.

MARCH 26, 1857

As I go through the woods by Andromeda Ponds though it is rather cool and windy in exposed places I hear a faint stertorous croak from a frog in the open swamp—at first one faint note only which I could not be sure that I had heard, but after listening long one or two more suddenly croaked in confirmation of my faith and all was silent again. When first in the spring—as you walk over the rustling leaves amid bare and ragged bushes—you hear this at first faint hard dry and short sound, it hardly sounds like the note of an animal. It may have been heard some days. [*Penciled addition: The next day at 2.30 P.M.*—or about the same time and about the same weather, our thermometer is at 48°.] I lay down on the fine dry sedge in the sun—in the deep and sheltered hollow a little further on—and when I had lain there ten or fifteen minutes, I heard one fine faint peep from over the windy ridge between the hollow in which I lay and the swamp which at first I referred to a bird—and looked round at the bushes which crowned the brim of this hollow to find it—but ere long a regularly but faintly repeated *phe-phe phe phe* revealed the *Hylodes pickeringii*. It was like the light reflected from the mountain ridges within the shaded portion of the moon—forerunner and herald of the spring.

MARCH 27, 1853

Tried to see the faint-croaking frogs at J. P. Brown's pond in the woods. They are remarkably timid and shy—had their noses and eyes out, croaking, but all ceased, dove and concealed themselves before I got within a rod of the shore. Stood perfectly still amid the bushes on the shore before one showed himself. Finally five or six and all eyed me—gradually approached me within three feet to reconnoiter and though I waited about half an hour would not utter a sound nor take their eyes off me. Were plainly affected by curiosity. Dark brown—and some perhaps dark green about two inches long. Had their noses and eyes out when they croaked. If described at all must be either young of *R. pipiens* [northern leopard frog] or the *R. palustris* [pickerel frog].

MARCH 27, 1857
Heard a lark in that meadow—twitters over it on quivering wing and awakes the slumbering life of the meadow. The turtle and the frog peep stealthily out and see the first lark go over.

MARCH 27, 1858
The sheldrake [common merganser] has a peculiar long clipper look often moving rapidly straight forward over the water. It sinks to various depths in the water. Sometimes, as when apparently alarmed, showing only its head and neck and the upper part of its back—and at others when at ease, floating buoyantly on the surface as if it had taken in more air, showing all its white breast and the white along its sides. Sometimes it lifts itself up on the surface and flaps its wings revealing its whole rosaceous breast and its lower parts and looking in form like a penguin.

When I first saw them fly upstream I suspected that they had gone to Fair Haven Pond and would alight under the lee of the cliff. Creeping slowly down through the woods four or five rods, I was enabled to get a fair sight of them—and finally we sat exposed on the rocks within twenty-five rods. They appear not to observe a person so high above them.

It was a pretty sight to see a pair of them tacking about—always within a foot or two of each other and heading the same way—now on this short tack now on that, the male taking the lead, sinking deep and looking every way. When the whole twelve had come together they would soon break up again, and were continually changing their ground—though not diving—now sailing slowly this way a dozen rods, and now that, and now coming in near the shore. Then they would all go to preening themselves—thrusting their bills into their backs—and keeping up such a brisk motion that you could not get a fair sight of one's head. From time to time you heard a slight titter not of alarm but perhaps a breeding note— for they were evidently selecting their mates. I see one scratch its ear or head with its foot. Then it was surprising to see how briskly sailing off one side they went to diving. As if they had suddenly come across a school of minnows a whole company would disappear at once, never rising as high as before. Now for nearly a minute there is not a feather to be seen—and the next minute you see a part of half a dozen there chasing one another and making the water fly far and wide.

When returning we saw near the outlet of the pond seven or eight sheldrakes standing still in a line on the edge of the ice and others swimming close by. They evidently love to stand on the ice for a change.

MARCH 28, 1853

My Aunt Maria asked me to read the life of Dr. Chalmers—which however I did not promise to do. Sunday, she was heard through the partition shouting to my Aunt Jane, who is deaf—"Think of it, he stood half an hour today to hear the frogs croak, and he wouldn't read the life of Chalmers."

MARCH 28, 1853

The woods ring with the cheerful jingle of the *F. hyemalis* [dark-eyed junco]. This is a very trig and compact little bird and appears to be in good condition. The straight edge of slate on their breasts contrasts remarkably with the white from beneath. The short light-

dark-eyed junco

colored bill is also very conspicuous amid the dark slate and when they fly from you the two white feathers in their tails are very distinct at a good distance. They are very lively pursuing each other, from bush to bush.

MARCH 28, 1857

At Lee's Cliff and this side I see half a dozen buff-edged butterflies, *Vanessa antiopa* [mourning cloak], and pick up three dead or dying, two together, the edges of their wings gone. Several are fluttering over the dry rock debris under the cliff—in whose crevices probably they have wintered. Two of the three I pick up are not dead—though they will not fly. Verily their day is a short one. What has checked their frail life? Within the buff edge is black with bright sky-blue spots—and the main part within is a purplish brown. Those little oblong spots on the black ground are light as you look directly down on them but from one side they vary through violet to a crystalline rose purple....

The broad buff edge of the *Vanessa antiopa*'s wings harmonizes with the russet ground it flutters over. And as it stands concealed in the winter with its wings folded above its back—in a cleft in the rocks—the gray-brown underside of its wings prevents its being distinguished from the rocks themselves.

MARCH 28, 1859

As we were paddling over the Great Meadows I saw at a distance high in the air above the middle of the meadow a very compact flock of blackbirds advancing against the sun. Though there were more than a hundred, they did not appear to occupy more than six feet in breadth—but the whole flock was dashing first to the right and then to the left. When advancing straight toward me and the sun they made but little impression on the eye—so many fine dark points merely seen against the sky—but as often they wheeled to the right or left, displaying their wings flatwise and the whole length of their bodies they were a very conspicuous black mass. This fluctuation in the amount of dark surface was a very pleasing phenomenon. It reminded me [of] those blinds whose sashes are made to move all together by a stick, now admitting nearly all the light and now entirely excluding it—so the flock of blackbirds opened and shut.

MARCH 29, 1852

Saw two wood tortoises at the bottom of the brook one upon another. The upper and larger one was decidedly bronze on the back—the under one with more sharply grooved scales. The former perhaps the male with a decided depression of the sternum. Their legs a reddish orange.

MARCH 29, 1853

What are these common snails[4] in the mud in ditches, with their feet out, for some time past?

This cold wind is refreshing to my palate, as the warm air of summer is not methinks. I love to stand there and be blown on as much as a horse in July.

As I sit two thirds the way up the sunny side of the Pine Hill looking over the meadows—which are now almost completely bare—the crows by their swift flight and scolding reveal to me some large bird of prey [rough-legged hawk] hovering over the river. I perceive by its markings and size that it cannot be a hen hawk—and now it settles on the topmost branch of a white maple bending it down. Its great armed and feathered legs dangle helplessly in the air for a moment as if feeling for the perch, while its body is tipping this way and that. It sits there facing me some forty or fifty rods off—pluming itself—but keeping a good lookout. At this distance and in this light it appears to have a rusty brown head and breast and is white beneath, with rusty leg feathers and a tail black beneath. When it flies again it is principally black varied with white—regular light spots on its tail and wings beneath—but chiefly a conspicuous white space on the forward part of the back. Also some of the upper side of the tail or tail coverts is white. It has broad ragged buzzard-like wings—and from the white of its back as well as the shape and shortness of its wings and its not having a gull-like body, I think it must be an eagle. It lets itself down with its legs somewhat helplessly dangling—as if feeling for something on the bare meadow—and then gradually flies away soaring and circling higher and higher until lost in the downy clouds. This lofty soaring is at least a grand recreation, as if it were nourishing sublime ideas. I should like to know why it soars higher and higher so, whether its thoughts are really turned to earth—for it seems to be more nobly as well as highly employed than the laborers ditching in the meadow beneath, or any others of my fellow townsmen.

MARCH 30, 1853

The motions of a hawk correcting the flaws in the wind by raising his shoulder—from time to time—are much like those of a leaf yielding to them. For the little hawks are hunting now. You have not to sit long on the cliffs before you see one.

MARCH 30, 1855

He must have a great deal of life in him to draw upon, who can pick up a subsistence in November and March. Man comes out of his winter quarters this month as lean as a woodchuck. Not till late could the skunk find a place where the ground was thawed on the surface.

MARCH 31, 1852

The song sparrow and the transient fox-colored sparrow—have they brought me no message this year? Do they lead heroic lives in Rupert's Land. They are so small I think their destinies must be large. Have I heard what this tiny passenger has to say while it flits thus from tree to tree? Is not the coming of the fox-colored sparrow something more earnest and significant than I have dreamed of? Can I forgive myself if I let it go to Rupert's Land before I have appreciated it. God did not make this world in jest—no, nor in indifference. These migrating sparrows all bear messages that concern my life. I do not pluck the fruits in their season. I love the birds and beasts because they are mythologically in earnest. I see that the sparrow cheeps and flits and sings adequately to the great design of the universe—that man does not communicate with it, understand its language because he is not at one with nature. I reproach myself because I have regarded with indifference the passage of the birds—I have thought them no better than I.

MARCH 31, 1857

As I rise the east side of the Hill I hear the distant faint peep of hylodes and the *tut tut* of croaking frogs from the west of the Hill. How gradually and imperceptibly the peep of the hylodes mingles with and swells the volume of sound which makes the voice of awakening nature! If you do not listen carefully for its first note you probably will not hear it—and not having heard that your ears become used to the sound so that you will hardly notice it at last, however loud and universal. I hear it now faintly from through and over the bare gray twigs and the sheeny needles of an oak and pine wood—and from over the russet fields beyond—and it is so intimately mingled with the murmur or roar of the wind as to be well nigh inseparable from it. It leaves such a lasting trace on the ear's memory that often I think I hear their peeping when I do not. It is a singularly emphatic and ear-piercing proclamation of animal life, when with a very few and slight exceptions vegetation is yet dormant. The dry croaking *tut tut* of the [wood] frogs (a sound which ducks seem to imitate—a kind of *quacking*—and they are both of the water!) is plainly enough down there in some pool in the woods. But the shrill peeping of the hylodes locates itself nowhere in particular, but seems to take its rise at an indefinite distance over wood and hill and pasture from clefts or hollows in the March wind. It is a wind-born sound.

APRIL 1, 1853

Now at night the scent of muskrats is very strong in particular localities. Next to the skunk its odor is perceived further than that of any of our animals that I think of. I perceive no difference between this and the musk with which ladies scent themselves—though here I pronounce it a strong rank odor. In the faint reflected twilight I distinguish one rapidly swimming away from me leaving a widening ripple behind, and now hear one plunge from some willow or rock.

APRIL 1, 1854

Yesterday and today I hear the cackle of the flicker so agreeable from association. It brings the year about.

APRIL 1, 1858

At Hemlock Brook a dozen or more rods from the river I see on the wet mud a little snapping turtle evidently hatched last year. It does not open its eyes nor mouth while I hold it. Its eyes appear as if sealed up by its long sleep. In our ability to contend with the elements, what feeble infants we are to this one. Talk of great heads, look at this one. Talk of Hercules' feats in the cradle. What sort of cradle and nursing has this infant had? It totters forth confident and victorious when it can hardly carry its shield. It looked so much like the mud or a wet muddy leaf—it was a wonder I saw it.

snapping turtle

APRIL 2, 1852

On the rocky point of this island where the wind is felt, the waves are breaking merrily—and now for half an hour our dog [belonging to Israel Rice] has been standing in the water and ceaselessly snapping at each wave as it broke as if it were a living creature. He regardless of cold and wet thrusts his head into each wave to gripe it. A dog snapping at the waves as they break on a rocky shore. He then rolls himself in the leaves for a napkin.

APRIL 2, 1856

Here is the broken shell of one of those large white snails, *Helix albolabris* [white-lipped snail], on the top of the Cliff. It is like a horn with ample mouth wound on itself. I am rejoiced to find anything so pretty. I cannot but think it nobler, as it is rarer, to appreciate some beauty than to feel much sympathy with misfortune.

APRIL 2, 1859

As I go down the street just after sunset, I hear many [Wilson's] snipe tonight.[5]

This sound is annually heard by the villagers but always at this hour, i.e. in the twilight—a hovering sound high in the air and they do not know what to refer it to. It is very easily imitated by the breath. A sort of shuddering with the breath. It reminds me of calmer nights. Hardly one in a hundred hears it, and perhaps not nearly so many know what creature makes it. Perhaps no one dreamed of snipe an hour ago—but the air seemed empty of such as they—but as soon as the dusk begins, so that a bird's flight is concealed, you hear this peculiar spirit-suggesting sound, now far now near, heard through and above the evening din of the village. I did not hear one when I returned up the street half an hour later.

APRIL 3, 1852

The bluebird carries the sky on his back.

APRIL 4, 1853

A warm dripping rain heard on one's umbrella as on a snug roof—and on the leaves without suggests comfort. We go abroad with a slow but sure contentment like turtles under their shells.

APRIL 4, 1859

I see several earthworms today under the shoe of the pump. On the platform. They may have come up through the cracks from the well where the warm air has kept them stirring.

APRIL 5, 1860

When I stand more out of the wind—under the shelter of the hill beyond Clamshell, where there is not wind enough to make a noise on my person—I hear or think that I hear a very *faint distant* ring of toads which though I walk and walk all the afternoon I never come nearer to. It is hard to tell if it is not a ringing in my ears. Yet I think it is a solitary and distant toad called to life by some warm and sheltered pool or hill—its note having as it were a chemical affinity with the air of the spring. It merely gives a slightly more ringing or sonorous sound to the general rustling of inanimate nature. A sound more ringing and articulate my ear detects, under and below the noise of the rippling wind. Thus gradually and moderately the year begins. It creeps into the ears so gradually that most do not observe it—and so our ears are gradually accustomed to the sound and perchance we do not perceive it when at length it has become very much louder and more general.

APRIL 6, 1853

All along under the south side of this hill on the edge of the meadow, the air resounds with the hum of honeybees, attracted by the flower of the skunk cabbage. I first heard the fine peculiarly sharp hum of the honeybee before I thought of them. Some hummed hollowly within the spathes, perchance to give notice to their fellows that

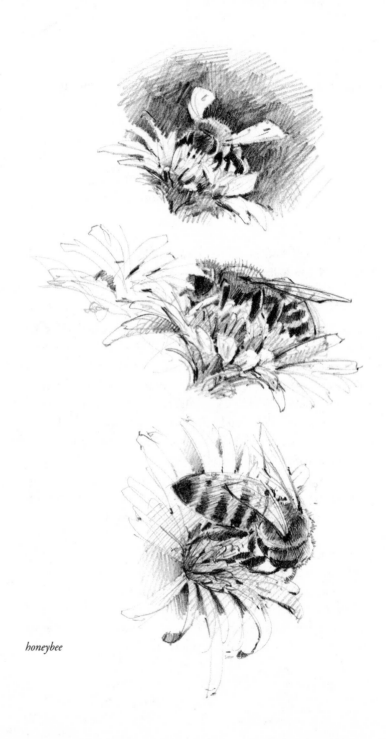

honeybee

plant was occupied—for they repeatedly looked in and backed out on finding another. It was surprising to see them, directed by their instincts to these localities, while the earth has still but a wintry aspect so far as vegetation is concerned—buzz around some obscure spathe close to the ground, well knowing what they were about. Then alight and enter. As the cabbages were very numerous for thirty or forty rods there must have been some hundreds of bees there at once at least. I watched many when they entered and came out and they all had little yellow pellets of pollen at their thighs. As the skunk cabbage comes out before the willow it is probable that the former is the first flower they visit.

APRIL 6, 1854

In clearing out the Assabet Spring, disturbed two small speckled (*palustris*) frogs just beginning to move.

APRIL 6, 1858

Talked a moment with two little Irish (?) boys eight or ten years old that were playing in the brook by the mill. Saw one catch a minnow. I asked him if he used a hook. He said no, it was a dolly *chunk* (?) or some such word. "*Dully* what?" [I] asked. "Yes, *dully*," said he, and he would not venture to repeat the whole word again. It was a small horsehair slip noose at the end of a willow stick four feet long. The horsehair was twisted two or three together. He passed this over the fish slowly and then jerked him out—the noose slipping and holding him. It seems they are sometimes made with wire to catch trout. I asked him to let me see the fish he had caught. It was a little [chain] pickerel five inches long, and appeared to me strange being *transversely* barred—and reminded me of the Wrentham pond pickerel—but I could not remember surely whether this was the rule or the exception, but when I got home I found that this was the one which Storer does not name nor describe—but only had heard of. Is it not the brook pickerel? Asking what other fish he had caught, he said a pike. That, said I, is a large pickerel. He said it had "a long, long neb like a duck's bill."

APRIL 7, 1853
Many spotted tortoises are basking amid the dry leaves in the sun along the side of a still warm ditch cut through the swamp. They make a great rustling a rod ahead as they make haste through the leaves to tumble into the water.

APRIL 8, 1854
Saw a large bird sail along over the edge of Wheeler's cranberry meadow just below Fair Haven, which I at first thought a gull—but with my glass found it was a hawk and had a perfectly white head and tail and broad black or blackish wings. It sailed and circled along over the low cliff and the crows dived at it in the field of my glass—and I saw it well both above and beneath as it turned—and then it passed off to hover over the Cliffs at a greater height. It was undoubtedly a white-headed [bald] eagle. It was to the eye but a large hawk.

APRIL 8, 1859
When the question of the protection of birds comes up, the legislatures regard only a low use and never a high use—the best-disposed legislators employ one perchance only to examine their crops and see how many grubs or cherries they contain, and never to study their dispositions, or the beauty of their plumage—or listen and report on the sweetness of their song. The legislature will preserve a bird professedly not because it is a beautiful creature—but because it is a good scavenger or the like. This at least is the defense set up. It is as if the question were whether some celebrated singer of the human race—some Jenny Lind or another—did more harm or good, should be destroyed or not, and therefore a committee should be appointed, not to listen to her singing at all, but to ex-

amine the contents of her stomach and see if she devoured anything which was injurious to the farmers and gardeners, or which they cannot spare.

APRIL 9, 1853
A mid-sized orange copper [eastern comma] butterfly on the mill road at the clearing with deeply scalloped leaves. You see the buff-edged and this, etc. in warm sunny southern exposures on the edge of woods or sides of rocky hills and cliffs above dry leaves and twigs. Where the wood has been lately cut and there are many dry leaves and twigs about.

APRIL 9, 1856
In a leafy pool by railroad which will soon dry up I see large skater insects [water striders] —where the snow is not all melted. . . . The skaters are as forward to play on the first smooth and melted pool, as boys on the first piece of ice in the winter. It must be cold to their feet.

APRIL 9, 1856
I go off a little to the right of the railroad and sit on the edge of that sand crater near the spring by the railroad. Sitting there on the warm bank—above the broad shallow crystalline pool on the sand—amid russet banks of curled early sedge grass showing a little green at base and dry leaves, I hear one hyla peep faintly several times. This is then a degree of warmth sufficient for the hyla. He is the first of his race to awaken to the new year—and pierce the solitude with his voice. He shall wear the medal for this year.

You hear him but you will never find him. He is somewhere down amid the withered sedge and alder bushes there by the water's edge—but where? From that quarter his shrill blast sounded—but he is silent and a kingdom will not buy it again.

While I am looking at the hazel I hear from the old locality—the edge of the great pines and oaks in the swamp by the railroad—the note of the pine warbler. It sounds far off and faint—but coming out and sitting on the iron rail I am surprised to see it within three or four rods on the upper part of a white oak, where it is busily catching insects, hopping along toward the extremities of the limbs and looking off on all sides, twice darting off like a wood pewee two rods over the railroad after an insect and returning to the oak, and from time to time uttering its simple rapidly iterated cool-sounding notes. When heard a little within the wood as he hops to that side the oak they sound particularly cool and inspiring like a part of the evergreen forest itself—the trickling of the sap. Its bright yellow or golden throat and breast, etc. are conspicuous at this season— a greenish yellow above, with two white bars on its bluish brown wings. It sits often with loose-hung wings and forked tail.

APRIL 10, 1852

Having got into the Great Meadows—after grounding once or twice on low spits of grass ground—we begin to see ducks which we have scared flying low over the water—always with a striking parallelism in the direction of their flight. They fly like regulars. They are like rolling-pins with wings. . . . Ducks most commonly seen flying by twos or threes. . . .

From Carlisle Bridge we saw many ducks a quarter of a mile or more northward—black objects on the water—and heard them laugh something like a loon. Might have got near enough to shoot them. A fine sight to see them rise at last, about fifty of them, apparently black ducks.[6] While they float on the water they appear to preserve constantly their relative distance. Their note not exactly like that of a goose, yet resembling some domestic fowl's cry—you know not what one. Like a new species of goose.

APRIL 11, 1852

The song of a robin on an oak in Hubbard's Grove sounds far off—
so I have heard a robin within three feet in a cage in a dark bar
room (how unstained by all the filth of that place!) with a kind of
ventriloquism so singing that his song sounded far off on the elms.
It was more pathetic still for this. The robins are singing now on all
hands while the sun is setting.

APRIL 11, 1857

This is the critical season of a river—when it is fullest of life, its
flowering season, the wavelets or ripples on its surface answering
to the scales of the fishes beneath....

    Our Concord River is a *dead* stream in more senses than we
had supposed.[7] In what sense now does the spring ever come to
the river—when the sun is not reflected from the scales of a single
salmon, shad, or alewife! No doubt there is *some* compensation for
this loss—but I do not at this moment see clearly what it is. That
river which the aboriginal and indigenous fishes have not deserted
is a more primitive and interesting river to me. It is as if some vital
quality were to be lost out of a man's blood—and it were to circu-
late more lifelessly through his veins.

APRIL 11, 1858

I notice at the Conantum house, of which only the chimney and
frame now stands, a triangular mass of rubbish, more than half
a bushel, resting on the great mantel-tree against an angle in the
chimney. It being mixed with clay, I at first thought it a mass of
clay and straw mortar, to fill up with, but looking further I found
it composed of corn cobs, etc. and the excrement probably of rats,
of this form and size—and of pure clay. Looking like the cells of
an insect. ⟋ Either the wharf rat [black rat] or this country
rat [brown rat]. They had anciently chosen this warm place for their
nest, and carried a great store of eatables thither—and the clay of

43

the chimney washing down had incrusted the whole mass over. So this was an old rats' nest as well as human nest—and so it is with every old house. The rats' nest may have been a hundred and fifty years old. Wherever you see an old house there look for an old rats' nest. In hard times they had apparently been *compelled* to eat the clay—or it may be that they love it. It is a wonder they had not set the house on fire with their nest.

APRIL 12, 1856
There suddenly flits before me and alights on a small apple tree in Mackay's field as I go to my boat a splendid purple finch. Its glowing redness is revealed when it lifts its wings—as when the ashes are blown from a coal of fire. Just as the oriole displays its gold.

APRIL 13, 1860
At first I had felt disinclined to make this excursion up the Assabet—but it distinctly occurred to me that perhaps if I come against my will as it were to look at the sweet gale as a matter of business, I might discover something else interesting, as when I discovered the sheldrake. As I was paddling past the uppermost hemlocks I saw two peculiar and plump birds near me on the bank there—which reminded me of the cow blackbird [brown-headed cowbird] and of the oriole at first. I saw at once that they were new to me—and guessed that they were [red] crossbills, which was the case—*male* and *female*. The former was dusky greenish (through a glass), orange, and red, the orange, etc. on head, breast, and rump. The vent white. Dark large bill. The female more of a dusky slate color and yellow instead of orange and red. They were very busily eating the seeds of the hemlock, whose cones were strewn over the ground and they were very fearless, allowing me to approach quite near.

When I returned this way I looked for them again—and at the larger hemlocks heard a peculiar note *cheep, cheep, cheep, cheep,* in

44

the rhythm of a fish hawk [osprey] but faster and rather loud—and looking up saw them fly to the north side and alight on the top of a swamp white oak, while I sat in my boat close under the south bank. But immediately they recrossed and went to feeding on the bank within a rod of me. They were very parrot-like both in color (especially the male, greenish and orange, etc.) and in their manner of feeding—holding the hemlock cones in one claw and rapidly extracting the seeds with their bills. Thus trying one cone after another very fast. But they kept their bills a-going so that near as they were I did not distinguish the *cross*. I should have looked at them in *profile*. At last the two hopped within six feet of me and one within four feet—and they were coming still nearer, as if partly from curiosity, though nibbling the cones all the while when my chain fell down and rattled loudly for the wind shook the boat—and they flew off a rod.

APRIL 14, 1852

Going down the railroad at nine A.M. I hear the lark singing from over the snow. This for steady singing comes next to the robin now. It will come up very sweet from the meadows ere long.... The slate-colored snow bird's [dark-eyed junco] (for they are still about) is a somewhat shrill jingle like the sound of ramrods—when the order has been given to a regiment to "return ramrods" and they obey stragglingly....

I saw the first white-bellied swallows [tree swallows] (about the house) on the morning of the 10th, as I have said—and that day also I saw them skimming over the Great Meadows, as if they had come to all parts of the town at once.

APRIL 15, 1852

What a novel life to be introduced to a dead sucker floating on the water in the spring! Where was it spawned, pray? The sucker is so recent, so unexpected, so unrememberable, so unanticipatable a creation. While so many institutions are gone by the board and we are despairing of men and of ourselves there seems to be life even in a dead sucker — whose fellows at least are alive. The world never looks more recent or promising — religion, philosophy, poetry — than when viewed from this point. To see a sucker tossing on the spring flood — its swelling imbricated breast heaving up a bait to not-despairing gulls. It is a strong and a strengthening sight. Is the world coming to an end? Ask the chubs. As long as fishes spawn — glory and honor to the cold-blooded who despair. As long as ideas are expressed, as long as friction makes bright, as long as vibrating wires make music of harps — we do not want redeemers. What a volume you might [write] on the separate virtues of the various animals — the black duck and the rest.

How indispensable our one or two flocks of geese in spring and autumn. What would be a spring in which that sound was not heard. Coming to unlock the fetters of northern rivers. Those annual steamers of the air.

APRIL 15, 1854

I see the white undersides of many purple finches busily and silently feeding on the elm blossoms within a few feet of me — and now and then their bloody heads and breasts. They utter a faint clear chip. Their feathers are much ruffled.... The arrival of the purple finches appears to be coincident with the blossoming of the elm — on whose blossoms it feeds.

APRIL 15, 1855

The Great Meadows are covered, except a small island in their midst, but not a duck do we see there. On a low limb of a maple on the edge of the river, thirty rods from the present shore we saw a fish hawk eating a fish. Sixty rods off we could see his white crest. We landed and got nearer by stealing through the woods. His legs looked long as he stood up on the limb with his back to us — and his body looked black against the sky and by contrast with the white of his head. There was a dark stripe on the side of the head. He had got the fish under his feet on the limb, and would bow his head, snatch a mouthful, and then look hastily over his right shoulder in our direction—then snatch another mouthful and look over his left shoulder. At length he launched off and flapped heavily away. We found at the bottom of the water beneath where he sat numerous fragments of the fish he had been eating, parts of the fins, entrails, gills, etc. and some was dropped on the bough. From one fin which I examined, I judged that it was either a sucker or a pout [brown bullhead]. There were small leeches adhering to it.

APRIL 15, 1859

The bay-wing [vesper sparrow][8] now sings—the first I have been able to hear—both about the Texas[9] house and the fields this side of Hayden's, both of them similar dry and open pastures. I heard it just before noon when the sun began to come out, and at 3 P.M., singing loud and clear and incessantly. It sings with a pleasing de-liberation—contrasting with the spring vivacity of the song spar-row, whose song many would confound it with. It comes to revive with its song the dry uplands and pastures and grass fields about the skirts of villages. Only think how finely life is furnished in all its de-tails. Sweet wild birds provided to fill its interstices with song! It is provided that while we are employed in our corporeal or intellectual or other exercises we shall be lulled and amused—or cheered by the singing of birds. When the laborer rests on his spade today—the sun having just come out—he is not left wholly to the mercy of his thoughts. Nature is not a mere void to him, but he can hardly fail to hear the pleasing and encouraging notes of some newly arrived bird. The strain of the grass finch [vesper sparrow] is very likely to fall on his ear and convince him whether he is conscious of it or not that the world is beautiful and life a fair enterprise to engage in. It will make him calm and contented. If you yield for a moment to the impressions of sense—you hear some bird giving expression to its happiness in a pleasant strain. We are provided with singing birds and with ears to hear them. What an institution that. Nor are we obliged to catch and cage them, nor to be bird-fanciers in the common sense. Whether a man's work be hard or easy—whether he be happy or unhappy—a bird is appointed to sing to a man while he is at his work.

APRIL 15, 1859

The warm pine woods are all alive this afternoon with the jingle of the pine warbler. The for the most part invisible minstrel. That wood for example at the Punk Oak—where we sit to hear it. . . . That wood is now very handsome seen from the westerly side, the sun falling far through it—though some trunks are wholly in shade. This warbler impresses me as if it were calling the trees to life. I think of springing twigs. Its jingle rings through the wood at short intervals—as if like an electric shock it imparted a fresh spring life to them. You hear the same bird, now here now there, as it incessantly flits about—commonly invisible—and uttering its simple jingle on very different keys, and from time to time a companion is heard farther or nearer.

This is a peculiarly summer-like sound. Go to a warm pine woodside on a pleasant day at this season after storm, and hear it ring with the jingle of the pine warbler.

APRIL 16, 1852

As I turned around the corner of Hubbard's Grove saw a woodchuck—the first of the season, in the middle of the field six or seven rods from the fence which bounds the wood and twenty rods distant. I ran along the fence and cut him off or rather overtook him though he started at the same time. When I was only a rod and a half off, he stopped—and I did the same; then he ran again, and I ran up within three feet of him—when he stopped

again the fence being between us. I squatted down and surveyed him at my leisure. . . .

It appeared to tremble, or perchance shivered with cold. When I moved it gritted its teeth quite loud—sometimes striking the under jaw against the other chatteringly, sometimes grinding one jaw on the other. Yet as if more from instinct than anger. Whichever way I turned that way it headed. I took a twig a foot long and touched its snout—at which it started forward and bit the stick, lessening the distance between us to two feet—and still it held all the ground it gained. I played with it tenderly awhile with the stick trying to open its gritting jaws. Ever its long incisors two above and two below were presented. But I thought it would go to sleep if I stayed long enough. It did not sit upright as sometimes but *standing* on its fore feet with its head down, i.e. half sitting half standing.

We sat looking at one another about half an hour—till we began to feel mesmeric influences. When I was tired I moved away, wishing to see him run, but I could not start him. He would not stir as long as I was looking at him or could see him. I walked round him—he turned as fast and fronted me still. I sat down by his side within a foot. I talked to him *quasi* forest lingo, baby-talk, at any rate in a conciliatory tone and thought that I had some influence on him. He gritted his teeth less. I chewed checkerberry leaves and presented them to his nose at last without a grit. Though I saw that by so much gritting of the teeth he had worn them rapidly and they were covered with a fine white powder—which if you measured it thus would have made his anger terrible. He did not mind any noise I might make. With a little stick I lifted one of his paws to examine it and held it up at pleasure. I turned him over to see what color he was beneath (darker or more purely brown) though he turned himself back again sooner than I could have wished. His tail was also all brown though not very dark—rat-tail like with loose hairs standing out on all sides like a caterpillar brush. He had a rather mild look. I spoke kindly to him. I reached checkerberry leaves to his mouth. I stretched my hands over him—though he turned up his head and still gritted a little. I laid my hand on him, but immediately took it off again—instinct not being wholly overcome. If I had had a few fresh bean leaves thus in advance of the season I am sure I should have tamed him completely. It was a frizzly tail. His is a humble terrestrial color like the partridge's, well concealed where dead wiry grass rises above darker brown or chestnut dead leaves—a modest color. If I had had some food I should have ended with stroking him at my leisure. Could easily have wrapped him in my handkerchief. He was not fat—nor particularly lean. I finally had to leave him without seeing him move from the place.

A large clumsy burrowing squirrel. *Arctomys* (bear-mouse?). I respect him as one of the natives. He lies there by his color and habits so naturalized amid the dry leaves—the withered grass and the bushes. A sound nap too he has enjoyed in his native fields, the past winter. I think I might learn some wisdom of him. His ancestors have lived here longer than mine. He is more thoroughly acclimated and naturalized than I. Bean leaves the red man raised for him—but he can do without them.

APRIL 16, 1855
A striped snake rustles down a dry open hillside where the withered grass is long.

APRIL 16, 1855
Anon alights near us a flock of golden-eyes—*surely* with their great black (looking) heads and a white patch on the side, short stumpy bills (after looking at the mergansers). Much clear black—contrasting with much clear white. Their heads and bills look ludicrously short and parrot-like after the others. Our presence and a boat party on the pond [Flint's Pond] at last drove nearly all the ducks into the deep easterly cove.

APRIL 16, 1855
I am startled sometimes these mornings to hear the sound of [mourning] doves alighting on the roof just over my head—they come down so hard upon it, as if one had thrown a heavy stick on to it, and I wonder it does not injure their organization. Their legs must be cushioned in their sockets to save them from the shock.

APRIL 16, 1856
The robins sing with a will now—what a burst of melody! It gurgles out of all conduits now—they are choked with it. There is such a tide and rush of song as when a river is straightened between two rocky walls. It seems as if the morning's throat were not large enough to emit all this sound.

APRIL 17, 1852
When I was young and compelled to pass my Sunday in the house without the aid of interesting books, I used to spend many an hour till the wished-for sundown watching the [purple] martins soar (from an attic window)—and fortunate indeed did I deem myself when a hawk appeared in the heavens though far toward the

horizon against a downy cloud—and I searched for hours till I had found his mate. They at least took my thoughts from earthly things.

APRIL 17, 1854

Every shopkeeper makes a record of the arrival of the first martin or bluebird to his box. Dodd the broker told me last spring that he knew when the first bluebird came to his boxes—he made a memorandum of it. John Brown, merchant, tells me this morning that the martins first came to his box on the 13th—he "made a minute of it." Beside so many entries in their day books and ledgers—they record these things.

APRIL 17, 1856

I love to hear the voice of the first thunder as of the toad (though it returns irregularly like pigeons) far away in *his* moist meadow where he is warmed to life, and see the flash of his eye.

APRIL 17, 1859

How pleasing and soothing are some of the first and least audible sounds of awakened nature in the spring! As this first humming of bees, etc.—and the stuttering of frogs. They cannot be called musical—are no more even than a noise, so slight that we can endure it. But it is in part an expression of happiness—an ode that is sung, and whose burden fills the air. It reminds me of the increased genialness of nature. The air which was so lately void and silent begins to resound as it were with the breathing of a myriad fellow creatures, and even the unhappy man, on the principle that misery loves company is soothed by this infinite din of neighbors. I have listened for the notes of various birds—and now, in this faint hum of bees, I hear as it were the first twittering of the bird Summer.... The notes of birds are interrupted—but the hum of insects is incessant. I suppose that the motion of the wings of the small tipulidae [crane flies] which have swarmed for some weeks produced a humming appreciated by some ears. Perhaps the [eastern] phoebe heard and was charmed by it. Thus *gradually* the spaces of the air are filled. Nature has taken equal care to cushion our ears on this finest sound—and to inspire us with the strains of the wood thrush and poet. We may say that each gnat is made to vibrate its wings for man's fruition.

In short we hear but little music in the world which charms us more than this sound produced by the vibration of an insect's wing and in some still and sunny nook in spring.

APRIL 17, 1859

I heard lately the voice of a hound hunting by itself. What an awful sound to the denizens of the wood! That relentless voracious demonic cry—like the voice of a fiend! At hearing of which, the fox, hare, marmot, etc. tremble for their young and themselves, imagining the worst. This however is the sound which the lords of creation love to accompany and follow with their bugles and "mellow horns"—conveying a similar dread to the hearers—instead of whispering peace to the hare's palpitating breast.

APRIL 18, 1852

The sight of the sucker floating on the meadow at this season affects me singularly, as if it were a fabulous or mythological fish—realizing my *idea* of a fish. It reminds me of pictures of dolphins or of Proteus. I see it for what it is—not an actual terrene fish, but the fair symbol of a divine idea, the design of an artist. Its color and form, its gills and fins and scales, are perfectly beautiful—because they completely express to my mind what they were intended to express. It is as little fishy as a fossil fish.

For the first time I perceive this spring that the year is a circle. I see distinctly the spring arc thus far. It is drawn with a firm line. Every incident is a parable of the great teacher. The cranberries washed up in the meadows and into the road on the causeway now yield a pleasant acid.

Why should just these sights and sounds accompany our life? Why should I hear the chattering of blackbirds—why smell the skunk each year? I would fain explore the mysterious relation between myself and these things. I would at least know what these things unavoidably are—make a chart of our life, know how its shores trend, that butterflies reappear and when—know why just this circle of creatures completes the world. Can I not by expectation affect the revolutions of nature—make a day to bring forth something new?

APRIL 18, 1858

Frogs are strange creatures. One would describe them as peculiarly wary and timid—another as equally bold and imperturbable. All that is required in studying them is patience. You will sometimes walk a long way along a ditch—and hear twenty or more leap in one after another before you—and see where they rippled the water, without getting sight of one of them. Sometimes as this afternoon the two *R. fontinalis* [green frog], when you approach a pool or spring a frog hops in and buries itself at the bottom. You sit down on the brink and wait patiently for his reappearance. After a quarter of an hour or more he is seen to rise to the surface and put out his nose quietly without making a ripple—eying you steadily. At length he becomes as curious about you as you can be about him. He suddenly hops straight toward [you] pausing within a foot— and takes a near and leisurely view of you. Perchance you may now scratch its nose with your finger—and examine it to your heart's content for it is become as imperturbable as it was shy before. You conquer them by superior patience and immovableness—not by quickness but by slowness, not by heat but by coldness. You see only a pair of heels disappearing in the weedy bottom and saving a few insects the pool becomes as smooth as a mirror and apparently as uninhabited. At length, after half an hour you detect a frog's snout and a pair of eyes above the green slime, turned toward you—etc.

great blue heron

APRIL 19, 1852

Scared up three [great] blue herons in the little pond close by—
quite near us. It was a grand sight to see them rise. So slow and
stately—so long and limber with an undulating motion. From head
to foot undulating also their large wings—undulating in two directions and looking warily about them. 〰〰〰 With
this graceful limber undulating motion they arose—as if so they
got under way, their two legs trailing parallel far behind like an
earthy residuum to be left behind. They are large like birds of Syrian

lands and seemed to oppress the earth—and hush the hillside to silence as they winged their way over it—looking back toward us. It would affect our thoughts—deepen and perchance darken our reflections if such huge birds flew in numbers in our sky. They are few and rare.[10]

APRIL 19, 1852
Stopped in the barn on the Baker Farm. Sat in the dry meadow hay—where the mice nest. To sit there rustling the hay just beyond reach of the rain while the storm roars without—it suggested an inexpressible dry stillness, the quiet of the haymow in a rainy day. Such stacks of quiet and undisturbed thought, when there is not even a cricket to stir in the hay, but all without is wet and tumultuous, and all within is dry and quiet. Oh what reams of thought one might have here.

APRIL 19, 1855
From Heywood's Peak I thought I saw the head of a loon in the pond, thirty-five or forty rods distant. Bringing my glass to bear, it seemed sunk very low in the water—all the neck concealed—but I could not tell which end was the bill. At length I discovered that it was the whole body of a little duck—asleep with its head in its back exactly in the middle of the pond. It had a moderate-sized black head and neck, a white breast, and *seemed* dark brown above, with a white spot on the side of the head (not reaching to the outside, from base of mandibles) and another, perhaps, on the end of the wing—with some black there. It sat drifting round a little, but with ever its breast toward the wind—and from time to time it raised its head and looked round to see if it were safe. I think it was the smallest duck I ever saw. Floating buoyantly asleep on the middle of Walden Pond. Was it not a female of the buffle-headed or spirit duck? I believed the wings looked blacker when it flew—with some white beneath. It floated like a little casket, and at first I doubted

56

a good while if it possessed life—until I saw it raise its head and look around. It had chosen a place for its nap exactly equidistant between the two shores there—and with its breast to the wind swung round only as much as a vessel held by its anchors in the stream.

At length the [railroad] cars scared it.

APRIL 19, 1858

Spend the day hunting for my boat which was stolen. As I go up the riverside I see a male marsh hawk [northern harrier] hunting. He skims along exactly over the edge of the water on the meadowy side not more than three or four feet from the ground and winding with the shore—looking for frogs for in such a tortuous line do the frogs sit. They probably know about what time to expect his visits—being regularly decimated. Particular hawks farm particular meadows. It must be easy for him to get a breakfast. Far as I can see with a glass, he is still *tilting* this way and that over the water line.

APRIL 21, 1852

On the east side of Ponkawtasset I hear a robin singing cheerily from some perch in the wood—in the midst of the rain. Where the scenery is now wild and dreary. His song a singular antagonism and offset to the storm. As if nature said, "Have faith, these *two* things I can do." It sings with power—like a bird of great faith that sees the bright future through the dark present—to reassure the race of man, like one to whom many talents were given and who will improve its talents. They are sounds to make a dying man live. They sing not their despair. It is a pure immortal melody....

"Did he sing thus in Indian days?" I ask myself—for I have always associated this sound with the village and the clearing, but now I do detect the aboriginal wildness in his strain, and can imagine him a woodland bird—and that he sang thus when there was no civilized ear to hear him, a pure forest melody even like the wood thrush. Every genuine thing retains this wild tone—which no true culture displaces. I heard him even as he might have sounded to the Indian, singing at evening upon the elm above his wigwam — with which was associated in the red man's mind the events of an Indian's life. His childhood. Formerly I had heard in it only those strains which tell of the white man's village life — now I heard those strains which remembered the red man's life, such as fell on the ears of Indian children. As he sang when these arrowheads which the rain has made shine so on the lean stubble field were fastened to their shaft.

APRIL 21, 1855
At Cliffs, I hear at a distance a wood thrush.[11] It affects us as a part of our unfallen selves.

APRIL 22, 1857
Near Tall's Island rescued a little pale or yellowish brown snake that was coiled around a willow half a dozen rods from the shore — and was apparently chilled by the cold. Was it not Storer's "little brown snake"? It had a flat body.

APRIL 22, 1859
When setting the pines at Walden the last three days I was sung to by the field sparrow. For music I heard their jingle from time to time — that the music the pines were set to — and I have no doubt they will build many a nest under their shelter. It would seem as if such a field as this (a dry open or half open pasture in the woods, with small pines scattered in it) was well nigh, if not quite abandoned to this one alone among the sparrows. The surface of the earth is portioned out among them. By a beautiful law of distribution, one creature does not too much interfere with another. . . .

Yet as the walls of cities are fabled to have been built by music, so my pines were established by the song of the field sparrow. They commonly place their nests here under the shelter of a little pine in the field.

APRIL 22, 1860
See now hen hawks, a pair soaring high as for pleasure—circling ever further and further away, as if it were midsummer. The peculiar flight of a hawk thus fetches the year about. I do not see it soar in this serene and leisurely manner very early in the season methinks.

APRIL 23, 1854
Saw my white-headed eagle again, first at the same place, the outlet of Fair Haven Pond. It was a fine sight. He is mainly—i.e. his wings and body—so black against the sky, and they contrast so strongly with his white head and tail. He was first flying low over the water; then rose gradually and circled westward toward White Pond. Lying on the ground with my glass I could watch him very easily—and by turns he gave me all possible views of himself. When I observed him edgewise I noticed that the tips of his wings curved upward slightly the more like a stereotyped undulation. ⌒ ⌒ He rose very high at last—till I almost lost him in the clouds—circling or rather *looping* along westward high over river and wood and farm, effectually concealed in the sky. ⌒ᘓ ᘒ ᘓ

APRIL 23, 1856
A very handsome little beetle, deep, about a quarter of an inch long, with *pale* golden wing cases artificially and handsomely marked with burnished dark green marks and spots, one side answering to the other. Front and beneath burnished dark green—legs brown or cinnamon color. It was on the side of my boat. Brought it home in a clam's shells tied up—a good insect box.

The [belted] kingfisher flies with a *crack cr-r-r-ack* and a limping or flitting flight from tree to tree before us and finally after a third of a mile circles round to our rear. He sits rather low over the water. Now that he has come I suppose that the fishes on which he preys rise within reach.

APRIL 25, 1841

A momentous silence reigns always in the woods—and their meaning seems just ripening into expression. But alas! they make no haste. The rush sparrow [field sparrow]—nature's minstrel of serene hours—sings of an immense leisure and duration.

APRIL 25, 1854

Saw a ruby-crested wren[12] [ruby-crowned kinglet] in the woods near Goose Pond.... It sounded far off—and like an imitation of a robin—a long strain and often repeated. I was quite near it before I was aware of it, it sounding still like a faint imitation of a robin— and of a golden robin [oriole] which later I often mistook for him.

Some chickadees and yellow redpolls [palm warblers] were first apparent, then my wren on the pitch pines and young oaks. He appeared curious to observe me. A very interesting and active little fellow darting about amid the treetops, and his song quite remarkable and rich and loud for his size. Begins with a very fine note before its pipes are filled—not audible at a little distance—then *woriter weter*, etc., etc., winding up with *teter teter* all clear and round. His song is comical and reminds me of the [brown] thrasher. This was at 4 P.M. when most birds do not sing. I saw it yesterday pluming itself and stretching its little wings.

APRIL 25, 1854

The first partridge drums in one or two places. As if the earth's pulse now beat audibly with the increased flow of life. It slightly flutters all Nature and makes her heart palpitate. Also, as I stand listening for the wren, and sweltering in my greatcoat, I hear the woods filled with the hum of insects—as if my hearing were affected—and thus the summer's quire begins.

APRIL 25, 1855
Hear a faint cheep and at length detect the white-throated sparrow—the handsome and well-marked bird, the largest of the sparrows with a yellow spot on each side of the front. Hopping along under the rubbish left by the woodchopper.... I first saw the white-throated sparrow at this date last year.

APRIL 25, 1859
Methinks I hear through the wind today, and it was the same yesterday—a very faint low ringing of toads, as if distant and just begun. It is an indistinct undertone—and I am *far from sure* that I *hear* anything. It may be all imagination.

APRIL 26, 1857
See on the water over the meadow north of the boat's place twenty rods from the nearest shore and twice as much from the opposite shore a very large striped snake [eastern ribbon snake] swimming. It swims with great ease and lifts its head a foot above the water darting its tongue at us.... This one when we approached swam toward the boat apparently to rest on it and when I put out my paddle at once coiled itself partly around it and allowed itself to be taken on board. It did not hang down from the paddle like a dead snake—but stiffened and curved its body in a loose coil about it....

This snake was killed about 2 P.M.—i.e. the head was perfectly killed then—yet the posterior half of the body was apparently quite alive and would curl strongly around the hand at 7 P.M. It had been hanging on a tree in the meanwhile.

I have the same objection to killing a snake that I have to the killing of any other animal—yet the most humane man that I know never omits to kill one.

I see a great many beetles, etc. floating and struggling on the flood.

We sit on the shore at Wheeler's fence opposite Merriam's. At this season still we go seeking the sunniest most sheltered and warmest place. C. [Channing] says this is the warmest place he has been in this year. We are in this like snakes that lie out on banks. In sunny and sheltered nooks we are in our best estate. There our thoughts flow and we flourish most.

APRIL 27, 1852
Observed the spotted tortoise in the water of the meadow on J. Hosmer's land. By riverside. Bright yellow spots on both shell and head, yet not regularly disposed, but as if when they were finished in other respects—the maker had sprinkled them with a brush. This fact, that the yellow spots are common to the shell and the head—affected me considerably as evincing the action of an artist from without. Spotted with reference to my eyes.

APRIL 27, 1854
The wood thrush afar—so superior a strain to that of other birds. I was doubting if it would affect me as of yore but it did measurably. I did not believe there could be such differences. This is the gospel according to the wood thrush. He makes a sabbath out of a week day. I could go to hear him—could buy a pew in his church. Did he ever practice pulpit eloquence? He is right on the slavery question.

APRIL 28, 1856
As I was measuring along the Marlborough Road—a fine little blue-slate [spring azure] butterfly fluttered over the chain. Even its feeble strength was required to fetch the year about. How daring,

even rash Nature appears who sends out butterflies so early! Sardanapalus-like — she loves extremes and contrasts.

APRIL 28, 1860

As you stand by such a willow in bloom and resounding with the hum of bees in a warm afternoon like this you seem nearer to summer — than elsewhere.

Again I am advertised of the approach of a new season, as yesterday. The air is not only warmer and stiller — but has more of meaning or smothered voice to it, now that the hum of insects begins to be heard. You seem to have a great companion with you. Are reassured by the scarcely audible hum, as if it were the noise of your own thinking. It is a voiceful and significant stillness — such as precedes a thunderstorm or a hurricane. The boisterous spring winds cease to blow, the waves to dash — the migrating ducks to vex the air so much. You are sensible of a certain repose in nature.

APRIL 29, 1851

The very dogs and cats incline to affection in their relation to man. It often happens that a man is more humanely related to a cat or dog than to any human being. What bond is it relates us to any animal we keep in the house but the bond of affection. In a degree we grow to love one another.

APRIL 29, 1857

A steel blue black flattish beetle which handled imparted a very disagreeable carrion-like scent to fingers.

APRIL 30, 1852

I hear a wood thrush here [Saw Mill Run] with a fine metallic ring to his note. This sound most adequately expresses the immortal beauty and wildness of the woods. I go in search of him. He sounds no nearer. On a low bough of a small maple near the brook in the swamp he sits with ruffled feathers singing more low or with less power—as it were ventriloquizing for though I am scarcely more than a rod off, he seems further off than ever.

APRIL 30, 1852

Caught three little peeping frogs. When I approached and my shadow fell on the water I heard a peculiarly trilled and more rapidly vibrated note (somewhat in kind like that which a hen makes to warn her chickens when a hawk goes over) and most stopped peeping; another trill and all stopped. It seemed to be a note of alarm. I caught one. It proved to be two coupled. They remained together in my hand. This sound has connection with their loves probably. (I hear a trilled sound from a frog this evening. It is my dreaming midsummer frog, and he seems to be toward the depot.) I find them generally sitting on the dead leaves near the water's edge from which they leap into the water.

APRIL 30, 1856

A fine morning. I hear the first brown thrasher singing within three or four rods of me on the shrubby hillside in front of the Hadley place.... Surveying seemed a noble employment which brought me within hearing of this bird. I was trying to get the exact course of a wall thickly beset with shrub oaks and birches, making an opening through them with axe and knife—while the hillside seemed to quiver or pulsate with the sudden melody. Again it is with the side of the ear that you hear—the music or the beauty belong not to your work itself but some of its accompaniments. You would fain devote yourself to the melody, but you will hear more of it if you devote yourself to your work.

MAY 1, 1852

A smart frost in the night—the plowed ground and platforms white with it. I hear the little forked-tail chipping sparrow (*Frin-*

gilla socialis) shaking out his rapid *tchi-tchi-tchi-tchi-tchi-tchi*—a little jingle from the oak behind the Depot. I hear the note of the shy Savannah sparrow (*F. savanna*), that plump bird with a dark streaked breast that runs and hides in the grass, whose note sounds so like a cricket's in the grass. [*Penciled addition:* Probably have seen it before—seringo.][13] (I used to hear it when I walked by moonlight last summer.) I hear it now from deep in the sod—for there is hardly grass yet. The bird keeps so low you do not see it. You do not suspect how many there are till at length their heads appear. The word *seringo* reminds me of its note—as if it were produced by some kind of fine metallic spring. It is an earth sound.

MAY 1, 1857

First notice the ring of the toad. As I am crossing the Common in front of the Meeting House. There is a cool and breezy south wind—and the ring of the first toad leaks into the general stream of sound, unnoticed by most, as the mill brook empties into the river and the voyager cannot tell if he is above or below its mouth. The bell was ringing for town meeting—and everyone heard it—but none heard this older and more universal bell rung by more native Americans all the land over. It is a sound from amid the

American toad

waves of the aerial sea—that breaks on our ears with the surf of the air, a sound that is almost breathed with the wind taken into the lungs, instead of being heard by the ears. It comes from far over or through the troughs of the aerial sea—like a petrel—and who can guess by what pool the singer sits? whether behind the Meeting House horse-sheds, or over the Burying Ground Hill, or from the riverside. A new reign has commenced. Bufo the First has ascended to his throne, the surface of the earth, led into office by the south wind. Bufo the Double-chinned inflates his throat. Attend to his message. Take off your greatcoats, swains! and prepare for the summer campaign. Hop a few paces further toward your goals. The measures I shall advocate are warmth, moisture, and low-flying insects.

MAY 1, 1858

The old *Salix sericea* [silky willow] is now all alive with the hum of honeybees. This would show that it is in bloom. I see and hear one humblebee among them—inaugurating summer with his deep bass. May it be such a summer to me as it suggests. It sounds a little like mockery however to cheat me again with the promise of such tropical opportunities. I have learned to suspect him, as I do all fortune-tellers. But no sound so brings round the summer again. It is like the drum of May training. This reminds me that men and boys and the most enlightened communities still love to march after the beating of a drum as do the most aboriginal of savages.

MAY 1, 1859

Hear the ruby-crowned wren.

MAY 1, 1859

We accuse savages of worshipping only the Bad Spirit or Devil, though they may distinguish both a Good and a Bad—but they regard only that one which they fear and worship the Devil only.

We too are savages in this—doing precisely the same thing. This oc-curred to me yesterday—as I sat in the woods admiring the beauty of the blue butterfly....

The catechism says that the chief end of man is to glorify God—and enjoy him forever—which of course is applicable mainly to God as seen in his works. Yet the only account of its beautiful insects, butterflies, etc. which God has made and set before us—which the State ever thinks of spending any money on—is the ac-count of those which are injurious to vegetation! This is the way we glorify God and enjoy him forever. Come out here and be-hold a thousand painted butterflies and other beautiful insects—which people the air—then go to the libraries and see what kind of prayer and glorification of God is there recorded. Massachusetts has published her report on "Insects Injurious to Vegetation," and our neighbor the "Noxious Insects of New York." We have attended to the evil and said nothing about the good. This is looking a gift horse in the mouth with a vengeance. Children are attracted by the beauty of butterflies but their parents and legislators deem it an idle pursuit. The parents remind me of the Devil—but the children of God. Though God may have pronounced his work good, we ask, Is it not poisonous?

MAY 3, 1852
Heard some kind of dorbug [scarab beetle] approaching with a hum as I sat in a meadow this afternoon and it struck the ground near me with as much noise as a bullet—as if someone had fired at me with an air gun.

MAY 3, 1852
The moon is full. The air is filled with a certain luminous liquid white light.... Going through the Depot Field, I hear the dream frog at a distance; the little peeping frogs make a background of sound in the horizon which you do not hear unless you attend.

The former is a trembling note—some higher some lower along the edge of the earth, an all-pervading sound.

MAY 3, 1855
A butterfly [eastern tailed blue] one inch in alar extent—dark velvety brown with slate colored tips—on dry leaves.

MAY 3, 1857
In another pool in Warren's meadow I hear the ring of toads and the peep of hylodes—and taking off my stockings and shoes at length stand in their midst. There are a hundred toads close around me—copulating or preparing to. These look at a little distance precisely like the last, but no one utters the peculiar rough belching croak—only their common musical ring—and occasionally a short fainter interrupted quivering note as of alarm.... One that rings within a foot of me seems to make the earth vibrate—and I feel it and am thrilled to my very spine, it is so terrene a sound. It reminds me of many a summer night on the river....

When that nearest ringer sounded the very sod by my feet (whose spires rose above water) seemed to tremble—and the earth itself—and I was thrilled to my spine and vibrated to it. They like a rest for their toes when they ring. It is a sound as crowded with protuberant bubbles as the rind of an orange. A clear ringing note with a bubbling trill. It takes complete possession of you—for you vibrate to it, and can hear nothing else.

MAY 4, 1855
Sitting in Abel Brooks' Hollow, see a *small* hawk go over high in the air—with a long tail and distinct from wings. It advanced by a sort of limping flight yet rapidly—not circling, nor tacking, but flapping briskly at intervals and then gliding straight ahead with rapidity, controlling itself with its tail. It seemed to be going a journey. Was it not the sharp-shinned, or *Falco fuscus?*

MAY 4, 1855

Found a black snake's skeleton [North American racer] — remarked the globular protuberance on which the vertebrae revolve, and the four (?) sharp recurved teeth in the lower jaw.

MAY 4, 1858

I find hopping in the meadow a *Rana halecina* [northern leopard frog] — much brighter than any I have seen this year. There is not only a vivid green halo about each spot, but the *back is vivid light green between the spots.* I think this was not the case with any of the hundreds I saw a month ago!! Why?? The brassy lines along the sides of the back are narrower (only about 1/16 of an inch) and more prominent than the more fawn-colored lines of the *R. palustris.* In this one, which I carry home and compare with the palustris, there is a large spot on each orbit but none on the top of the head in front. It is *all white* beneath — except a *tinge* of greenish yellow on the abdomen.

MAY 4, 1859

Looking up through this soft and warm southwest wind I notice the conspicuous shadow of Middle Conantum Cliff now at 3 P.M., and elsewhere the shade of a few apple trees — their trunks and boughs.... This I *notice* at *the same time* with the first bumblebee, when the *Rana palustris* purrs in the meadow generally. The white willow and aspen display their tender green full of yellow light. The particolored warbler [northern parula] is first heard over the swamp. The woodchuck, who loves warmth, is out on the hillsides in numbers. The jingle of the chip-bird [chipping sparrow] is *incessantly* heard. The thrasher sings incessantly. The first [field] cricket is heard in a warm rocky place, and that scent of vernal flowers is in the air.

MAY 4, 1859

It would require a good deal of time and patience to study the habits of woodchucks. They are so shy—and watchful. They hear the least sound of a footstep on the ground—and are quick to see also. One should go clad in a suit somewhat like their own. The warp of tawny and the woof of green, and then with a painted or well-tanned face he might lie out on a sunny bank till they appeared.

MAY 5, 1857

Have dug up in the garden this season half a dozen of those great leather-colored pupae (with the tongue case bent round to breast like a long urn handle) of the sphinx moth.

MAY 5, 1860

See at Lee's a pewee (phoebe) building. She has just woven in, or laid on the edge, a fresh sprig of saxifrage in flower. I notice that phoebes will build in the same recess in a cliff year after year. It is a constant thing here, though they are often disturbed. Think how many pewees must have built under the eaves of this cliff since pewees were created and this cliff itself built! You can possibly find the crumbling relics of how many, if you should look carefully enough! It takes us many years to find out that Nature repeats herself annually. But how perfectly regular and calculable all her phenomena must appear to a mind that has observed her for a thousand years!

MAY 6, 1852

My dream frog turns out to be a toad. I watched half a dozen a long time at 3:30 this afternoon in Hubbard's Pool, where they were frogging (?) lustily. They sit in the shade, either partly in the water or on a stick looked darker and narrower in proportion to their length than toads usually do, and moreover are aquatic. I see them jump into the ditches as I walk. After an interval of silence one appeared to be gulping the wind into his belly, inflating himself so that he was considerably expanded, then he discharged it all into his throat while his body or belly collapsed suddenly—expanding his throat to a remarkable size. Was nearly a minute inflating itself— then swelled out its sac which is rounded and reminded me of the bag to a work table, holding its head up the while. It is whitish specked (the bag) on a dull bluish or slate ground. Much bigger than all the rest of the head and nearly an inch in diameter. It was a ludicrous sight with their so serious prominent eyes peering over it and a deafening sound when several were frogging at once as I was leaning over them.... The mouth to be shut always and perhaps the air was expelled through the nostrils. The strain appeared prolonged as long as the air lasted—and was sometimes quavered or made intermittent apparently by closing the orifice, whatever it was, on the blast.... Close by it is an unmusical monotonous deafening sound, a steady blast (not a peep nor a croak but a *kind* of piping) but far away it is a dreamy lulling sound, and fills well the crevices of nature....

The music of all creatures has to do with their loves, even of toads and frogs. Is it not the same with man?

MAY 7, 1852
The red-wing's shoulder seen in a favorable light throws all epaulets into the shade. It is General Abercrombie methinks when they wheel partly with the red to me.

MAY 8, 1857
The full moon rises—and I paddle by its light. It is an evening for the soft-snoring *purring* frogs (which I suspect to be *Rana palustris*). I get within a few feet of them as they sit along the edge of

the river and meadow but cannot see them. Their croak is very fine and rapid—and has a soft purring sound at a little distance. I see them paddling in the water like toads.

Within a week I have had made a pair of corduroy pants—which cost when done $1.60. They are of that peculiar clay color, reflecting the light from portions of their surface. They have this advantage, that beside being very strong they will look about as well three months hence as now—or as ill some would say. . . . The birds and beasts are not *afraid* of me now. A mink came within twenty feet of me the other day as soon as my companion had left me—and if I had had my gray sack on as well as my corduroys, it would perhaps have come quite up to me.

MAY 8, 1860
The night warbler's note.

MAY 9, 1853
I have devoted most of my day to Mr. [Bronson] Alcott. . . . We wade so gently and reverently—or we pull together so smoothly that the fishes of thought are not scared from the stream, but come and go grandly like yonder clouds that float peacefully through the western sky.

MAY 10, 1853
You hear the clear whistle—and see the red or fiery orange of the oriole darting through Hosmer's orchard. But its note is not melodious and rich. It is at most a clear tone—the healthiest of your city beaux and belles.

MAY 10, 1854
In Boston yesterday an ornithologist said significantly—If you held the bird in your hand—but I would rather hold it in my affections. . . .

Above the railroad bridge I saw a kingfisher twice sustain himself in one place about forty feet above the meadow by a rapid motion of his wings—somewhat like a devil's needle—not progressing an inch, apparently over a fish.

MAY 10, 1858

I hear in several places the low dumping notes of awakened [American] bullfrogs—what I call their *pebbly* notes, as if they were cracking pebbles in their mouths—not the plump *dont dont* or *ker dont,* but *kerdle dont dont.* As if they sat round mumbling pebbles. At length, near Ball's Hill I hear the first regular bullfrog's trump. Some fainter ones far off are very like the looing of cows. This sound heard low and far over meadows when the warmer hours have come grandly inaugurates the summer.... That season which is bounded on the north—on the spring side at least—by the trump of the bullfrog. This note is like the first colored petals within the calyx of a flower. It conducts us toward the germ of the flower *summer.* He knows no winter. I hear in his tone the rumors of summer heat. By this note he summons the season.... It reminds me at once of tepid waters—and of bathing. His trump is to the ear what the yellow lily or spatterdock is to the eye. He swears by the powers of mud.

It is enough for the day to have heard only the first half trump of an early awakened one—from far in some warm meadow bay. It is a certain revelation and anticipation of the livelong summer to come. It gives leave to the corn to grow and to the heavens to thunder and lighten. It gives leave to the invalid to take the air. Our climate is now as tropical as any. It says, Put out your fires and sit in the fire which the sun has kindled.

MAY 10, 1860

Going over the hill behind S. Brown's when we crossed the triangular space between the roads beyond the pump-maker's, I saw countless little heaps of sand like the small ant-hills—but looking more closely the size of the holes (a little less than ¼ of an inch) and the comparative irregularity of the heaps—as if the sand had been brought forth and dropped in greater quantity at once— attracted my attention and I found they were the work of bees. The bees were hovering low over the surface, and were continually entering and issuing from the holes. They were about the size of a honeybee—black bodied with I thought yellow thighs—if it was not pollen. Many of the holes appeared to have been freshly stopped up with granules of moist sand. These holes were made close together in the dry and sandy soil there with very little grass on it sloping toward the west—between the roads—and covered a triangular space some seven rods by three. I counted twenty-four in a square foot. There must have been some twenty-five thousand of these nests in all. The surface was yellowed with them. Evidently a kind of mining bee.

MAY 11, 1853

It must be the myrtle-bird [yellow-rumped warbler] which is now so common in Hubbard's meadow woods—or swamp. With a note somewhat like a yellowbird's [yellow warbler]. Striped olive yellow and black on back or shoulders, light or white beneath. Black chin—restless bird—sharp head.

MAY 11, 1853

I hear the distant drumming of a partridge. Its beat however distant and low falls still with a remarkably forcible, almost painful impulse on the ear—like veritable little drumsticks on our tympanum—as if it were a throbbing or fluttering in our veins or bones or the chambers of the ear and belonging to ourselves. As if it were produced by some little insect which had made its way up into the passages of the ear. So penetrating is it. It is as palpable to the ear as the sharpest note of a fife. Of course, that bird can drum with its wings on a log which can go off with such a powerful whir beating

ruffed grouse

the air. I have seen a thoroughly frightened hen and cockerel fly almost as powerfully—but neither can sustain it long. Beginning slowly and deliberately the partridge's beat sounds faster and faster from far away under the boughs and through the aisles of the wood until it becomes a regular roll—but is speedily concluded. How many things shall we not see and be and do when we walk there where the partridge drums!

MAY 11, 1854

Earliest gooseberry in garden open. Heard a Maryland yellow-throat about alders at Trillium Woods—where I first heard one last year—but it finds the alders cut down in the winter....

The willows on the Turnpike now resound with the hum of bees and I hear the yellowbird and Maryland yellow-throat amid them. These *yellow* birds are concealed by the yellow of the willows.

MAY 11, 1854

Now at last I see crow blackbirds [common grackles] without doubt—they have probably been here before for they are put down under April in the bird book (for '37). They fly as if carrying or dragging their precious long tails (broad at the end) through the air. Their note is like a great rusty spring and also a hoarse chuck. On the whole I think they must have been rusty grackles [rusty black-birds] which I mistook for this bird and I think I saw their silvery irides—look like red-wings without the red spot.

MAY 11, 1855
I trod on a large black snake which as soon as I stepped again went off swiftly down the hill toward the swamp with head erect like a racer. Looking closely I found another left behind, partly concealed by the dry leaves. They were lying amid the leaves in this open wood east of Beck Stow's amid the sweet fern and huckleberry bushes. The remaining one ran out its tongue at me—and vibrated its tail swiftly making quite a noise on the leaves—then darted forward, passed round an oak and *whipped* itself straight down into a hole at its base one and a half inches over. After its head had entered its tail was not long in following.

MAY 11, 1856
There are many swallows circling low over the river behind Mon-roe's—bank swallows, barn, republican [cliff swallow], chimney [chimney swift], and white-bellied. These are all circling together a foot or two over the water—passing within ten or twelve feet of me in my boat. It is remarkable how social the different species of swallow are one with another. They recognize their affinity more than usual.

MAY 11, 1859
Found in the path in the woods by the Mill Brook ditch, Flint's Pond—dead—the *Coluber punctatus* [ring-necked snake], 13¼ inches long—but no row of spots in *middle* of abdomen. The head above blackish with a blackish ring behind the yellow. Tail 3 inches long, breadth of body ⁵⁄₁₆, plates 162, scales 55. Above uniform

glossy slate color with a yellowish white band across the occiput—the head above blackish and a blackish band close behind the yellowish one. Beneath yellow or buff (whitish under head) with a row of small slanting black spots. One on each side of each abdominal plate except the first ¾ inch behind the head. In the midst of the path in the woods. I admired the iridescence from its glossy belly. It differs from Storer's *C. punctatus*[14]—for it is not *brown* above, nor "reddish yellow" beneath, and has no row of spots in middle of the abdomen.

MAY 12, 1857

While dropping beans in the garden at Texas just after sundown (May 13th)[15] I hear from across the fields the note of the bay-wing, *Come here here there there quick quick quick or I'm gone* (which I have no doubt sits on some fence post or rail there) and it instantly translates me from the sphere of my work—and repairs all the world that we jointly inhabit. It reminds me of so many country afternoons and evenings when this bird's strain was heard far over the fields—as I pursued it from field to field. The spirit of its earth song, of its serene and true philosophy was breathed into me and I saw the world as through a glass—as it lies eternally. Some of its aboriginal contentment—even of its domestic felicity—possessed me. What he suggests is permanently true. As the bay-wing sang many a thousand years ago so sang he tonight. In the beginning God heard his song and pronounced it good—and hence it has endured. It reminded me of many a summer sunset—of many miles of gray rails—of many a rambling pasture—of the farmhouse far in the fields—its milk pans and well sweep—and the cows coming home from pasture.

MAY 12, 1858

Found a large water adder [northern water snake]—by the edge of Farmer's large mud-hole, which abounds with tadpoles and frogs on which probably it was feeding. It was sunning on the bank and would face me and dart its head toward me when I tried to drive it from the water. It is barred above—but indistinctly when out of water—so that it then appears almost uniformly dark brown but in the water broad reddish brown bars are seen very distinctly alternating with very dark brown ones. The head was very flat and suddenly broader than the neck behind. Beneath it was whitish and reddish flesh color. It was about two inches in diameter at the thickest part. They are the biggest and most formidable looking snakes that we have. The inside of its mouth and throat was pink. It was awful to see it wind along the bottom of the ditch at last—raising wreaths of mud—amid the tadpoles to which it must be a very sea serpent. I afterward saw another running under Sam Barrett's grist mill the same afternoon. He said that he saw a water snake—which he distinguished from a black snake—in an apple tree nearby last year with a young robin in its mouth, having taken it from the nest. There was a cleft or fork in the tree which enabled it to ascend.

MAY 14, 1853
The still dead-looking willows and buttonbushes are alive with redwings—now perched on a yielding twig, now pursuing a female swiftly over the meadow, now darting across the stream. No two have epaulets equally brilliant. Some are small and almost white— others a brilliant vermilion.

MAY 14, 1854
A St. Domingo cuckoo [black-billed cuckoo], black-billed with red round eye—a silent long slender graceful bird, dark cinnamon (?) above, pure white beneath. It is in a leisurely manner picking the young caterpillars out of a nest (now about 1/3 of an inch long) with its long curved bill. Not timid.

MAY 14, 1858

Picked up floating an *Emys picta* [painted turtle] hatched last year. It is 1½0 of an inch long in the upper shell—and agrees with Agassiz's description at that age. Agassiz says he could never obtain a specimen of the *insculpta* [wood turtle] only one year old, it is so rarely met with and young *Emydidae* are so aquatic. I have seen them frequently.

MAY 16, 1852

The muskrat has piled his shells high up the bank this year on account of the freshet. Even our river shells will have some lilac purple or green tints telling of distant skies—like shells from the Indies. How did these beautiful rainbow tints get into the shell of the fresh-water clam buried in the mud at the bottom of our dark river? Even the sea-bottom tells of the upper skies.

MAY 16, 1853

The sprayey dream of the toad has a new sound from the meadow—the hylodes are heard more distinctly—and the tree toad [gray tree frog] chirrups often from the elms (?). The sultry warmth and moister air has called him into life.

gray tree frog

MAY 16, 1854

On Hubbard's meadow, saw a motion in the water as if a pickerel had darted away—approached and saw a mid-sized snapping turtle on the bottom. Managed at last after stripping off my coat and rolling up my shirt sleeve, by thrusting in my arm to the shoulder to get him by the tail and lift him aboard. He tried to get under the boat. He snapped at my shoe and got the toe in his mouth. His back was covered with green moss (?) or the like mostly concealing the scales. In this were small leeches. Great rough but not hard scales on his legs. He made a pretty loud hissing like a cross dog by his breathing. It was wonderful how suddenly this sluggish creature would snap at anything. As he lay under the seat I scratched his back—and filling himself with air and rage his head would suddenly fly upward, his shell striking the seat—just as a steel trap goes off—and though I was prepared for it it never failed to startle me it was so swift and sudden. He slowly inflated himself and then suddenly went off like a percussion lock snapping the air. Thus undoubtedly he catches fishes as a toad catches flies. His carinated tail and great triangular points in the rear edge of his shell. Nature does not forget beauty of outline even in a mud turtle's shell.

MAY 16, 1858

A [ruby-throated] hummingbird yesterday came into the next house and was caught. Flew about our parlor today and tasted Sophia's flowers. In some lights you saw none of the colors of its throat. In others in the shade the throat was a clear bright scarlet—but in the sun it glowed with splendid metallic *fiery* reflections about the neck and throat. It uttered from time to time as it flew a faint squeaking chirp or chirrup. The hum sounded more hollow when it approached a flower. Its wings fanned the air so forcibly that you felt the cool wind they raised a foot off—and nearer it was very remarkable. Does not this very motion of the wings keep a bird cool in hot weather?

MAY 17, 1856

In the dry lupine bank pasture, about fifteen rods from the river—
apparently traveling up the hill—I see a box tortoise, the first I have
found in Concord. Beside being longer (its upper shell 5½ by 4¼
inches), it is much flatter and more oblong, less oval, than the one
I found on Cape Cod last July. Especially it is conspicuously

broader and flatter forward. The two rear marginal plates have a triangular sinus between them while the Cape Cod ones come to a point.

The fifth and sixth marginal plates do not project by their edges beyond the shell.

The yellow marks are much narrower and more interrupted and like Oriental characters than on the Cape Cod one.

The sternum also is less oval, uniformly blackish brown except a few slight bone-[?] or horn-colored blotches—while the Cape Cod one is light yellow with a few brown blotches. The scales of the sternum in this are much less sharp angled than in the Cape Cod one.

The sternum more hollow or depressed—the tail about ⅜ of an inch long only, beyond the anus (?).

The bill is very upright somewhat like this: A beak like any Caesar's. Fore legs covered with orange-colored scales. Hind ones mostly brown or bronze with a few orange spots. Beside the usual hiss, uttered in the evening as I was carrying it, a single, as it were involuntary, squeak much like a croaking frog. Iris bright light red or rather vermilion—remarkable. Head brown above with yellow spots—orange beneath and neck.

MAY 17, 1856

Meanwhile I hear a loud hum and see a splendid male humming-bird coming zigzag in long tacks like a bee but far swifter along the edge of the swamp—in hot haste. He turns aside to taste the honey of the *Andromeda calyculata* [leatherleaf, now *Chamaedaphne calyculata*] (already visited by bees) within a rod of me. This golden green gem. Its burnished back looks as if covered with green scales dusted with gold. It hovers as it were stationary in the air with an intense humming before each little flower bell of the humble *Andromeda calyculata*—and inserts its long tongue in each, turning toward me that splendid ruby on its breast, that glowing ruby.

Even this is coal black in some lights! There along with me in the deep wild swamp above the andromeda amid the spruce. Its hum was heard afar at first like that of a large bee—bringing a larger summer. This sight and sound would make me think I was in the tropics—in *Demerara* or *Maracaibo*.

MAY 18, 1852

This afternoon the brown thrashers are very numerous and musical. They plunge downward when they leave their perch in a peculiar way. It is a bird that appears to make a business of singing for its own amusement. There is great variety in its strains. It is not easy to detect any repetition.

MAY 18, 1856

R.W.E. says that Agassiz tells him he has had turtles six or seven years which grew so little compared with others of the same size killed at first, that he thinks they may live four or five hundred years.

MAY 18, 1856

On the surface of the water amid the maples on the Holden Wood shore where I landed, I noticed some of the most splendid iridescence or opalescence from some oily matter—where the water was smooth amid the maples—that I ever saw. It was where some sucker or other fish perchance had decayed. The colors are intense blue and crimson—with dull golden. The whole at first covering seven or eight inches—but broken by the ripples I have made into polygonal figures like the fragments of a most wonderfully painted mirror. These fragments drift and turn about apparently as stiffly on the surface as if they were as thick and strong as glass. The colors are in many places sharply defined in fine lines—making unaccountable figures, as if they were produced by a sudden crystallization. How much color or expression can reside in so thin a substance. With such accompaniments does a sucker die and mix his juices with the river. This beauty like the rainbow and sunset sky marks the spot where his body has mingled with the elements. A somewhat similar beauty reappears painted on the clam's shell. Even a dead sucker suggests a beauty—and so a glory of its own. I leaned over the edge of my boat and admired it, as much as ever I did a rainbow or sunset sky. The colors were not faint but strong and fiery—if not angry.

MAY 18, 1860

The night warbler is a *powerful* singer for so small a bird. It launches into the air above the forest—or over some hollow or open space in the woods—and challenges the attention of the woods by its rapid and impetuous warble and then drops down swiftly into the tree-tops like a performer withdrawing behind the scenes—and he is very lucky who detects where it alights.

MAY 19, 1856

Hear and see a yellow-throated vireo which methinks I have heard before. Going and coming he is in the top of the same swamp white oak—singing indolently, *ullia—eelya* and sometimes varied to *eelyee.*

MAY 19, 1860

See a [smooth] green snake a very vivid yellow green of the same color with the tender foliage at present—and as if his colors had been heightened by the rain.

MAY 20, 1853

Saw a [scarlet] tanager in Sleepy Hollow. It most takes the eye of any bird. You here have the red-wing reversed—the deepest scarlet of the red-wing spread over the whole body, not on the wing-coverts merely while the wings are black. It flies through the green foliage as if it would ignite the leaves.

MAY 20, 1856

I now see distinctly the chestnut-sided warbler (of the 18th and 17th) — by Beck Stow's. It is very lively on the maples, birches, etc. over the edge [of] the swamp — sings *eech eech, eech | wichy wichy | tchea* or *itch itch itch | witty witty | tchea*. Yet this note I represented on the 18th by *tche tche tche | tchut tchutter we.*

MAY 22, 1853

When yesterday Sophia and I were rowing past Mr. Prichard's land where the river is bordered by a row of elms and low willows at 6 P.M. — we heard a singular note of distress as it were from a [gray] catbird. A loud vibrating catbird sort of note — as if the catbird's mew were imitated by a smart vibrating spring. Blackbirds and others were flitting about, apparently attracted by it.

At first thinking it was merely some peevish catbird or red-wing I was disregarding it but on second thought turned the bows to the shore — looking into the trees as well as over the shore, thinking some bird might be in distress, caught by a snake or in a forked twig. The hovering birds dispersed at my approach — the note of distress sounded louder and nearer as I approached the shore covered with low osiers. The sound came from the ground not from the trees. I saw a little black animal making haste to meet the boat under the osiers — a young muskrat? a mink?

No, it was a little dot of a kitten. It was scarcely six inches long from the face to the base — or I might as well say the tip of the tail, for the latter was a short sharp pyramid perfectly perpendicular but not swelled in the least. It was a very handsome and very precocious kitten — in perfectly good condition — its breadth being considerably more than one third of its length. Ceasing its mewing it came scrambling over the stones as fast as its weak legs would permit straight to me. I took it up and dropped it into the boat — but while I was pushing off it ran the length of the boat to Sophia, who held it while we rowed homeward.

Evidently it had not been weaned—was smaller than we remembered that kittens ever were—almost infinitely small. Yet it had hailed a boat, its life being in danger, and saved itself. Its performance, considering its age and amount of experience, was more wonderful than that of any young mathematician or musician that I have read of. Various were the conjectures as to how the kitten came there—a quarter of a mile from a house. The possible solutions were finally reduced to three. First, it must either have been born there or secondly, carried there by its mother—or thirdly by human hands. In the first case it had possibly brothers and sisters, one or both, and its mother had left them to go a-hunting on her own account and might be expected back. In the second she might equally be expected to return.

At any rate, not having thought of all this till we got home we found that we had got ourselves into a scrape. For this kitten though exceedingly interesting required one nurse to attend it constantly for the present and of course, another to spell the first—and beside we had already a cat well-nigh grown who manifested such a disposition toward the young stranger that we had no doubt it would have torn it in pieces in a moment if left alone with it. As nobody made up his or her mind to have it drowned and still less to drown it—having once looked into its innocent extremely pale blue eyes (as of milk thrice skimmed) and had his finger or his chin sucked by it, while its eyes being shut its little paws played a soothing tune—it was resolved to keep it till it could be suitably disposed of.

It rested nowhere—in no lap, under no covert—but still faintly cried for its mother and its accustomed supper. It ran toward every sound or movement of a human being and whoever crossed the room it was sure to follow at a rapid pace. It had all the ways of a cat of the maturest years, could purr divinely and raised its back to rub at boots and shoes. When it raised its foot to scratch its ear, which by the way it never hit, it was sure to fall over and roll on the floor. It climbed straight up the sitter faintly mewing all the way and sucked his chin. In vain at first its head was bent down into saucers of milk which its eyes did not see and its chin was wetted. But soon it learned to suck a finger that had been dipped in it—and better still a rag. And then at last it slept and rested.

The street was explored in vain to find its owner—and at length an Irish family took it into their cradle. Soon after we learned that a neighbor who had heard the mewing of kittens in the partition had sent for a carpenter, taken off a board and found two the very day at noon that we sailed. That same hour it was first brought to the light a coarse Irish cook had volunteered to drown it—had carried it to the river and without bag or sinker had cast it in. It saved itself and hailed a boat! What an eventful life—what a precocious kitten. We feared it owed its first plump condition to the water. How strong and effective the instinct of self-preservation.

MAY 23, 1854

The first yellow dorbug struggling in the river.

MAY 23, 1854

We soon get through with Nature. She excites an expectation which she cannot satisfy. The merest child which has rambled into a copse wood dreams of a wilderness so wild and strange and inexhaustible as Nature can never show him. The red-bird which I saw on my companion's string on election days[16] I thought but the outmost sentinel of the wild immortal camp—of the wild and dazzling infantry of the wilderness—that the deeper woods abounded with redder birds still. But now that I have threaded all our woods and waded the swamps I have never yet met with his compeer—still less his wilder kindred. The red-bird which is the last of Nature is but the first of God.... That forest on whose skirts the red-bird flits is not of earth. I expected a fauna more infinite and various—birds of more dazzling colors and more celestial song. How many springs

87

shall I continue to see the common sucker (*Catostomus Bostoniensis*) floating dead on our river. Will not Nature select her types from a new fount? The vignette of the year. This earth which is spread out like a map around me is but the lining of my inmost soul exposed. In me is the sucker that I see. No wholly extraneous object can compel me to recognize it. I am guilty of suckers.

MAY 23, 1854
Saw in Dakin's land near the road at the bend of the river, fifty-nine bank swallows' holes in a small upright bank—within a space of 20 by 1½ feet (in the middle) part above and part below the sand-line. This would give over a hundred birds to this bank. They continually circle about over the meadow and river in front—often in pairs, one pursuing the other and filling the air with their twittering.

MAY 23, 1856
Dorbugs hum in the yard (and were heard against the windows some nights ago). The cat is springing into the air for them.

MAY 25, 1855
The golden robin keeps whistling something like *Eat it Potter—eat it!*

MAY 26, 1854
In Nathan Stow's sproutland every black cherry is completely stripped of leaves by the [tent] caterpillars and they look *as if* dead—only their great triangular white nests being left in their forks.

MAY 26, 1855
See a beautiful blue-backed and long-tailed [passenger] pigeon sitting daintily on a low white pine limb.

MAY 26, 1855

In the meanwhile hear another note—very *smart* and somewhat sprayey rasping—*tshrip tshrip tshrip tshrip* or five or six times with equal force each time. The bird hops near directly over my head. It is black with a large *white* mark forward on wings—and a fiery orange throat above and below eye and line on crown—yellowish beneath, white vent, forked tail, dusky legs and bill. Holds its wings (which are light beneath) loosely. It inclines to examine about the lower branches of the white pines or midway up. The Blackburnian warbler very plainly—whose note Nuttall knows nothing about.

MAY 27, 1841

I sit in my boat on Walden—playing the flute this evening—and see the [yellow] perch, which I seem to have charmed, hovering around me—and the moon traveling over the ribbed bottom—and feel that nothing but the wildest imagination can conceive of the manner of life we are living. Nature is a wizard. The Concord nights are stranger than the Arabian nights.

yellow perch

MAY 27, 1853

The reign of insects commences this warm evening after the rains. They could not come out before. I hear from the pitch pine woods beyond E. Wood's a vast faint hum—as of a factory far enough off to be musical. I can fancy it something ambrosial from starlit mansions—a faint murmuring harp music rising from all groves—and soon insects are felt on the hands and face, and dorbugs are heard humming by or entangled in the pines like winged bullets. I suppose that those dorbugs which I saw the other day just beginning to stir under the dead leaves have now first issued forth. They never mistake their time.

MAY 28, 1854

Saw that common snake—*Coluber eximius* of De Kay, checkered adder, etc., etc.—forty-one inches long [milk snake]. A rather light brown above with large dark brown irregularly quadrangular blotches margined with black, and similar small ones on the sides; abdomen light salmon white—whitest toward the head—checkered with quadrangular blotches, very light bluish slate in some lights and dark slate or black in others. Abdominal plates 201, caudal scales 45. I should think from Storer's description that his specimen had lost its proper colors in spirits. He describes not the colors of a living snake—but those which alcohol might impart to it. It is as if you were to describe the white man as very red in the face—having seen a drunkard only....

The inhumanity of science concerns me as when I am tempted to kill a rare snake that I may ascertain its species. I feel that this is not the means of acquiring true knowledge.

MAY 29, 1853

How still the hot noon; people have retired behind blinds. Yet the kingbird—lively bird, with white belly and tail edged with white, and with its lively twittering—stirs and keeps the air brisk.

dragonfly

MAY 29, 1854
There are myriads of shad-flies [mayflies] fluttering over the dark
and still water under the hill, one every yard or two continually
descending, almost falling to the surface of the water as if to drink
and then with perhaps a little difficulty rising again—again to fall
upon it and so on. I see the same one fall and rise five or six feet
thus four or five times—others rise *much* higher. And now comes
along a large dragonfly and snatches one. This two or three times.

MAY 29, 1860
We proceeded to the Cooper's hawk nest in an oak and pine wood
(Clark's) north of Ponkawtasset. I found a fragment of one of the
eggs which he had thrown out. Farmer's egg by the way was a dull
or dirty white—i.e. a rough white with large dirty spots *perhaps* in
the grain but not surely, of a regular oval form and a little larger

than his marsh hawk's egg. I climbed to the nest—some thirty to thirty-five feet high in a white pine against the main stem. It was a mass of bark fiber and sticks about 2½ feet long by eighteen inches wide and sixteen high. The lower and main portion was a solid mass of fine bark fiber such as a red squirrel uses. This was surrounded and surmounted by a quantity of dead twigs of pine and oak etc. generally the size of a pipestem or less. The concavity was very slight, not more than 1½ inches and there was nothing soft for a lining, the bark fibers being several inches beneath the twigs but the bottom was floored for a diameter of six inches or more with flakes of white oak and pitch pine bark one to two inches long each—a good handful of them—and on this the eggs had lain. We saw nothing of the hawk.

MAY 30, 1854
Wood frogs skipping over the dead leaves whose color they resemble.

MAY 30, 1855
In the thick of the wood between railroad and Turnpike hear the *evergreen forest note,* and see *probably* the bird—black throat, greenish yellow or yellowish green head and back, light slate (?) wings with two white bars. Is it not the black-throated green warbler? I find *close by* a small fresh egg on the forest floor with a slight perforation, white (with perhaps a tinge of flesh color (?) when *full*) and brown spots and black marks at the larger end. In Brewer's synopsis the egg of the black-throat is described as "light flesh color with purple spots." But these spots are not purple. I could find no nest.

MAY 30, 1857
In the midst of the shower, though it was not raining very hard, a black and white creeper [black and white warbler] came and inspected the limbs of a tree before my rock—in his usual zigzag, prying way, head downward often—and when it thundered loud-

est, heeded it not. Birds appear to be but little incommoded by the rain. Yet they do not often sing in it.

MAY 31, 1850

Today May 31st a red and white cow being uneasy broke out of the steam mill pasture and crossed the bridge and broke into Elijah Wood's grounds. When he endeavored to drive her out by the bars she boldly took to the water, wading first through the meadows full of ditches, and swam across the river about forty rods wide at this time and landed in her own pasture again. She was a buffalo crossing her Mississippi. This exploit conferred some dignity on the herd in my eyes—already dignified—and reflectedly on the river, which I looked on as a kind of Bosphorus.

I love to see the domestic animals reassert their native rights—any evidence that they have not lost their original wild habits and vigor.

MAY 31, 1854

Saw a greater telltale [greater yellow-legs] — and this is the only one I have seen probably—distinguished by its size. It is very watchful but not timid—allowing me to come quite near, while it stands on the lookout at the water's edge. It keeps nodding its head with an awkward jerk—and wades in the water to the middle of its yellow legs. It acts the part of the telltale though there are no birds here, as if it were with a flock—goes off with a loud and sharp *phe phe phe phe* or something like that. Remarkable as a sentinel for other birds.

MAY 31, 1858

I see, running along on the flat side of a railroad rail on the causeway, a wild mouse—with an exceedingly long tail [meadow jumping mouse]. Perhaps it would be called the long-tailed meadow mouse. It has no white, only the feet are light flesh color—but it is uniformly brown as far as I can see for it rests a long time on the rail within a rod—but when I look at it from behind in the sun it is a very tawny almost golden brown, quite handsome. It finally runs with a slight hop (the tarsus of the hind legs being very long while the fore legs are short and its head accordingly low) down the bank to the meadow.

JUNE 1, 1853

Walking up this side hill I disturbed a nighthawk eight or ten feet from me, which went half fluttering half hopping, the mottled creature—like a winged toad, as Nuttall says the French of Louisiana (?) call them, down the hill as far as I could see. Without moving I looked about and saw its two eggs on the bare ground on a slight shelf of the hill on the dead pine needles and sand without any cavity or nest whatever, very obvious when once you had detected them but not easily detected from their color, a coarse gray formed of white spotted with a bluish or slaty brown or umber—a stone—granite—color, like the places it selects. I advanced and put my hand on them and while I stooped, seeing a shadow on the ground, looked up and saw the bird which had fluttered down the hill so blind and helpless, circling low and swiftly past over my head showing the white spot on each wing in true nighthawk fashion. When I had gone a dozen rods it appeared again higher in the air, with its peculiar flitting limping kind of flight, all the while noiseless, and suddenly descending it dashed at me within ten feet of my head like an imp of darkness, then swept away high over the pond dashing now to this side now to that on different tacks as if in pursuit of its prey. It had already forgotten its eggs on the earth. I can see how it might easily come to be regarded with superstitious awe.

JUNE 1, 1857

A red-wing's nest, four eggs—low in a tuft of sedge in an open meadow. What Champollion can translate the hieroglyphics on these eggs. It is always writing of the same character though much diversified. While the bird picks up the material and lays the egg, who determines the style of the marking.

JUNE 1, 1857

I hear the note of a bobolink concealed in the top of an apple tree behind me. Though this bird's full strain is ordinarily somewhat trivial, this one appears to be meditating a strain as yet unheard in meadow or orchard. *Paulo majora canamus.*[17] He is just touching the strings of his theorbo—his glassichord, his water organ—and one or two notes globe themselves and fall in liquid bubbles from his teeming throat. It is as if he touched his harp within a vase of liquid melody—and when he lifted it out the notes fell like bubbles from the trembling strings. Methinks they are the most *liquidly* sweet and melodious sounds I ever heard.

JUNE 2, 1853

The birds are wide awake as if knowing that this fog presages a fair day. I ascend Nawshawtuct from the north side. I am aware that I yield to the same influence which inspires the birds and the cockerels whose hoarse courage I hear now vaunted. So men should crow in the morning. I would brag like the chanticleer in the morning—with all the lustiness that the new day imparts—without thinking of the evening when I and all of us shall go to roost. With all the humility of the cock that takes his perch upon the highest rail and wakes the country with his clarion. Shall not men be inspired as much as cockerels?

JUNE 2, 1855

From that cocoon of the *Attacus cecropia* which I found—I think it was on the 24th of May—on a red maple shrub three or four feet from the ground on the edge of the meadow by the new Bedford road just this side of Beck Stow's—came out this forenoon a splendid moth.

I had pinned the cocoon to the sash at the upper part of my window and quite forgotten it. About the middle of the forenoon Sophia came in and exclaimed that there was a moth on my window.

At first I supposed that she meant a cloth-eating moth—but it turned out that my *A. cecropia* had come out and dropped down to the window sill, where it hung on the *side* of a slipper (which was inserted into another) to let its wings hang down and develop themselves. At first the wings were not only not unfolded laterally—but not longitudinally, the thinner ends of the forward ones for perhaps ¾ of an inch being very feeble and occupying very little space. It was surprising to see the creature unfold and expand before our eyes—the wings gradually elongating as it were by their own gravity and from time to time the insect assisted this operation by a slight shake. It was wonderful how it waxed and grew, revealing some new beauty every fifteen minutes—which I called Sophia to see—but never losing its hold on the shoe. It looked like a young emperor just donning the most splendid ermine robes that ever emperor wore. At first its wings appeared double one within the other. At last it advanced so far as to spread its wings completely but feebly when we approached. The wings every moment acquiring greater expansion and their at first wrinkled edge becoming more tense. This occupied several hours. It continued to hang to the shoe with its wings ordinarily closed erect behind its back the rest of the day—and at dusk, when apparently it was waving its wings preparatory to its evening flight, I gave it ether—and so saved it in a perfect state. As it lies not spread to the utmost it is 5⁹⁄₁₀ by 2¼ inches.

JUNE 2, 1856
Agassiz tells his class that the intestinal worms in the mouse are not developed except in the stomach of the cat.

JUNE 3, 1856

While running a line in the woods, close to the water on the southwest side of Loring's Pond, I observed a chickadee sitting quietly within a few feet. Suspecting a nest, I looked and found it in a small hollow maple stump which was about five inches in diameter and two feet high. I looked down about a foot and could just discern the eggs. Breaking off a little I managed to get my hand in and took out some eggs. There were seven, making by their number an unusual figure as they lay in the nest—a sort of egg rosette—a circle around with one (or more) in the middle. In the meanwhile the bird sat silent though rather restless within three feet. The nest was very thick and warm—of average depth and made of the bluish slate rabbit's (?) fur. The eggs were a perfect *oval*—⅝ inch long, white with small reddish brown or rusty spots especially about larger end, partly developed. The bird sat on the remaining eggs next day. I called off the boy in another direction that he might not find it.

JUNE 3, 1859

A *large* yellow butterfly (somewhat Harris *Papilio asterias* like but not *black*-winged) 3½ to 4 inches in expanse [eastern tiger swallowtail]. Pale yellow—the front wings crossed by three or four black bars—rear or outer edge of all wings widely bordered with black and some yellow behind it—a short black tail to each hind one. With two blue spots in front of two red-brown ones on the tail.

JUNE 4, 1854

These warm and dry days which put spring far behind—the sound of the cricket at noon has a new value and significance, so serene and cool. It is the *iced*-cream of song. It is modulated shade.

JUNE 4, 1855

In the clintonia swamp I hear a smart brisk loud and clear whistling warble—quite novel and remarkable—something like *te chit a wit, te chit a wit, tchit a wit, tche tche.* It is all bright yellow or ochreous *orange* (?) below except vent and a dark or black crescent on breast—with a white line about eye. Above it appears a nearly uniform dark blue slate, legs light, bill dark (?), tail long and forked. I think it must be the Canada warbler seen in '37 though that seems *short* for this. It is quite different from the warbler of May 30.

JUNE 4, 1860

A catbird has her nest in our grove. We cast out strips of white cotton cloth—all of which she picked up and used. I saw a bird fly-

gray catbird

ing across the street with so long a strip of cloth, or the like, the other day and so slowly — that at first I thought it was a little boy's kite with a long tail. The catbird sings less now — while its mate is sitting or maybe taking care of her young and probably this is the case with robins and birds generally.

JUNE 5, 1854
I see at a distance a kingbird or blackbird pursuing a crow — lower down the hill — like a satellite revolving about a black planet. I have come to this hill to see the sun go down — to recover sanity and put myself again in relation with Nature.

JUNE 5, 1857
In that first apple tree at Wyman's an apparent hairy woodpecker's nest (from the size of the bird) about ten feet from ground. The bird darts away with a shrill loud chirping of alarm incessantly repeated long before I get there and keeps it up as long as I stay in the neighborhood. The young keep up an incessant fine breathing peep which can be heard across the road and is much increased when they hear you approach the hole — they evidently expecting the old bird. I perceive no offensive odor. I saw the bird fly out of this hole May 1st and probably the eggs were laid about that time.

JUNE 6, 1854
Sphinx moths about the flowers — honeysuckles — at evening, a night or two.

JUNE 6, 1856
In the large circular hole or cellar at the turntable on the railroad — which they are repairing — I see a star-nosed mole endeavoring in vain to bury himself in the sandy and gravelly bottom. Some inhuman fellow has cut off his tail. It is blue black with much fur — a

very thick plump animal apparently some four inches long, but he occasionally shortens himself a third or more. Looks as fat as a fat hog. His fore feet are large and set sidewise or on their edges and with these he shovels the earth aside, while his large long starred snout is feeling the way and breaking ground. I see deep indentations in his fur where his eyes are situated and once I saw distinctly his eye open — a dull blue (?)-black bead, not so very small — and he very plainly noticed my movements two feet off. He was using his eye as plainly as any creature that I ever saw. Yet [Ebenezer] Emmons says it is a question whether their eyes are not merely rudimentary. I suppose this was the *Condylura macroura* — since that is most common — but only an inch of its tail was left and that was quite stout. I carried him along to plowed ground where he buried himself in a minute or two.

JUNE 6, 1857

As I sit on Lee's Cliff, I see a pe-pe [olive-sided flycatcher] on the topmost dead branch of a hickory eight or ten rods off. Regularly, at short intervals, it utters its monotonous note like *till-till-till*—or *pe-pe-pe*. Looking round for its prey and occasionally changing its perch, it every now and then darts off (phoebe-like) even five or six rods toward the earth to catch an insect—and then returns to its favorite perch. If I lose it for a moment, I soon see it settling on the dead twigs again and hear its *till, till, till*. It appears through the glass mouse-colored above and head (which is perhaps darker), white throat and narrow white beneath, with no white on tail.

JUNE 7, 1853

The ovenbird runs from her covered nest, so close to the ground under the lowest twigs and leaves, even the loose leaves on the ground, like a mouse, that I cannot get a fair view of her. She does not fly at all. Is it to attract me, or partly to protect herself?

JUNE 7, 1853

Visited my nighthawk on her nest. Could hardly believe my eyes when I stood within seven feet and beheld her sitting on her eggs, her head to me. She looked so Saturnian, so one with the earth—so sphinx-like, a relic of the reign of Saturn which Jupiter did not destroy, a riddle that might well cause a man to go dash his head against a stone. It was not an actual living creature, far less a winged creature of the air—but a figure in stone or bronze, a fanciful production of art, like the gryphon or phoenix. In fact, with its breast toward me, and owing to its color or size no bill perceptible, it looked like the end [of] a brand—such as are common in a clearing—its breast mottled or alternately waved with dark brown and gray, its flat grayish weatherbeaten crown, its eyes nearly closed purposely lest those bright beads should betray it with the stony cunning of the sphinx.

JUNE 7, 1858

As I was wading in this Wyman meadow—looking for bullfrog-spawn—I saw a hole at the bottom where it was six or eight inches deep by the side of a mass of mud and weeds which rose just to the surface three or four feet from the shore. It was about five inches in diameter with some sand at the mouth just like a musquash's hole. As I stood there within two feet, a pout put her head out, as if to see who was there and directly came forth and disappeared under the target weed—but as I stood perfectly still waiting for the water which I had disturbed to settle about the hole she circled round and round several times between me and the hole—cautiously, stealthily approaching the entrance but as often withdrawing and at last mustered courage to enter it. I then noticed another similar hole in the same mass, two or three feet from this. I thrust my arm into the first, running it in and downward about fifteen inches. It was a little more than a foot long and enlarged somewhat at the end—the bottom also being about a foot beneath the surface—for it slanted downward, but I felt nothing within. I only felt a pretty regular and rounded apartment with firm walls of weedy or fibrous mud. I then thrust my arm into the other hole which was longer and deeper, but at first discovered nothing—but trying again I found that I had not reached the end for it turned a little and descended more than I supposed. Here I felt a similar apartment or enlargement, some six inches in diameter horizontally but not quite so high nor nearly so wide at its throat. There to my surprise I felt something soft like a gelatinous mass of spawn—but feeling a little further felt the horns of a pout. I deliberately took hold of her by the head and lifted her out of the hole and the water—having run my arm in two thirds its length. She offered not the slightest resistance from first to last—even when I held her out of water before my face—and only darted away suddenly when I dropped her in the water. The entrance to her apartment was so narrow that she could hardly have escaped if I had tried to prevent her. Putting in my arm again I felt under where she had been a flattish mass of ova several inches in diameter resting on the mud—and took out some. Feeling again in the first hole I found as much more there. Though I had been stepping round and over the second nest for several minutes I had not scared the pout. The ova of the first nest already contained *white* wiggling young. I saw no motion in the others. The ova in each case were dull yellowish and the size of small buckshot. These nests did not communicate with each other and had no other outlet.

Pouts, then, make their nests in shallow mud holes or bays in masses of weedy mud—or probably in the muddy bank—and the old pout hovers over the spawn or keeps guard at the entrance. Where do the Walden pouts breed when they have not access to this meadow? The first pout, whose eggs were most developed, was the largest and had some slight wounds on the back—the other *may have* been the male in the act of fertilizing the ova. [*Penciled addition:* The ova in jar had mostly turned quite white and dead on the 8th—perhaps could not bear the light.]

JUNE 9, 1857
In the sproutland beyond the red huckleberry, an indigo-bird [indigo bunting]—which *chips* about me as if it had a nest there. This is a splendid and marked bird—high-colored as is the tanager, looking strange in this latitude. Glowing indigo. It flits from top of one bush to another, chirping as if anxious. Wilson says it sings—not like most other birds in the morning and evening chiefly, but

also in the middle of the day. In this I notice it is like the tanager, the other fiery-plumaged bird. They seem to love the heat. It probably had its nest in one of those bushes.

Saw a hog-pasture of a dozen acres in the woods, with thirty or forty large hogs and a shelter for them at night—half-mile east of the last house—something rare in these days hereabouts.... The hogs I saw this afternoon all busily rooting without holding up their heads to look at us—the whole field looked as if it had been most miserably plowed or scarified with a harrow—with their shed to retreat to in rainy weather, affected me as more human than other quadrupeds. They are comparatively clean about their lodgings and their shed with its litter bed was on the whole cleaner than an Irishman's shanty. I am not certain what there was so very human about them.

A painted tortoise laying her eggs ten feet from the wheel track on the Marlborough road. She paused at first, but I sat down within two feet and she soon resumed her work. Had excavated a hollow about five inches wide and six long in the moistened sand—and cautiously with long intervals she continued her work, resting always on the same spot her fore feet—and never looking round, her eye shut all but a narrow slit. Whenever I moved, perhaps to brush off a mosquito, she paused. A wagon approached—rumbling afar off—and then there was a pause till it had passed and long long after—a tedious *naturlangsam* pause of the slow-blooded creature—a sacrifice of time such as those animals are up to which slumber half a year and live for centuries. It was twenty minutes before I discovered that she was not making the hole but filling it up slowly—having laid her eggs. She drew the moistened sand under herself, scraping it along from behind with both feet brought together—the claws turned inward. In the long pauses the ants troubled her (as the mosquitoes me) by running over her eyes—which made her snap or dart out her head suddenly, striking the shell. She did not dance on the sand—nor finish covering the hollow quite so carefully as the one observed last year. She went off suddenly (and quickly at first) with a slow but sure instinct through the woods toward the swamp.

JUNE 10, 1857

In Julius Smith's yard a striped snake (so called) was running about this forenoon and in the afternoon it was found to have shed its slough—leaving it halfway out a hole, which probably it used to confine it in. It was about in its new skin. Many creatures—devil's needles, etc., etc.—cast their sloughs now. Can't I?

JUNE 10, 1860

There is much handsome interrupted fern in the Painted Cup Meadow—and near the top of one of the clumps we noticed something like a large cocoon, the color of the rusty cinnamon fern wool. It was a red bat—the New York bat, so called. It hung suspended head directly downward with its little sharp claws or hooks caught through one of the divisions at the base of one of the pinnae, above the fructification. It was a delicate rusty brown—in color very like the wool of the cinnamon fern with the whiter bare spaces seen through it early in the season. I thought at first glance it was a broad brown cocoon—then that it was the plump body of a monstrous emperor [imperial] moth. It was rusty or reddish brown, white or hoary within or beneath the tips with a white apparently triangular spot beneath about the insertion of the wings. Its wings were very compactly folded up—the principal bones (darker reddish) lying flat along the underside of its body—and a hook on each meeting its opposite under the chin of the creature.

It did not look like fur but more like the plush of the ripe cattail head though more loose—all trembling in the wind and with the pulsations of the animal. I broke off the top of the fern and let the bat lie on its back in my hand. I held it and turned it about for ten or fifteen minutes but it did not awake. Once or twice it opened its eyes a little—and even it raised its head, opened its mouth, but soon drowsily dropped its head and fell asleep again. Its ears were rounded and nearly bare. It was more attentive to sounds than to motions. Finally, by shaking it, and especially by hissing or whistling I thoroughly awakened it—and it fluttered off twenty or thirty rods to the woods. I cannot but think that its instinct taught it to cling to the interrupted fern—since it might readily be mistaken for a mass of its fruit. Raised its old haggish head. Unless it showed its head wide awake, it looked like a tender infant.

JUNE 11, 1840
We stole noiselessly down the stream, occasionally driving a pickerel from the covert of the pads—or a bream [bluegill] from her nest—and the small green bittern [green heron] would now and then sail away on sluggish wings from some recess of the shore. With its patient study by rocks and sandy capes, has it wrested the whole of her secret from nature yet? It has looked out from its dull eye for so long, standing on one leg—on moon and stars sparkling through silence and dark—and now what a rich experience is its. What says it of stagnant pools—and reeds—and damp night fogs? It would be worth while to look in the eye which has been open and seeing at such hours and in such solitudes.

When I behold that dull yellowish green I wonder if my own soul is not a bright invisible green. I would fain lay my eye side by side with its—and learn of it.

JUNE 11, 1851
The whippoorwill suggests how wide asunder [are] the woods and the town. Its note is very rarely heard by those who live on the

street, and then it is thought to be of ill omen. Only the dwellers on the outskirts of the village hear it occasionally. It sometimes comes into their yards. But go into the woods in a warm night at this season, and it is the prevailing sound. I hear now five or six at once. It is no more of ill omen therefore here than the night and the moonlight are. It is a bird not only of the woods, but of the night side of the woods....

I hear some whippoorwills on hills—others in thick wooded vales—which ring hollow and cavernous like an apartment or cellar with their note. As when I hear the working of some artisan from within an apartment.

JUNE 11, 1851

I hear the night-singing bird breaking out as in his dreams, made so from the first for some mysterious reason.

JUNE 11, 1854

Saw in and near some woods four or five cow blackbirds—with their light-brown heads—their strain an imperfect milky gurgling *conqueree,* an unsuccessful effort. It made me think—for some reason—of streams of milk bursting out a sort of music between the staves of a keg.

JUNE 11, 1856

A beautiful grass-green snake about fifteen inches long—light beneath with a yellow space under the eyes along the edge of the upper jaw.

JUNE 12, 1852

Small white-bellied (?) swallows in a row (a dozen) on the telegraph wire over the water by the bridge. This perch is little enough departure from unobstructed air to suit them, pluming themselves.

tree swallow

If you could furnish a perch aerial enough even birds of paradise would alight.

JUNE 13, 1851

As I climbed the hill again toward my old bean-field, I listened to the ancient familiar immortal dear cricket sound under all others, hearing at first some distinct chirps—but when these ceased I was aware of the general earth song which my hearing had not heard amid which these were only taller flowers in a bed—and I wondered if behind or beneath this there was not some other chant yet more universal. Why do we not hear when this begins in the spring? And when it ceases in the fall! Or is it too gradual.

JUNE 13, 1852

No doubt woodchucks in their burrows hear the steps of walkers through the earth and come not forth.... Saw four cunning little woodchucks nibbling the short grass about one third grown that live under Conant's old house. Mistook one for a piece of rusty iron.

JUNE 13, 1853

What was that rare and beautiful bird in the dark woods under the Cliffs with black above and white spots and bars—a large triangular blood-red spot on breast, and sides of breast and beneath white? Note a warble like the oriole but softer and sweeter. It was quite tame. I cannot find this bird described—and think it must be a [rose-breasted] grosbeak.

At first I thought I saw a chewink [eastern towhee]. It sat within a rod sideways to me and I was going to call Sophia to look at it— but then it turned its breast full toward me and I saw the blood-red breast—a *large* triangular painted spot, occupying the greater part of the breast. It was in the cool shaded underwood by the old path just under the cliff. It is a memorable event to meet with so rare a bird. Birds answer to flowers both in their abundance and in their rareness. The meeting with a rare and beautiful bird like this is like meeting with some rare and beautiful flower, which you may never find again perchance—like the great purple fringed orchis at least. How much it enhances the wildness and the richness of the forest to see in it some beautiful bird which you never detected before.

JUNE 13, 1855

C. finds a pigeon woodpecker's nest in an apple tree, five of those pearly eggs about six feet from ground—could squeeze your hand in. Also a peetweet's [spotted sandpiper]—with four eggs in Hubbard's meadow beyond the old swamp oak site—and two [eastern] kingbirds' nests with eggs in an apple and in a willow by riverside.

JUNE 13, 1858

I see a song sparrow's nest here in a little spruce just by the mouth of the ditch [at Ledum Swamp]. It rests on the thick branches fifteen inches from the ground, firmly made of coarse sedge without, lined with finer, and then a little hair, small within—a very thick firm and portable nest, an inverted cone—four eggs. They build this in a peculiar manner in these sphagnous swamps—elevated apparently on account of water and of different materials. Some of the eggs have quite a blue ground.

JUNE 14, 1851

And now having proceeded a little way down this road, the sun having buried himself in the low cloud in the west and hung out his crimson curtains, I hear while sitting by the wall the sound of the stake driver [American bittern] at a distance—like that made by a man pumping in a neighboring farmyard, watering his cattle, or like chopping wood before his door on a frosty morning—and I can imagine him driving a stake in a meadow. The pumper. I immediately went in search of the bird—but after going a third of a mile it did not sound much nearer, and the two parts of the sound did not appear to proceed from the same place. What is the peculiarity of these sounds which penetrate so far on the keynote of nature. At last I got near to the brook in the meadow behind Hubbard's wood, but I could not tell if [it] were further or nearer than that. When I got within half a dozen rods of the brook, it ceased—and I heard it no more. I suppose that I scared it. As before I was further off than I thought—so now I was nearer than I thought. It is not easy to understand how so small a creature can make so loud a sound by merely sucking in or throwing out water with pump-like lungs.

JUNE 14, 1853

C. says his dog chased a woodchuck yesterday, and it climbed up into an oak and sat on a limb ten or twelve feet high.

JUNE 14, 1855

I told C. to look into an old mortise hole in Wood's Bridge for a white-bellied swallow's nest—as we were paddling under—but he laughed incredulous. I insisted—and when he climbed up he scared out the bird. Five eggs. "You see the feathers about, do you not?" "Yes," said he.

JUNE 14, 1855
Looked at the peetweet's nest which C. found yesterday. It was very difficult to find again in the broad open meadow—no nest but a mere hollow in the dead cranberry leaves, the grass and stubble ruins, under a little alder. The old bird went off at last from under us—low in the grass at first and with *wings up* making a worried sound which attracted other birds. I frequently noticed others afterward flying low over the meadow—and alighting and uttering this same note of alarm. There were only four eggs in this nest yesterday and today to C.'s surprise, there are the two eggs which he left and a young peetweet beside—a gray pinch of down with a black center to its back—but already so old and precocious that it runs with its long legs swiftly off from squatting beside the two eggs and hides in the grass. We have some trouble to catch it. How came it here with these eggs—which will not be hatched for some days? C. saw nothing of it yesterday. J. Farmer says that young peetweets run at once like partridges and quails [bobwhites], and that they are the only birds he knows that do. These eggs *were not addled* (I had opened one, C. another). Did this bird come from another nest—or did it belong to an earlier brood?

JUNE 15, 1850
I picked up today the lower jaw of a hog with white and sound teeth and tusks—which reminded me that there was an animal health and vigor distinct from the spiritual health. This animal succeeded by other means than temperance and purity.

JUNE 15, 1852
Golden and coppery reflections from a yellow dorbug's coat of mail in the water.

JUNE 15, 1852

It is candlelight, the fishes leap. The meadows sparkle with the coppery light of fireflies. The evening star multiplied by undulating water is like bright sparks of fire continually ascending.

JUNE 15, 1860

As I stood there I heard that peculiar hawk-like (for rhythm) but more resonant or clanging kind of scream which I may have heard before this year—plover-like, indefinitely far—over the Clamshell plain. After proceeding half a dozen rods toward the hill I heard the familiar willet note of the upland plover [upland sandpiper]—and looking up saw one standing erect (like a large telltale—or chicken with its head stretched up) on the rail fence. After a while it flew off southwest and low, then wheeled and went a little higher down the river. Of pigeon size—but quick quivering wings. Finally rose higher and flew more or less zigzag as if uncertain where it would alight—and at last when almost out of sight it pitched down into a field near Cyrus Hubbard's.

JUNE 16, 1852

The bullfrogs lie on the very surface of the pads showing their great yellow throats, color of the yellow breeches of the old school, and protuberant eyes. His whole back out revealing a vast expanse of belly. His eyes like ranunculus or yellow lily buds—winking from time to time—and showing his large dark-bordered tympanum. Imperturbable looking. His yellow throat swells up like a small moon at a distance over the pads when he croaks.

JUNE 16, 1853

Coming along near the celtis I heard a singular sound as of a bird in distress amid the bushes—and turned to relieve it. Next thought it a squirrel in an apple tree barking at me. Then found that it came from a hole in the ground under my feet—a loud sound between a grunting and a wheezing, yet not unlike the sound a red squirrel sometimes makes but louder. Looking down the hole I saw the tail and hind quarters of a woodchuck which seemed to be contending with another further down. Reaching down carefully I took hold of the tail, and though I had to pull very hard indeed I drew him out between the rocks—a bouncing great fat fellow—and tossed him a little way down the hill. As soon as he recovered from his bewilderment he made for the hole again, but I barring the way he ran off elsewhere.

JUNE 16, 1853

Coming down the river heard opposite the new houses where I stopped to pluck the tall grass a sound as of young blackbirds amid the buttonbushes. After a long while gazing, standing on the roots of the buttonbushes I detected a couple of meadow or mud hens, *Rallus virginianus* [Virginia rail], gliding about under the buttonbushes over the mud and through the shallow water and uttering a squeaking or squawking note as if they had a nest there or young. Bodies about the size of a robin—short tail—wings and tail white-edged—bill about 1½ inches long—orange beneath in one bird. Brown deepening into black spots above. Turtle-dove color on breasts and beneath. Ashy about eyes and cheeks. Seemed not willing to fly—and for a long time unwilling to pass me—because it must come near to keep under the buttonbushes.

JUNE 17, 1852

The sound of the crickets at dawn after these first sultry nights seems like the dreaming of the earth still continued into the daylight. I love that early twilight hour when the crickets still creak right on with such dewy faith and promise as if it were still night— expressing the innocence of morning. When the creak of the cricket is fresh and bedewed. While the creak of the cricket has that ambrosial sound no crime can be committed.

JUNE 17, 1853

I did not mention yesterday the great devil's needle with his humped back,[18] which hovered over the boat and though headed across its course, and not appearing to fly in the direction in which the boat was moving, yet preserved his relation to the boat perfectly. What steamer can reverse its paddle wheels as he can.

JUNE 18, 1852

The hornet's nest is built with many thin layers of his paper with an interval of about ⅛ of an inch between them so that his wall is one or two inches thick.[19] This probably for warmth dryness and lightness. So sometimes the carpenter has learned to build double walls.

JUNE 18, 1853

Saw tonight Lewis the blind man's horse which works on the sawing machine at the Depot—now let out to graze along at the road, but at each step he lifts his hind legs convulsively high from the ground, as if the whole earth were a treadmill, continually slipping away from him while he climbed its convex surface. It was painful to witness—but it was symbolical of the moral condition of his master and of all artisans in contradistinction from artists—all who are engaged in any routine—for to them also the whole earth is a treadmill, and the routine results instantly in a similar painful deformity. The horse may bear the mark of his servitude on the muscles of his legs—the man on his brow.

JUNE 18, 1853

Moon not quite full. Going across Depot Field. The western sky is now a crescent of saffron inclining to salmon, a little dunnish, perhaps. The grass is wet with dew. The evening star has come out, but no other. There is no wind. I see a nighthawk in the twilight, flitting near the ground. I hear the hum of a beetle going by. The greenish fires of lightning-bugs are already seen in the meadow. I almost lay my hand on one amid the leaves as I get over the fence at the brook.

JUNE 18, 1853

The distant village sounds are the barking of dogs, that animal with which man has allied himself, and the rattling of wagons. For the farmers have gone into town a-shopping this Saturday night. The dog is the tamed wolf—as the villager is the tamed savage. But near the crickets are heard in the grass chirping from everlasting to everlasting, a mosquito sings near my ear—and the humming of a dorbug drowns all the noise of the village. So roomy is the universe.

JUNE 19, 1853

In the middle of the path to Wharf Rock at Flint's Pond, the nest of a Wilson's thrush [veery]—five or six inches high between the green stems of three or four goldenrods, made of dried grass or fibers of bark, with dry oak leaves attached loosely making the whole nine or ten inches wide to deceive the eye. Two blue eggs. Like an accidental heap. Who taught it to do thus?

JUNE 19, 1859

A flying squirrel's nest and young on Emerson's hatchet path—south of Walden—on hilltop, in a covered hollow in a small old stump at base of a young oak, covered with fallen leaves and a portion of the stump—nest apparently of dry grass. Saw three young run out after the mother and up a slender oak. The young half-grown, very tender-looking and weak-tailed—yet one climbed quite to the top of an oak twenty-five feet high, though feebly. Claws must be very sharp and early developed. The mother rested quite near on a small projecting stub big as a pipestem, curled crosswise on it. Have a more rounded head and snout than our other squirrels. The young in danger of being picked off by hawks.

JUNE 19, 1860

Observe a nest crowded full with four young brown thrashers half fledged. You would think they would die of heat, so densely packed and overflowing. Three head one way, and the other lies across. How quickly a fox would gobble them up!

JUNE 20, 1840

Something like the woodland sounds will be heard to echo through the leaves of a good book. Sometimes I hear the fresh emphatic note of the ovenbird, and am tempted to turn many pages—sometimes the hurried chuckling sound of the squirrel when he dives into the wall.

JUNE 20, 1852

Lying with my window open—these warm even sultry nights—I hear the sonorously musical trump of the bullfrogs from time to time, from some distant shore of the river. As if the world were given up to them. By those villagers who live on the street they are never seen and rarely heard by day—but in the quiet sultry nights their notes ring from one end of the town to another. It is as if you had waked up in the infernal regions. I do not know for a time in what world I am.

JUNE 20, 1853

Saw a little skunk coming up the riverbank in the woods at the White Oak. A funny little fellow about six inches long and nearly as broad. It faced me and actually compelled me to retreat before it for five minutes. Perhaps I was between it and its hole.

Its broad black tail tipped with white was erect like a kitten's. It had what looked like a broad white band drawn tight across its forehead or top-head—from which two lines of white ran down, one on each side of its back—and there was a narrow white line down its snout. It raised its back, sometimes ran a few feet forward, sometimes backward, and repeatedly turned its tail to me—prepared to discharge its fluid like the old. Such was its instinct—and all the while it kept up a fine grunting like a little pig or a squirrel. It reminded me that the red squirrel, the woodchuck, and the skunk all make a similar sound. Now there are young rabbits, skunks, and probably woodchucks.

JUNE 21, 1852

Cherry birds [cedar waxwings]. I have not seen though I think I have heard them before—their *fine* seringo note, like a vibrating spring

cedar waxwing

in the air. They are a handsome bird with their crest—and chestnut breasts. They are ready for the cherries, when they shall be ripe.

JUNE 21, 1853
Where the other day I saw a pigeon woodpecker tapping and enlarging a hole in the dead limb of an apple tree, when as yet probably no egg was laid, today I see two well-grown young woodpeckers about as big as the old, looking out at the hole showing their handsome spotted breasts and calling lustily for something to eat—or it may be suffering from the heat. Young birds in some situations must suffer greatly from heat these days—so closely packed in their nests and perhaps insufficiently shaded. It is a wonder they remain so long there patiently.

JUNE 22, 1852
More thunder showers threaten—and I still can trace those that are gone by. The fireflies in the meadows are very numerous, as if they had replenished their lights from the lightning. The far-retreated thunder clouds low in the southeast horizon and in the north, emitting low flashes which reveal their forms, appear to lift their wings like fireflies—or it is a steady glare like the glow-worm. Wherever they go, they make a meadow.

JUNE 22, 1853
I looked for the nest of the Maryland yellow-throat [common yellowthroat], but could not find it. Some animal has carried it off from the tuft of sedge—but I found one little egg which had dropped out. How many tragedies of this kind in the fields!

JUNE 23, 1852
The wood thrush sings at all hours. I associate it with the cool morning, sultry noon, and serene evening. At this hour it suggests a cool vigor.

JUNE 24, 1852

The dog worried a woodchuck half grown—which did not turn its back and run into its hole but backed into it and faced him and us gritting its teeth and prepared to die. But even this little fellow was able to defend himself against the dog with his sharp teeth. That fierce gritting of their teeth is a remarkable habit with these animals.

JUNE 24, 1857

Went to Farmer's Swamp to look for the [eastern] screech owl's[20] nest Farmer had found. You go about forty-five rods on the first path to the left in the woods and then turn to the left a few rods. I found the nest at last near the top of a middling-sized white pine about thirty feet from the ground.

As I stood by the tree the old bird dashed by within a couple of rods uttering a peculiar mewing sound which she kept up amid the bushes, a blackbird in close pursuit of her. I found the nest empty on one side of the main stem but close to it resting on some limbs. It was made of twigs rather less than an eighth of an inch thick and was almost flat above—only an inch lower in the middle than at the edge—about sixteen inches in diameter and six or eight inches thick. With the twigs in the midst and beneath was mixed sphagnum and sedge from the swamp beneath, and the lining or flooring was coarse strips of grape-vine bark, the whole pretty firmly matted together. How common and important a material is grape-vine bark for birds' nests! Nature wastes nothing. There were white droppings of the young on the nest and one large pellet of fur and small bones 2½ inches long. In the meanwhile the old bird was uttering that hoarse worried note from time to time—somewhat like a partridge's—flying past from side to side and alighting amid the trees or bushes. When I had descended I detected one young one two-thirds grown perched on a branch of the next tree about fifteen feet from the ground—which was all the while staring at me with its great yellow eyes. It was gray with gray horns and a dark beak. As I walked past near it, it turned its head steadily always facing me, without moving its body, till it looked directly the opposite way over its back—but never offered to fly. Just then I thought surely that I heard a puppy faintly barking at me four or five rods distant amid the bushes having tracked me into the swamp—*what what, what what what.* It was exactly such a noise as the barking of a very small dog or perhaps a fox. But it was the old owl for I presently saw her making it.

JUNE 26, 1840
When a dog runs at you whistle for him.

JUNE 26, 1852
A skater insect casts seven flat globular shades— four smaller in front, two larger behind, and the smallest of all in the center. From the shadow on the bottom you cannot guess the form on the surface—everything is transmuted by the water. The shadow however small is black within, edged with a sunny halo corresponding to the day's twilights—and a certain liquidness is imparted to the whole by the incessant motion from the undulation of the surface.

JUNE 28, 1857
Observed tonight a yellow [paper] wasps' (?) nest made of the same kind of paper with the hornets'—in horizontal strips some brownish some white. It was broad cone shape, some two inches in its smallest diameter with a hole at the apex beneath about ½ inch diameter and was suspended to the sheathing overhead within the recess at Mrs. Brown's front door. She was afraid of the wasps and so I brushed it off for her. It was apparently the same kind of nest that I observed first a few days since of the same size, under the peak of our roof just over my chamber windows. (The last is now five

inches in diameter, July 7th.) It contained only one comb about 1⅛ inches in diameter suspended from above and this was surrounded by about two thin coverings of paper ⅛ of an inch or more apart. The wasps looked at first like bees—with yellow rings on the abdomen. The cells contain what look and move like white grubs.

JUNE 29, 1851
At a distance in the meadow I hear still at long intervals the hurried commencement of the bobolink's strain, the bird just dashing into song—which is as suddenly checked as it were by the warder

of the seasons, and the strain is left incomplete forever. Like human beings they are inspired to sing only for a short season.

JUNE 29, 1852

The *Rana halecina* (?) shad frog is our handsomest frog—bronze striped with brown spots edged and intermixed with *bright* green; does not regard the fly that sits on him. The frogs and tortoises are striped and spotted for their concealment. The painted tortoise's throat held up above the pads, streaked with yellowish, makes it the less obvious. The mud turtle is the color of the mud—the wood frog and the hylodes of the dead leaves—the bullfrogs of the pads—the toad of the earth, etc., etc. The tree toad of the bark.

JUNE 30, 1860

See in the garden the hole in which a toad sits by day. It is a round hole about the width of his body across, and extending under one side about the length of my little finger. In the main indeed shaped like a turtle's nest—but not so broad beneath and not quite so deep.
There sits the toad in the shade and concealed completely under the ground—with its head toward the entrance waiting for evening.

JULY 1, 1852

A young man in Sudbury told me he had heard woodchucks whistle.

JULY 2, 1858

The wood thrush sings almost wherever I go, eternally reconsecrating the world morning and evening for us. And again it seems habitable and more than habitable to us.

JULY 3, 1853

The ovenbird's nest in Laurel Glen is near the edge of an open pine wood under a fallen pine twig and a heap of dry oak leaves. Within these on the ground is the nest with a dome-like top and an arched entrance of the whole height and width on one side. Lined within with dry pine needles.

JULY 3, 1854

The clams are so thick on the bottom at Hubbard's bathing place that standing up to my neck in water I brought my feet together and lifted up between them so as to take off in my hand without dipping my head, three clams the first time, though many more dropped off.

When you consider the difficulty of carrying two melons under one arm—and that this was in the water—you may infer the number of the clams.

JULY 3, 1860

Looked for the marsh hawk's nest (of June 16th) in the Great Meadows. It was in the very midst of the sweet gale (which is three feet high) occupying an opening only a foot or two across. We had much difficulty in finding it again—but at last nearly stumbled on to a young hawk. There was one as big as my fist resting on the bare flat nest in the sun, with a great head, staring eyes, and open gaping or panting mouth, yet mere down, grayish white down as yet—but I detected another which had crawled a foot one side amid the bushes for shade or safety more than half as large again, with small feathers and a yet more angry hawk-like look. How naturally anger sits on the young hawk's head. It was 3:30 P.M. and the old birds were gone—and saw us not. Meanwhile their callow young lie panting under the sweet gale and rose bushes in the swamp—waiting for their parents to fetch them food.

JULY 4, 1852

What means this endless motion of water bugs collected in little groups on the surface—and ceaselessly circling about their center (as if they were a family hatched from the eggs on the underside of a pad). Is not this motion intended partly to balk the fishes? Methinks they did not begin to move till sunrise—where were they?

JULY 4, 1853

The beauty of some butterflies,—dark steel blue with a light blue edge.[21]

JULY 5, 1852

I see many devil's needles zigzagging along the Second Division Brook—some green, some blue, both with black and perhaps velvety wings. They are confined to the brook. How lavishly they are painted! How cheap was the paint—how free the fancy of their creator!

JULY 5, 1852

I caught a handful of small water bugs, fifteen or twenty about as large as apple seeds. Some country people call them apple seeds it is said from their scent. I perceived a strong scent—but I am not sure it was like apples. I should rather think they were so called from their shape.

JULY 5, 1857

There came out this morning, apparently from one of those hard *stem-wound* cocoons on a black birch in my window a moth whose wings are spread 4¼ inches and it is about 1¾ inches long. It is black, wings and body—with two short broad feathery antennae. The wings all have a clay-colored border behind, with a distinct black waving line down the middle of it—and about midway the wings a less distinct clay-colored line. Near the point of each forward wing a round black spot or eye with a bluish crescent within its forward edge—and beyond this spot a purple tinge with a short whitish waving line continued through it from the crescent. The rear wings have a row of oblong roundish black spots along the clay-colored border within the black line. There is a very faint light line on the fore wings on each side of the head. Beneath on wings and body dark purplish brown takes the place of the black above. It is rather handsomer and higher colored beneath than above. There is a very small light or clay-colored triangular spot near the middle of wing beneath. Also a row of brown spots on a white band along each side of the body. This is evidently the male *Attacus promethea.*

The rich purplish brown beneath (a sort of chocolate purple) makes the figure of a smaller moth of different form. The cocoon about an inch long is surrounded by the now pale withered leaf of the birch which is wrapped almost quite around it and extends beneath — and it is very hard and firm, the light silk being wound thickly about the petiole, and also afterward the twig itself for half an inch or more both above and beneath the petiole. Sometimes there is no real petiole for a core — but the silky sheath can be slid up and down the twig.

JULY 8, 1852

Under the *Salix nigra* var. *falcata* [black willow], near that handsomest one, which now is full of scythe-shaped leaves ... I found a remarkable [luna] moth lying flat on the still water as if asleep (they appear to sleep during the day), as large as the smaller birds. Five and a half inches in alar extent and about three inches long, something like the smaller figure in one position of the wings — with a remarkably narrow lunar-cut tail — of a sea green color with four conspicuous spots whitish within — then a red line, then yellowish border below or toward the tail, but brown, brown orange, and black above toward head. A very robust hardy body covered with a kind of downy plumage 1¼ inches long by ⅝ thick.

The sight affected me as tropical — and I suppose it is the northern verge of some species. It suggests into what productions Nature would run if all the year were a July. By night it is active—for though I thought it dying at first it made a great noise in its prison, a cigar box, at night. When the day returns it apparently drops wherever it may be, even into the water, and dozes till evening again.

JULY 8, 1855
See the killdeer a dozen rods off in pasture anxious about its eggs or young—with its shrill squeaking note, its ring of white about its neck and two black crescents on breast. They are not so common and noisy as in June.

JULY 11, 1851
And now at half-past 10 o'clock I hear the cockerels crow in Hubbard's barns—and morning is already anticipated. It is the feathered wakeful thought in us that anticipates the following day. This sound is wonderfully exhilarating at all times. These birds are worth far more to me for their crowing and cackling than for their drumsticks and eggs.

JULY 12, 1852
The turtle dove [mourning dove] flutters before you in shady wood paths or looks out with extended neck—losing its balance, slow to leave its perch.

JULY 12, 1852
Now for another fluvial walk…. It is an objection to walking in the mud that from time to time you have to pick the leeches off you.

JULY 12, 1857
It is exceedingly sultry this afternoon, and few men are abroad. The cows stand up to their bellies in the river—lashing their sides with their tails from time to time.

I see at 9:30 P.M. a little brood of four or five barn swallows which have quite recently left the nest—perched close together for the night on a dead willow twig in the shade of the tree about four feet above the water. Their tails not yet much grown. When I passed up the old bird twittered about them in alarm. I now float within four feet and they do not move or give sign of awaking. I could take them all off with my hand. They have been hatched in the nearest barn or elsewhere and have been led at once to roost here for coolness and security. There is no cooler nor safer place for them. I observe that they take their broods to the telegraph wires for an aerial perch—where they teach them to fly.

Heard yesterday a sharp and loud *ker-pheet*—I think from a surprised woodchuck, amid bushes—the *siffleur*. Reminds me somewhat of a peetweet—and also of the squeak of a rabbit, but much louder and sharper. And all is still.

Saw today for the first time this season fleets of yellow [clouded sulphur] butterflies dispersing before us [as] we rode along berrying on the Walden road.

Their yellow fleets are in the offing. Do I ever see them in numbers off the road? They are a yellow flower that blossoms generally about this time. Like a mackerel fleet with their small hulls and great sails. Collected now in compact but gorgeous assembly in the road, like schooners in a harbor, a haven—now suddenly dispersing on our approach and filling the air with yellow snowflakes in their zigzag flight, or as when a fair wind calls those schooners out and disperses them over the broad ocean.

JULY 15, 1854

My thoughts are driven inward—even as clouds and trees are reflected in the still smooth water. There is an inwardness even in the mosquitoes' hum—while I am picking blueberries in the dank wood.

JULY 16, 1851

The angelica with its large umbels is gone to seed. On it I find one of those slow-moving green worms [caterpillar of the eastern tiger swallowtail] with rings spotted black and yellow—like an East Indian production. What if these grew as large as elephants. The honest and truly fair is more modestly colored.

JULY 16, 1851

The rush sparrow [field sparrow] jingles her small change—pure silver on the counter of the pasture.

JULY 16, 1857

As I walked through the pasture side of the hill, saw a [deer] mouse or two glance before me in faint galleries in the grass. They are sel-

white-footed deer mouse

dom seen, for these small deer, like the *larger*, disappear suddenly as if they had exploded before your eyes.

JULY 17, 1854

The stinging spotted flies [deer flies] are very troublesome now. They settle in the hollows of the face and pester us like imps.

JULY 17, 1856

Bathed at Clamshell. See great schools of minnows, apparently [golden] shiners hovering in the clear shallow next the shore. They seem to choose such places for security. They take pretty good care of themselves—and are harder to catch with the hands than you expect, darting out of the way at last quite swiftly. Caught three however between my hands. They have brighter golden irides, all the abdomen conspicuously pale golden—the back and half down the sides pale brown, a broad distinct black band along sides (which methinks marks the shiner) and comparatively transparent beneath behind vent. When the water is gone I am surprised to see how they can skip or spring from side to side in my cup-shaped two hands— for a long time. This to enable them to get off floating planks or pads on the shore when in fright they may have leaped on to them. But they are very tender and the sun and air *soon* kill them. If there is any water in your hand they will pass out through the smallest crack between your fingers. They are about ¾ of an inch long generally though of various sizes.

JULY 17, 1856

Stooping to drink at the Hosmer Spring, I saw a hundred caddis cases of light-colored pebbles at the bottom—and a dozen or twenty crawled halfway up the side of the tub—apparently on their way out to become perfect insects.

JULY 18, 1852

It is a sabbath within the water as well as in the air and on the land—and even the little pickerels not half so long as your finger appear to be keeping it holy among the pads.

JULY 18, 1860

The *Asclepias cornuti* [milkweed, *A. syriaca*] is abundantly visited nowadays by a large orange brown butterfly with dark spots and with *silver* spots beneath [monarch butterfly]. Wherever an asclepias grows you see them.

JULY 20, 1860

Great numbers of pollywogs have apparently just changed into frogs. At the pondlet on Hubbard's land, now separated from the main pond by a stony bar, hundreds of small frogs are out on the shore, enjoying their new state of existence—masses of them, which with constant plashing go hopping into the water a rod or more before me, where they are very swift to conceal themselves in the mud at the bottom. Their bodies may be 1½ inches long or more. I have rarely seen so many frogs together. Yet I hardly see one pollywog left in this pool.

JULY 21, 1851

The quail—invisible—whistles, and who attends.

JULY 22, 1853

Observed on the wild basil on Annursnack small reddish [American copper] butterflies which looked like a part of the plant. It has a singularly soft velvety leaf....

    Yellow butterflies on the road.

JULY 22, 1860

In the path through Hosmer's pines beyond the Assabet, see a wood turtle (whose shell has apparently had one or two mouthfuls taken out of it on the sides) eating in a leisurely manner a common pink-topped toadstool some two inches in diameter—which it had knocked down and half consumed. Its jaws were covered with it.

JULY 23, 1852

Every man says his dog will not touch you. Look out nevertheless.

JULY 25, 1852

This early twitter or breathing of chip-birds in the dawn sounds like something organic in the earth. This is a morning celebrated by birds. Our bluebird sits on the peak of the house and warbles as in the spring—but as he does not now by day.

JULY 26, 1852

Went to Cambridge and Boston today. Dr. Harris says that my great moth is the *Attacus luna*—may be regarded as one of several emperor moths. They are rarely seen, being very liable to be snapped up by birds. Once, as he was crossing the college yard, he saw the wings of one coming down which reached the ground just at his feet. What a tragedy! The wings came down as the only evidence that such a creature had soared—wings large and splendid which were designed to bear a precious burthen through the upper air. So most poems even epics are like the wings come down to earth while the poet whose adventurous flight they evidence has been snapped up [by] the ravenous vulture of this world. If this moth ventures abroad by day some bird will pick out the precious cargo and let the sails and rigging drift—as when the sailor meets with a floating spar and sail and reports a wreck seen in a certain latitude and longitude.

JULY 27, 1860

I see running on the muddy shore under the pontederia [pickerel-weed] a large flat and thin-edged brown bug (with six legs) [water scorpion] some ⅞ of an inch long pointed behind with apparently its eggs — fifty or sixty in number, large and dark-colored standing side by side on their ends and forming a very conspicuous patch which covers about a third of its flat upper surface. I remove one with my knife and it appears to stand in a thick glutinous matter. It runs through the water and mud, and falls upon its back a foot or more from my hand without dislodging them.

JULY 29, 1853

Butterflies of various colors are now more abundant than I have seen them before — especially the small reddish or coppery ones. I counted ten yesterday on a single *Sericocarpus conyzoides* [probably white wood aster]. They were in singular harmony with the plant — as if they made a part of it. The insect that comes after the honey or pollen of a plant is necessary to it and in one sense makes a part of it — being constantly in motion and as they moved opening and closing their wings to preserve their balance, they presented a very lifesome scene. Today I see them on the early goldenrod, *Solidago stricta* [*S. juncea*].

JULY 29, 1856

Pratt gave me a chimney swallow's nest which he says fell down Wesson's chimney with young in it two or three days ago. As it comes to me it is in the form of the segment of the circumference of a sphere whose diameter is 3½ inches — the segment being two plus wide, one side of course longer than the other. (It bears a little soot on the inner side.) It may have been placed against a slanting part of the chimney — or perhaps some of the outer edge is broken off. It is composed wholly of stout twigs, one to two inches long,

¹⁄₁₆ to ⅛ inch in diameter piled quasi cob fashion, so as to form a sort of basketwork ⅓ to ½ inch thick without any lining—at least in this—but very open to the air. These twigs, which are quite knubby, seem to be of the apple, elm, and the like and are firmly fastened together by a very conspicuous whitish semi-transparent glue which is laid on pretty copiously—sometimes extending continuously one inch. It reminds me of the edible nests of the Chinese swallow [edible-nest swiftlet]. Who knows but their edibleness is due to a similar glue secreted by the bird and used still more profusely in building its nests. The chimney swallow is said to break off the twigs as it flies.

JULY 30, 1852

What a gem is a bird's egg, especially a blue or a green one—when you see one broken or whole in the woods! I noticed a small blue egg this afternoon washed up by Flint's Pond and half buried by white sand—and as it lay there alternately wet and dry no color could be fairer, no gem could have a more advantageous or favorable setting. Probably it was shaken out of some nest which overhung the water. I frequently meet with broken egg shells where a crow perchance or some other thief has been marauding. And is not that shell something very precious that houses that winged life?

JULY 30, 1853

Saw some green galls on a goldenrod (?) ¾ an inch in diameter, shaped like a fruit or an Eastern temple ⬡ with two or three little worms inside—completely changing the destiny of the plant, showing the intimate relation between animal and vegetable life. The animal signifies its wishes by a touch and the plant instead of going on to blossom and bear its normal fruit devotes itself to the service of the insect and becomes its cradle and food. It suggests that nature is a kind of gall—that the Creator stung her and man is the grub she is destined to house and feed. The plant rounds off and paints the gall with as much care and love as its own flower and fruit—adorning it perchance even more.

JULY 31, 1855
Mr. Samuel Hoar tells me that about forty-eight years ago, or some two or three years after he came to Concord, where he had an office in the yellow store—there used to be a great many bullfrogs in the mill-pond which by their trumping in the night disturbed the apprentices of a Mr. Joshua Jones who built and lived in the brick house nearby—and soon after set up the trip-hammer. But as Mr. H was going one day to or from his office (he boarded this side the mill-dam) he found that the apprentices had been round the pond in a boat knocking the frogs on the head, got a good-sized tub nearly full of them. After that scarcely any were heard, and the trip-hammer being set up soon after, they all disappeared as if frightened away by the sound. But perhaps the cure was worse than the disease. For I know of one—then a young minister study-ing divinity who boarded in that very brick house—who was so much disturbed by that trip-hammer that out of compassion he was taken in at the old parsonage.

AUGUST 2, 1854
A few fireflies in the meadows. I am uncertain whether that so large and bright and high was a firefly or a shooting star. Shooting stars are but fireflies of the firmament.

AUGUST 2, 1856
A green bittern comes noiselessly flapping with stealthy and in-quisitive looking to this side the stream and then that, thirty feet above the water. This antediluvian bird—creature of the night—is a fit emblem of a dead stream like this Musketicook. This especially is the bird of the river. There is sympathy between its sluggish flight

and the sluggish flow of the stream—its slowly lapsing flight even like the rills of Musketicook and my own pulse sometimes.

AUGUST 2, 1859

That fine z-ing of locusts in the grass which I have heard for three or four days is methinks an August sound—and is very inspiriting. It is a certain maturity in the year, which it suggests. My thoughts are the less crude for it. There is a certain moral and physical sluggishness and standstill at midsummer.

AUGUST 4, 1841

The rush sparrow sings still unintelligible as from beyond a depth in me which I have not fathomed—where my future lies folded up.

AUGUST 4, 1851

As my eye rested on the blossom of the meadowsweet in a hedge I heard the note of an autumnal cricket—and was penetrated with the sense of autumn. Was it sound? or was it form? or was it scent? or was it flavor? It is now the royal month of August. When I hear this sound I am as dry as the rye which is everywhere cut and housed—though I am drunk with the season's wine.

AUGUST 4, 1852

The little bees have gone to sleep amid the clethra blossoms in the rain and are not yet aroused.

AUGUST 4, 1856

This favorable moist weather has expanded some of the huckleberries to the size of bullets. Each patch, each bush seems fuller and blacker than the last. Such a profusion—yet you see neither birds nor beasts eating them unless ants and the huckleberry-bug [shield bug]!!

AUGUST 5, 1851

The air that has swept over Caucasus and the sands of Arabia comes to breathe on New England fields. The dogs bark—they are not as much stiller as man. They are on the alert suspecting the approach of foes. The darkness perchance affects them—makes them mad and wild.

AUGUST 6, 1845

I sit here at my window like a priest of Isis—and observe the phenomena of three thousand years ago, yet unimpaired. The tantivy of wild pigeons, an ancient race of birds, gives a voice to the air—flying by twos and threes athwart my view or perching restless on the white pine boughs occasionally. A fish hawk dimples the glassy surface of the pond and brings up a fish. And for the last half hour I have heard the rattle of railroad cars conveying travelers from Boston to the country.

AUGUST 6, 1852

I find a bumblebee asleep in a thistle blossom (a pasture thistle), the loiterer, having crowded himself in deep amid the dense florets—out of the reach of birds while the sky was overcast. What a sweet couch!

AUGUST 7, 1853

I think that within a week I have heard the alder cricket[22]—a clearer and shriller sound from the leaves in low grounds, a clear shrilling out of a cool moist shade. An autumnal sound. The year is in the grasp of the crickets and they are hurling it round swiftly on its axle.

AUGUST 8, 1856

When I came forth, thinking to empty my boat and go a-meditating along the river, for the full ditches and drenched grass forbade other routes except the highway (and this is one advantage of a boat), I learned to my chagrin that Father's pig was gone. He had leaped out of the pen some time since his breakfast — but his dinner was untouched. Here was an ugly duty not to be shirked — a wild shoat that weighed but ninety to be tracked caught and penned — an afternoon's work at least (if I were lucky enough to accomplish it so soon) prepared for me, quite different from what I had anticipated. I felt chagrined it is true but I could not ignore the fact — nor shirk the duty that lay so near to me. Do the duty that lies nearest thee. I proposed to Father to sell the pig as he was running (somewhere) to a neighbor who had talked of buying him — making a considerable reduction. But my suggestion was not acted on, and the responsibilities of the case all devolved on me — for I could run faster than Father. Father looked to me, and I ceased to look to the river.

Well, let us see if we can track him. Yes, this is the corner where he got out — making a step of his trough. Thanks to the rain, his tracks are quite distinct. Here he went along the edge of the garden over the water and muskmelons — then through the beans and potatoes — and even along the front yard walk I detect the print of his divided hoof, his two sharp toes (*ungulae*). It's a wonder we did not see him. And here he passed out under the gate, across

pig

the road—how naked he must have felt!—into a grassy ditch and whither next. Is it of any use to go hunting him up unless you have devised some mode of catching him when you have found? Of what avail to know where he has been, even where he is? He was so shy the little while we had him—of course he will never come back, he cannot be tempted by a swill-pail. Who knows how many miles off he is—perhaps he has taken the back track and gone to Brighton or Ohio! At most probably we shall only have the satisfaction of glimpsing the nimble beast at a distance from time to time as he trots swiftly through the green meadows and cornfields.

But, now I speak—what is that I see pacing deliberately up the middle of the street forty rods off? It is *he*. As if to tantalize, to tempt us to waste our afternoon—without further hesitation, he thus offers himself. He roots a foot or two and then lies down on his belly in the middle of the street. But think not to catch him a-napping. He has his eyes about—and his ears too. He has already been chased. He gives that wagon a wide berth, and now seeing me he turns and trots back down the street. He turns into a front yard. Now if I can only close that gate upon him $99/100$ of the work is done—but ah! he hears me coming afar off, he foresees the danger—and with swinish cunning and speed he scampers out. My neighbor in the street tries to head him—he jumps to this side the road, then to that, before him—but the third time the pig was there first and went by. "Whose is it?" he shouts. "It's ours." He bolts into that neighbor's yard and so across his premises. He has been twice there before it seems—he knows the road—see what work he has made in his flower-garden! He must be fond of bulbs. Our neighbor picks up one tall flower with its bulb attached, holds it out at arm's length. He is excited about the pig—it is a subject he is interested in. But where is [he] gone now? The last glimpse I had of him was as he went through the cow yard—here are his tracks again in this cornfield, but they are lost in the grass. We lose him—we beat the bushes in vain—he may be far away. But hark!

I hear a grunt. Nevertheless for half an hour I do not see him that grunted. At last I find fresh tracks along the river—and again lose them. Each neighbor whose garden I traverse tells me some anecdote of losing pigs, or the attempt to drive them, by which I am not encouraged. Once more he crosses our first neighbor's garden and is said to be in the road.

But I am not there yet—it is a good way off. At length my eyes rest on him again, after three quarters of an hour's separation. There he trots with the whole road to himself—and now again drops on his belly in a puddle. Now he starts again, seeing me twenty rods [off] deliberates, considers which way I want him to go—and goes the other. There was some chance of driving him along the sidewalk—or letting him go rather—till he slipped under our gate again, but of what avail would that be. How corner and catch him who keeps twenty rods off.

He never lets the open side of the triangle be less than half a dozen rods wide. There was one place where a narrower street turned off at right angles with the main one just this side our yard—but I could not drive him past that. Twice he ran up the narrow street—for he knew I did not wish it—but though the main street was broad and open and no traveler in sight, when I tried to drive him past this opening he invariably turned his piggish head toward me, dodged from side to side and finally ran up the narrow street or *down* the main one as if there were a high barrier erected before him. But really he is no more obstinate than I—I cannot but respect his tactics and his independence. He will be he—and I may be I. He is not unreasonable because he thwarts me—but only the more reasonable. He has a strong will. He stands upon his idea. There is a wall across the path not where a man bars the way—but where he is resolved not to travel. Is he not superior to man therein? Once more he glides down the narrow street, deliberates at a corner, chooses wisely for him, and disappears through an openwork fence. Eastward. He has gone to fresh gardens and

pastures new. Other neighbors stand in the doorways but half sym-
pathizing. Only observing, "Ugly thing to catch." "You have a job
on your hands."

I lose sight of him—but hear that he is far ahead in a large field
and there we try to let him alone a while giving him a wide berth.

At this stage an Irishman was engaged to assist. "I can catch
him," says he with Buonapartean confidence. He thinks him a
family Irish pig. His wife is with him, bare-headed—and his little
flibbertigibbet of a boy seven years old. "Here Johnny, do you run
right off there" (at the broadest possible angle with his own course).
"Oh but he can't do anything." "Oh but I only want him to tell me
where he is—to keep sight of him." Michael soon discovers that
he is not an Irish pig—and his wife and Johnny's occupation are
soon gone. Ten minutes afterward I am patiently tracking him step
by step through a cornfield—a near-sighted man helping me—and
then into garden after garden far eastward, and finally into the
highway, at the graveyard—but hear and see nothing. One suggests
a dog to track him. Father is meanwhile selling him to the black-
smith—who also is trying to get sight of him. After fifteen minutes since he disappeared eastward I hear that he has been to the
river twice far in the north—through the first neighbor's premises.
I wend that way. He crosses the street far ahead, Michael behind—
he dodges up an avenue. I stand in the gap there, Michael at the
other end—and now he tries to corner him. But it is a vain hope
to corner him in a yard. I see a carriage manufactory door open.
"Let him go in there, Flannery." For once the pig and I are of one
mind—he bolts in and the door is closed. It is a large barn crowded
with carriages. The rope is at length obtained—the windows are
barred with carriages lest he bolt through. He is resting quietly on
his belly in the further corner thinking unutterable things.

Now the course recommences within narrower limits—bump
bump bump he goes, against wheels and shafts. We get no hold
yet. He is all ear and eye. Small boys are sent under the carriages to

drive him out—he froths at the mouth and deters them. At length he is stuck for an instant between the spokes of a wheel and I am securely attached to his hind leg. He squeals deafeningly—and is silent. The rope is attached to a hind leg. The door is opened, and the *driving* commences. Roll an egg as well. You may drag him, but you cannot drive him. But he is in the road—and now another thunder shower greets us. I leave Michael with the rope in one hand and a switch in the other and go home. He seems to be gaining a little westward. But, after long delay—I look out and find that he makes but doubtful progress. A boy is made to face him with a stick and it is only when the pig springs at him savagely that progress is made homeward. He will be killed before he is driven home. I get a wheelbarrow and go to the rescue. Michael is alarmed. The pig is rabid, snaps at him. We drag him across the barrow—hold him down—and so at last get him home.

If a wild shoat like this gets loose, first track him if you can, or otherwise discover where he is. Do not scare him more than you can help. Think of some yard or building or other inclosure that will hold him—and by showing your forces (yet as if uninterested parties) fifteen or twenty rods off, let him of his own accord enter it. Then slightly shut the gate. Now corner and tie him and put him into a cart or barrow.

All progress in driving at last was made by facing and endeavoring to switch him from home. He rushed upon you and made a few feet in the desired direction. When I approached with the barrow he advanced to meet it with determination.

So I get home at dark—wet through and supperless—covered with mud and wheel grease, without any rare flowers.

AUGUST 8, 1859
The river, now that it is so clear and sunny, is better than any aquarium. Standing up and pushing gently up the stream or floating yet more quietly down it, I can in some places see the secrets of

half the river and its inhabitants—the common and familiar bream with the dusty light reflected from its fins, the vigorous-looking perch (tiger-like among fishes). I notice that *many* of the perch are poised head downward peeping under the rocks. The motionless pickerel with reticulated back and sides—as it were the seed vessel of a water plant—eyes set far back. It is an enchanter's wand ready to surprise you with life.

AUGUST 9, 1858
Edward Bartlett shows me this morning a nest which he found yesterday. It is saddled on the lowest horizontal branch of an apple tree in Abel Heywood's orchard—against a small twig—and answers to Nuttall's description of the [American] goldfinch's nest, which it probably is. The eggs were five pure white—or with a faint bluish green tinge—just begun to be developed. I did not see the bird.

AUGUST 10, 1860
Saw this evening, behind a picture in R.W.E.'s dining-room, the *hoary bat*. First heard it fluttering at *dusk*—it having hung there all day. Its rear parts covered with a fine hoary down.

AUGUST 12, 1851
The chewinks make a business now of waking each other up with their low "yorrick" in the neighboring low copse.

AUGUST 12, 1854
On Conantum saw a cow looking steadily up into the sky for a minute. It gave to her face an unusual almost human or wood god faunlike expression—and reminded me of some frontispieces to Virgil's Bucolics. She was gazing upward steadily at an angle of about 45°. There were only some downy clouds in that direction. It was so unusual a sight that anyone would notice it. It suggested adoration.

AUGUST 12, 1858

As I stand on the [Clamshell] bank there I find suddenly that I hear, low and steady—under all other sounds—the creak of the mole cricket by the riverside. It has a peculiarly *late* sound—suggestive of the progress of the year.... *Creak creak, creak creak, creak creak, creak creak.* It is a sound associated with the declining year—and recalls the moods of that season. It is so unobtrusive yet universal a sound, so underlying the other sounds which fill the air—the song of birds, rustling of leaves, dry hopping sound of grasshoppers, etc.—that now in my chamber I can hardly be sure whether I hear it still, or remember it, it so rings in my ears.

AUGUST 13, 1840

When I listen to the faint creaking of the crickets, it seems as if my course for the future lay that way.

AUGUST 14, 1856

Meet a little boy with six young blind mice in his hat—which Horatio Watts has given. He did not find them till he came to fork over and turn the hay. There were six of these little brown blind meadow mice (I suppose *Arvicola hirsutus?*) [meadow vole, *Microtus pennsylvanicus*] with short tails and blunt muzzles and great heads—looking like little bulldogs. The nest was open on the surface—amid the roots of the grass, of dried grass—like a bird's 3½ inches diameter, with a gallery or two leading from it. Watts said these were the kind that clung to the mother! But why did they not? Sometimes find nine of them.

AUGUST 15, 1852

Some birds fly in flocks. I see a dense compact flock of bobolinks going off in the air over a field. They cover the rails and alders, and go rustling off with a brassy tinkling note like a ripe crop as I approach—revealing their yellow breasts and bellies. This is an

bobolink

autumnal sight—that small flock of grown birds in the afternoon sky.

AUGUST 15, 1853

The leaves of a rubus [blackberry or raspberry] scored by some worm or insect—i.e. eaten half through leaving whitish serpentine ribbon-like lines doubling on themselves. Some have looked [to] find some mystic alphabet in such things.

AUGUST 16, 1853

How earthy old people become—moldy as the grave. Their wisdom smacks of the earth—there is no foretaste of immortality in it. They remind me of earthworms and mole crickets.

AUGUST 16, 1858

In my boating of late I have several times scared up a couple of summer ducks [wood ducks] of this year—bred in our meadows. They allowed me to come quite near—and helped to people the river. I have not seen them for some days. Would you know the end of our intercourse? Goodwin shot them, and Mrs.——, who never sailed on the river *ate* them. Of course, she knows not what she did. I shall *not* eat her canary.... They belonged to me, as much as to anyone when they were alive—but it was considered of more importance that Mrs.—— should taste the flavor of them dead— than that I should enjoy the beauty of them alive.

AUGUST 18, 1841

I sit here in the barn this flowing afternoon weather, while the school bell is ringing in the village, and find that all the things immediate to be done are very trivial. I could postpone them to hear this locust sing.

AUGUST 18, 1851

Some dogs I have noticed have a propensity to worry cows. They go off by themselves to distant pastures and ever and anon like four-legged devils they worry the cows—full of the devil. They are so full of the devil they know not what to do. I come to interfere between the cows and their tormentors. Ah I grieve to see the devils escape so easily by their swift limbs, imps of mischief. They are the dog state of those boys who pull down handbills in the street. Their next migration perchance will be into such dogs as these—ignoble fate. The dog whose office it should be to guard the herd turned its tormentor. Some courageous cow endeavoring in vain to toss the nimble devil.

AUGUST 18, 1853

What means this sense of lateness that so comes over one now—as if the rest of the year were downhill, and if we had not performed anything before, we should not now.... How early in the year it begins to be late. The sound of the crickets even in the spring makes our hearts beat with its awful reproof—which it encourages with its seasonable warning. It matters not by how little we have fallen behind—it seems irretrievably late. The year is full of warnings of its shortness—as is life. The sound of so many insects and the sight of so many flowers affects us so. The creak of the cricket and the sight of the prunella and autumnal dandelion. They say—for the night cometh in which no man may work.

AUGUST 18, 1854

In a ditch behind Peter's a small *Cistuda blandingii* [Blanding's turtle] swimming off rapidly. Its shell is 4¼ inches long by 3¼ wide in rear, three wide in front. And its depth is nearly two inches, with a slight dorsal ridge—which the large one has not. I distinguished it from the *Emys guttata* [spotted turtle, *Clemmys guttata*] at first glance by its back being sculptured concentrically about the rear side—leaving a smooth space within ½ inch in diameter. My large one is almost entirely smooth on back being sculptured only ⅛ inch wide on circumference of each scale. It has small rather indistinct yellow spots somewhat regularly arranged in the middle of each scale. Head peppered with dull yellow spots above. Head light yellow beneath—and also legs about roots passing into a dirty white. It is a very restless and active turtle. Not once inclosing itself or using its valve at all, at once walking off when put down, keeping its head, legs, and tail out—continually running out its neck to its full extent and often bending it backward over the shell. Its neck with the loose skin about it has a squarish form. Readily turns itself over with its head when on its back. Upper shell black. Sternum light brown with a large black blotch on the outside after part of each scale—and about half its area. Five claws on fore feet, four and a rudiment or concealed one on hind feet. In this small one the sculptured part occupies nearly the whole scale and is from ½ to ¾ inch wide, while in the large one it is only ⅛ of an inch wide—a mere border. Apparently as it grows the smooth rear is extended or shoves forward and a portion of the sculptured part scales off....

I have just been through the process of killing the cistudo for the sake of science—but I cannot excuse myself for this murder, and see that such actions are inconsistent with the poetic perception, however they may serve science, and will affect the quality of my observations. I pray that I may walk more innocently and serenely through nature. No reasoning whatever reconciles me to this act. It affects my day injuriously. I have lost some self respect. I have a murderer's experience in a degree.

AUGUST 18, 1854
I think I saw a [northern] mockingbird on a black cherry near Pedrick's.[23] Size of and like a catbird, bluish black side head, a white

spot on closed wings, lighter breast and beneath—but he flew before I had fairly adjusted my glass. There were brown thrashers with it making their clicking note.

AUGUST 20, 1851

I hear a cricket in the Depot Field—walk a rod or two and find the note proceeds from near a rock. Partly under a rock between it and the roots of the grass he lies concealed—for I pull away the withered grass with my hands—uttering his night-like creak, with a vibratory motion of his wings and flattering himself that it is night because he has shut out the day. He was a black fellow nearly an inch long with two long slender feelers. They plainly avoid the light and hide their heads in the grass. At any rate they regard this as the evening of the year. They are remarkably secret and unobserved considering how much noise they make. Every milkman has heard them all his life—it is the sound that fills his ear as he drives along—but what one has ever got off his cart to go in search of one? I see smaller ones moving stealthily about whose note I do not know. Who ever distinguished their various notes? Which fill the crevices in each other's song. It would be a curious ear indeed that distinguished the species of the crickets which it heard—and traced even the earth song home, each part to its particular performer. I am afraid to be so knowing. They are shy as birds, these little bodies. Those nearest me continually cease their song as I walk so that the singers are always a rod distant—and I cannot easily detect one. It is difficult moreover to judge correctly whence the sound proceeds. Perhaps this wariness is necessary to save them from insectivorous birds—which would otherwise speedily find out so loud a singer. They are somewhat protected by the universalness of the sound, each one's song being merged and lost in the general concert—as if it were the creaking of earth's axle. They are very numerous in oats and other grain which conceals them and yet affords a clear passage.

I never knew any drought or sickness so to prevail as to quench the song of the crickets—it fails not in its season, night or day.

AUGUST 21, 1851
It is remarkable that animals are often obviously manifestly related to the plants which they feed upon or live among—as caterpillars—butterflies—tree toads—partridges—chewinks—and this afternoon I noticed a yellow spider [goldenrod crab spider] on a goldenrod. As if every condition might have its expression in some form of animated being.

AUGUST 21, 1852
Young [domestic] turkeys are straying in the grass which is alive with grasshoppers.

AUGUST 22, 1859
At the factory where they were at work on the dam, they showed large and peculiar insects [water scavenger beetles] which they were digging up amid the gravel and water of the dam—nearly two inches long and half an inch wide, with six legs, two large shield-like plates on the forward part of the body—under which they apparently worked their way through wet sand, and two large claws somewhat lobster-like forward. The abdomen long—of many rings—and fringed with a kind of bristles on each side.

AUGUST 23, 1851
I saw a snake by the roadside and touched him with my foot to see if he were alive. He had a toad in his jaws which he was preparing to swallow with his jaws distended to three times his width, but he relinquished his prey in haste and fled, and I thought as the toad jumped leisurely away with his slime-covered hindquarters glistening in the sun—as if I his deliverer wished to interrupt his medi-

tations, without a shriek or fainting—I thought what a healthy indifference he manifested. Is not this the broad earth still, he said.

AUGUST 24, 1852
The ghost horse [northern walkingstick] on a goldenrod—a real caricature of Flying Childers like a light green seed vessel, three or four inches long and one tenth of an inch in diameter—with four slender legs more than an inch long in two pairs, springing from within an inch of each other in the middle of his body—and an eye more than an inch behind its snout. A caricature on the horse, one or more of its legs in the air as if arrested while taking a step. You can hardly believe it is an insect—and if you handle it it is so sluggish in its motions that you might not discover it if not bent on it. Thus I thought of it till I disturbed it, took it into my hand—and then found it had six legs, and no long snout at all, but only two slender feelers. That it had laid its two fore legs and feelers together so as exactly to resemble a long snout and also a seed vessel the more—with its eye far in the rear.

AUGUST 25, 1854
Tortoise eggs are nowadays dug up in digging potatoes.

AUGUST 25, 1855
In Dennis's field this side the river, I count about one hundred and fifty cowbirds about eight cows—running before their noses and in odd positions awkwardly walking with a straddle, often their heads down and tails up a long time at once—occasionally flying to keep up with a cow, over the heads of the others, and following off after a single cow. They keep close to the cow's head and feet and she does not mind them. But when all went off in a whirring (rippling?) flock at my approach the cow (about whom they were all gathered) *looked off after them* for some time as if she felt deserted.

AUGUST 25, 1856

I paddle directly across the meadow—the river is so high, and land east of the elm on the third or fourth row of potatoes.... Almost every stem which rises above the surface has a grasshopper or caterpillar upon it. Some have seven or eight grasshoppers, clinging to their masts, one close and directly above another—and like shipwrecked sailors now the third or fourth day exposed. Whither shall they jump? It is a quarter of a mile to shore—and countless sharks lie in wait for them. They are so thick that they are like a crop which the grass bears—some stems are bent down by their weight. This flood affects other inhabitants of these fields than men—not only the owners of the grass but its inhabitants much more. It drives them to their upper stories—to take refuge in the rigging. Many that have taken an imprudent leap are seen struggling in the water. How much life is drowned out! That inhabits about the roots of the meadow-grass. How many a family perchance of short-tailed meadow mice has had to scamper or swim!

AUGUST 26, 1851

Woodchucks are seen tumbling into their holes on all sides.

AUGUST 26, 1854

I hear part of a phoebe's strain, as I go over the railroad bridge. It is the voice of dying summer.

AUGUST 26, 1854

Opened one of my snapping turtle's eggs. The egg was not warm to the touch. The young is now larger and dark-colored shell and all— more than a hemisphere, and the yolk which maintains it is much reduced. Its shell very deep, hemispherical, fitting close to the shell of the egg—and if you had not just opened the egg you would say it could not contain so much. Its shell is considerably hardened— its feet and claws developed and also its great head, though held in for want of room. Its eyes are open — it puts out its head — stretches forth its claws — and liberates its tail though all were enveloped in a gelatinous fluid. With its great head it has already the ugliness of the full grown and is already a hieroglyphic of snappishness. It may take a fortnight longer to hatch it.

How much lies quietly buried in the ground that we wot not of. We unconsciously step over the eggs of snapping turtles slowly hatching the summer through. Not only was the surface perfectly dry and trackless there but blackberry vines had run over the spot where these eggs were buried and weeds had sprung up above. If Iliads are not composed in our day, snapping turtles are hatched and arrive at maturity. It already thrusts forth its tremendous head (for the first time in this sphere) and slowly moves from side to side (opening its small glistening eyes for the first time to the light) expressive of dull rage as if it had endured the trials of this world for a century. When I behold this monster thus steadily advancing toward maturity — all nature abetting — I am convinced that there must be an irresistible necessity for mud turtles. With what tenacity Nature sticks to her idea! These eggs not warm to the touch — buried in the ground — so slow to hatch — are like the seeds of vegetable life. . . .

Even the hinder part of a mud turtle's shell is scalloped one would say rather for beauty than use.

AUGUST 26, 1860
The shrilling of the alder locust is the solder that welds these autumn days together. All bushes (*arbusta*) resound with their song, and you wade up to your ears in it. Methinks the burden of their song is the countless harvests of the year — berries, grain, and other fruits.

When I awake in the morning, I remember what I have seen and heard of snapping turtles and am in doubt whether it was dream or reality. I slowly raise my head and peeping over the bedside see my great mud turtle shell lying bottom up under the table—showing its prominent ribs—and realize into what world I have awaked. Before I was in doubt how much prominence my good Genius would give to that fact. That the first object you see on awakening should be an empty mud turtle's shell!! Will it not make me of the earth earthy? Or does it not indicate that I am of the earth earthy? What life—what character this has shielded—which is now at liberty to be turned bottom upward. I can put specimens of all our other turtles into this cavity. This too was once an infant in its egg. When I see this, then I am sure that I am not dreaming, but am awake to this world. I do not know any more terrene fact. It still carries the earth on its back. Its life is between the animal and vegetable—like a seed it is planted deep in the ground, and is all summer germinating. Does it not possess as much the life of the vegetable as the animal?

AUGUST 28, 1854

The meadow is drier than ever—and new pools are dried up. The breams from one to 2½ inches long lying on the sides—and quirking from time to time, a dozen together where there is but a pint of water on the mud, are a handsome but sad sight—pretty green jewels, dying in the sun. I saved a dozen or more by putting them into deeper pools.

AUGUST 28, 1856

I open the painted tortoise nest of June 10th—and find a young turtle partly out of his shell. He is roundish and the sternum clear uniform pink. The marks on the sides are pink. The upper shell is $15/16$ of an inch plus by $13/16$. He is already wonderfully strong and precocious. Though those eyes never saw the light before—he watches me very warily, even at a distance. With what vigor he crawls out of the hole I have made over opposing weeds. He struggles in my fingers with great strength. Has none of the tenderness of infancy. His whole snout is convex and curved like a beak. Having attained the surface he pauses and warily watches me. In the meanwhile another has put his head out of his shell—but I bury the latter up and leave them....

June—July—and August—the tortoise eggs are hatching, a few inches beneath the surface in sandy fields. You tell of active labors—of works of art and wars the past summer. Meanwhile the tortoise eggs underlie this turmoil. What events have transpired on the lit and airy surface three inches above them! Sumner knocked down—Kansas living an age of suspense. Think what is a summer to them. How many worthy men have died and had their funeral sermons preached—since I saw the mother turtle bury her eggs here. They contained an undeveloped liquid then, they are now turtles. June July and August—the livelong summer—what are they with their heats and fevers, but sufficient to hatch a tortoise in. Be not in haste—mind your private affairs. Consider the turtle. A whole summer—June July and August—is not too good nor too much to hatch a turtle in.

AUGUST 28, 1860
Hear the night warbler and the whippoorwill.

AUGUST 29, 1855
Saw two green-winged teal—somewhat pigeon-like on a flat low rock in the Assabet.

AUGUST 29, 1858

Before bathing at the Pokelogan—I see and hear a school of large suckers which have come into this narrow bay—and are swiftly dashing about and rising to the surface with a bubbling sound as if to snatch something from the surface. They agitate the whole bay. They [are] great ruddy-looking fellows limber with life. How intelligent of all watery knowledge. They seem to measure the length, breadth, and depth of that cove—which perhaps they never entered before—with every wave of their fins. They feel it all at once. With what superfluous vigor they seem to move about restlessly in their element. Lift them but six inches and they would quirk their tails in vain. They are poor soft fish however, large as they are, and taste when cooked at present much like boiled brown paper.

AUGUST 30, 1856

Those small gray sparrow-egg cranberries lay so prettily in the recesses of the sphagnum, I could wade for hours in the cold water gazing at them, with a swarm of mosquitoes hovering about my bare legs, but at each step the friendly sphagnum in which I sank protected my legs like a buckler—not a crevice by which my foes could enter.

AUGUST 30, 1859

The pasture thistle though past its prime is quite common—and almost every flower (i.e. thistle) wherever you meet with it, has one or more bumblebees on it clambering over its mass of florets. One such bee which I disturb has much ado before he can rise from the grass and get under weigh—as if he were too heavily laden—and at last he flies but low. Now that flowers are rarer—almost every one of whatever species has bees or butterflies upon it.

bumblebee

AUGUST 31, 1852

Landed near the bee tree. A bumblebee on a cow wheat blossom
sounded like the engine's whistle far over the woods—then like an
Aeolian harp.

SEPTEMBER 1, 1850

Now about the first of September you will see flocks of small birds
forming compact and distinct masses, as if they were not only animated by one spirit but actually held together by some invisible
fluid or film—and will hear the sound of their wings rippling or
fanning the air as they flow through it, flying, the whole mass, rico-

chet like a single bird—or as they flow over the fence. Their mind must operate faster than man's in proportion as their bodies do.

SEPTEMBER 1, 1859

Saw this afternoon, on a leaf in the Saw Mill wood path, a very brilliant beetle ¼ or ⅓ inch in length—with brilliant green and copper reflections [dogbane leaf beetle]. The same surface, or any part of the upper surface of the bug was green from one point of view and burnished copper from another. Yet there was nothing in its form to recommend this bug.

SEPTEMBER 2, 1856

One man's mind running on pigeons will sit thus in the midst of a village—many of whose inhabitants never see nor dream of a pigeon except in the pot, and where even naturalists do not observe—and he looking out with expectation and faith from morning till night, will surely see them.

SEPTEMBER 3, 1851

I had always instinctively regarded the horse as a free people somewhere—living wild. Whatever has not come under the sway of man is wild. In this sense original and independent men are wild—not tamed and broken by society. Now for my part I have such a respect for the horse's nature as would tempt me to let him alone—not to interfere with him—his walks, his diet, his loves. But by mankind he is treated simply as if he was an engine which must have rest and is sensible of pain. Suppose that every squirrel were made to turn a coffee mill! Suppose that the gazelles were made to draw milk carts!

SEPTEMBER 4, 1851

Saw what I thought a small red dog in the road—which cantered along over the bridge this side the powder mills, and then turned into the woods. This decided me—this turning into the woods—

that it was a [red] fox. The dog of the woods. The dog that is more at home in the woods than in the roads and fields. I do not often see a dog turning into the woods.

SEPTEMBER 4, 1854

I have provided my little snapping turtle with a tub of water and mud—and it is surprising how fast he learns to use his limbs and this world. He actually runs with the yolk still trailing from him, as if he had got new vigor from contact with the mud. The insensibility and toughness of his infancy make our life with its disease and low spirits ridiculous. He impresses me as the rudiment of a man worthy to inhabit the earth. He is born with a shell. That is symbolical of his toughness. His shell being so rounded and sharp on the back at this age he can turn over without trouble.

SEPTEMBER 4, 1856

The crackling flight of grasshoppers. The grass also is all alive with them and they trouble me, by getting into my shoes which are loose—and obliging me to empty them occasionally.

SEPTEMBER 6, 1857

I see one of those peculiarly green locusts with long and slender legs on a grass stem—which are often concealed by their color. What green herbaceous graminivorous ideas he must have! I wish that my thoughts were as *seasonable* as his.

SEPTEMBER 7, 1854

This seems the first autumnal sunset. The small skaters seem more active than by day—or their slight dimpling is more obvious in the lit twilight. A stray white cat sits on the shore looking over the water. This is her hour. A nighthawk dashes past low over the water.

SEPTEMBER 9, 1851

On the first top of Conantum. I hear the farmer harnessing his horse and starting for the distant market, but no man harnesses himself, and starts for worthier enterprises. One cock-crow tells the whole story of the farmer's life. The moon is now sinking into clouds in the horizon. I see the glow-worms deep in the grass by the brookside in midst of Conantum. The moon shines dun and red. A solitary whippoorwill sings.

SEPTEMBER 9, 1854

This morning I find a little hole ¾ of an inch or an inch over above my small tortoise eggs—and find a young tortoise coming out (apparently in the rainy night) just beneath. It is the *Sternothaerus odoratus* [musk turtle]—already has the strong scent—and now has drawn in its head and legs. I see no traces of the yolk, or what-not, attached. It may have been out of the egg some days. *Only one* as yet. I buried them in the garden June 15th.

I am affected by the thought that the earth nurses these eggs. They are planted in the earth, and the earth takes care of them—she is genial to them and does not kill them. It suggests a certain vitality and intelligence in the earth—which I had not realized. This mother is not merely inanimate and inorganic. Though the immediate mother turtle abandons her offspring, the earth and sun are kind to them. The old turtle on which the earth rests takes care of them while the other waddles off. Earth was not made poisonous and deadly to them. The earth has some virtue in it—when seeds are put into it, they germinate, when turtles' eggs they hatch in due time. Though the mother turtle remained and brooded them—it would still nevertheless be the universal world turtle which through her cared for them as now. Thus the earth is the mother of all creatures.

SEPTEMBER 12, 1851

Saw a pigeon place on George Heywood's cleared lot—the six dead trees set up for the pigeons to alight on, and the brush house close by to conceal the man. I was rather startled to find such a thing going now in Concord. The pigeons on the tree looked like fabulous birds with their long tails and their pointed breasts. I could hardly believe they were alive and not some wooden birds used for decoys—they sat so still—and even when they moved their necks I thought it was the effect of art. As they were not catching them I approached and scared away a dozen birds who were perched in the trees and found that they were freshly baited there—though the net was carried away, perchance to some other bed. . . . As I stood there, I heard a rushing sound and looking up saw a flock of thirty or forty pigeons dashing toward the *trees,* who suddenly whirled on seeing me and circled round and made a new dash toward the bed as if they would fain alight if I had not been there—then steered off.

SEPTEMBER 12, 1854

I scare pigeons from Hubbard's oaks beyond. How like the creaking of trees the slight sounds they make! Thus they are concealed. Not only their *prating* or *quivet* is like a sharp creak—but I heard a sound from them like a dull grating or cracking of bough on bough. . . .

On a white oak beyond Everett's orchard by the road I see quite a flock of pigeons and their blue black droppings and their feathers spot the road. The bare limbs of the oak apparently attracted them—though its acorns are thick on the ground. These are found whole in their crops. They swallow them whole. I should think from the droppings that they had been eating berries. I hear that Wetherbee caught ninety-two dozen last week.

SEPTEMBER 12, 1857

In an open part of the swamp, started a very large *wood frog* which gave one leap and squatted still. I put down my finger and though it shrank a little at first it permitted me to stroke it as long as I pleased. Having passed, it occurred to me to return and cultivate its acquaintance. To my surprise, it allowed me to slide my hand under it and lift it up, while it squatted cold and moist on the middle of my palm, panting naturally. I brought it close to my eye and examined it. It was very beautiful seen thus nearly, not the dull dead leaf color which I had imagined — but its back was like burnished bronze armor defined by a varied line on each side, where as it seemed the plates of armor united. It had four or five dusky bars which matched exactly when the legs were folded — showing that the painter applied his brush to the animal when in that position — and reddish orange soles to its delicate feet. There was a conspicuous dark brown patch along the side of the head, whose upper edge passed directly through the eye horizontally just above its center, so that the pupil and all below were dark and the upper portion of the iris golden. I have since taken up another in the same way. Indeed they can generally be treated so. Some are reddish, as burnished copper.

SEPTEMBER 12, 1858

In Hubbard's ditched meadow this side his grove, I see a great many large spider webs stretched across the ditches — about two feet from bank to bank, though the thick woven part is ten or twelve inches.

They are parallel a few inches or a foot or more apart and more or less vertical and attached to a main cable stretched from bank to bank. They are the yellow backed spider [yellow garden spider] — commonly large and stout but of various sizes. I count sixty-four such webs there — and in each case the spider occupies the center, head downward. This is enough methinks to establish the rule.

yellow garden spider

They are not afraid of turning their brains then. Many insects must be winging their way over this small river. It reminds me of the Indians catching ducks at Green Bay with nets in "old times."

SEPTEMBER 15, 1859

Pigeons dart by on every side—a dry slate color, like weather-stained wood (the weather-stained birds) fit color for this aerial traveler—a more subdued and earthy blue than the sky, as its field (or path) is between the sky and the earth. Not black or brown, as is the earth—but a terrene or slaty blue suggesting their aerial resorts and habits.

SEPTEMBER 16, 1859

Grasshoppers have been very abundant in dry fields for two or three weeks. Sophia walked through the Depot Field a fortnight ago and when she got home picked fifty or sixty from her skirts—for she wore hoops and crinoline. Would not this be a good way to clear a field of them. To send a bevy of fashionably dressed ladies across a field and leave them to clean their skirts when they get home. It would supplant anything at the patent office—and the motive power is cheap.

SEPTEMBER 18, 1860

The toadstools in wood paths are perforated (almost like pepper boxes) by flattish slippery insects bronze and black [thrips]—which are beneath and within it. Or you see their heads projecting and the *dust* (or exuviae) they make like a curb about the holes.

SEPTEMBER 21, 1859

I sat near Coombs's pigeon place by White Pond. The pigeons sat motionless on his bare perches—from time to time dropping down into the bed—and uttering a *quivet* or two. Some stood on the perch—others squatted flat. I could see their dove-colored breasts.

Then all at once, being alarmed, would take to flight but ere long return in straggling parties.

He tells me that he has fifteen dozen baited—but does not intend to catch any more at present or for two or three weeks, hoping to attract others. Rice says that white oak acorns pounded up shells and all make the best bait for them.

SEPTEMBER 24, 1855

I suppose it was the solitary sandpiper (*Totanus solitarius*) which I saw feeding at the water's edge on Cardinal Shore—like a snipe. It was very tame—we did not scare it even by shouting. I walked along the shore to within twenty-five feet of it ... and it still ran toward me in feeding—and when I flushed it, it flew round and alighted between me and C. who was only three or four rods off. It was about as large as a snipe, had a bluish dusky bill about 1¼ inches long apparently straight which it kept thrusting into the shallow water with a nibbling motion—a perfectly white belly, dusky green legs, bright *brown* and black above with duskier wings. When it flew, its wings which were uniformly dark hung down much and I noticed no white above—and heard no note.

SEPTEMBER 24, 1857

I saw a red squirrel run along the bank under the hemlocks with a nut in its mouth. He stopped near the foot of a hemlock, and hastily pawing a hole with his fore feet, dropped the nut, covered it up and retreated partway up the trunk of the tree—all in a few moments. I approached the shore to examine the deposit—and he descending betrayed no little anxiety for his treasure and made two or three motions to recover the nut before he retreated. Digging there I found two pignuts joined together with their green shells on— buried about 1½ inches in the soil under the red hemlock leaves.

This then is the way forests are planted. This nut must have been brought twenty rods at least—and was buried at just the right depth. If the squirrel is killed or neglects its deposit—a hickory springs up. [*Penciled addition:* These nuts were there Oct. 8th. Gone Nov. 21st.]

SEPTEMBER 24, 1860

See two very handsome butterflies on the Flint's Pond road in the woods at Gourgas lot which C. had not seen before. I find that they are quite like the *Vanessa atalanta*—or red admiral of England.

SEPTEMBER 25, 1840

As I sat on the cliff today the crows, as with one consent, began to assemble from all parts of the horizon—from river and pond and field, and wood, in such numbers as to darken the sky—as if a netting of black beads were stretched across it. After some tacking and wheeling the center of the immense cohort was poised just over my head. Their cawing was deafening, and when that ceased the winnowing of their wings was like the rising of a tempest in the forest. But their silence was more ominous than their din. At length they departed sullenly as they came.

SEPTEMBER 25, 1851

Examined the [bald-faced] hornets' nest near Hubbard's Grove—suspended from contiguous huckleberry bushes. The tops of the bushes appearing to grow out of it, little leafy sprigs, had a pleasing effect. An inverted cone eight or nine inches by seven or eight. I found no hornets now buzzing about it. Its entrance appeared to have been enlarged—so I concluded it had been deserted—but looking nearer I discovered two or three dead hornets, men of war, in the entryway. Cutting off the bushes which sustained it I proceeded to open it with my knife. First there were half a dozen layers of waved brownish paper resting loosely on one another—occupying nearly an inch in thickness—for a covering. Within were the six-sided cells in three stories, suspended from the roof and from one another by one or two suspension rods only—the lower story much smaller than the rest. And in what may be called the attic garret of the structure were two live hornets apparently partially benumbed with cold, which in the sun seemed rapidly recovering themselves, their faculties. Most of the cells were empty, but in some were young hornets still, their heads projecting— apparently still-born. Perhaps overtaken unexpectedly by cold weather. These insects appear to be very sensible to cold. The inner circles of cells were made of whitish, the outer of grayish paper. It was like a deserted castle of the Mohawks. A few dead ones at the entrance of their castle. . . .

The hornets' nest not brown but gray, two shades whitish and dark, alternating on the outer layers or the covering—giving it a waved appearance.

SEPTEMBER 25, 1857
In an old grist mill the festoons of cobwebs revealed by the white dust on them are an ornament. Looking over the shoulder of the miller I drew his attention to a mouse running up a brace. "Oh, yes," said he, "we have plenty of them. Many are brought to the mill in barrels of corn and when the barrel is placed on the platform of the hopper they scamper away."

SEPTEMBER 27, 1860
Monroe's tame ducks sail along and feed close to me as I am working there. Looking up I see a little dipper [horned grebe] about one half their size in the middle of the river—evidently attracted by these tame ducks, as to a place of security. I sit down and watch it. The tame ducks have paddled four or five rods downstream along the shore. They soon detect the dipper, three or four rods off, and betray alarm by a tittering note—especially when it dives, as it does continually. At last, when it is two or three rods off and approaching them by diving, they all rush to the shore and come out on it in

their fear—but the dipper shows itself close to the shore and when they enter the water again joins them within two feet, still diving from time to time and threatening to come up in their midst. They return upstream—more or less alarmed and pursued in this wise by the dipper who does not know what to make of their fears—and soon the dipper is thus tolled along to within twenty feet of where I sit and I can watch it at my leisure. It has a dark bill and considerable white on the sides of the head or neck with black between it—no tufts, and no observable white on back or tail.

When at last disturbed by me it suddenly sinks low (all its body) in the water without diving. Thus it can float at various heights. (So on the 30th I saw one suddenly dash along the surface from the meadow ten rods before me to the middle of the river there and then dive, and though I watched fifteen minutes and examined the tufts of grass, I could see no more of it.)

SEPTEMBER 29, 1858
Brushed a *spectrum* ghost horse off my face in a birch wood—by the J. P. Brown Cold Heart Leaf Pond.

SEPTEMBER 30, 1852
10 A.M. To Fair Haven Pond bee hunting—Pratt, Rice, Hastings, and myself—in a wagon. A fine clear day after the coolest night and severest frost we have had. The apparatus was first a simple round tin box about 4½ inches in diameter and 1½ inches deep, containing a piece of empty honeycomb.... By the roadside at Walden—on the sunny hillside sloping to the pond—we saw a large mass of goldenrod and aster several rods square and comparatively fresh. Getting out of our wagon we found it to be resounding with the hum of bees. (It was about 1 o'clock.) There were far more flowers than we had seen elsewhere. Here were bees in great numbers, both bumblebees and honeybees as well as butterflies and wasps and flies. So pouring a mixture of honey and water into the empty comb

in the tin box, and holding the lid of the tin box in one hand and the wooden box with the slides shut in the other, we proceeded to catch the honeybees by shutting them in suddenly between the lid of the tin box and the large circular bottom of the wooden one—cutting off the flower stem with the edge of the lid at the same time. Then, holding the lid still against the wooden box we drew the slide in the bottom and also the slide covering the window at the top that the light might attract the bee to pass up into the wooden box. As soon as he had done so and was buzzing against the glass—the lower slide was closed and the lid with the flower removed, and more bees were caught in the same way. Then placing the open tin box containing the comb filled with honeyed water close under the wooden one, the slide was drawn again—and the upper slide closed making it dark—and in about a minute they went to feeding as was ascertained by raising slightly the wooden box. Then the latter was wholly removed and they were left feeding or sucking up the honey in broad daylight. In from two to three minutes one had loaded himself and commenced leaving the box. He would buzz round it back and forth a foot or more, and then perhaps finding that he was too heavily loaded alight to empty himself or clean his feet. ◯ ⌒ ⌒ Then, starting once more, he would begin to circle round irregularly at first in a small circle only a foot or two in diameter as if to examine the premises that he might know them again till at length rising higher and higher and circling wider and wider and swifter and swifter till his orbit was ten or twelve feet in diameter and as much from the ground—though its center might be moved to one side so that it was very difficult to follow him—especially if you looked against a wood or the hill, and you had to lie low to fetch him against the sky. (You must operate in an open space, not in a wood.) All this as if to ascertain the course to his nest. Then in a minute or less from his first starting he darts off in a bee line—that is as far as I could see him which might be eight or ten rods looking against the sky (and you had to follow his whole career very attentively indeed to see when and where he went off at a tangent), in a waving or sinuous line toward his nest.

We sent forth as many as a dozen bees—which flew in about three directions—but all toward the village or where we knew there were hives. They did not fly so almost straight as I had heard but within three or four feet of the same course for half a dozen rods or as far as we could see. Those belonging to one hive all had to digress to get round an apple tree. As none flew in the right direction for us we did not attempt to line them. In less than half an hour the first returned to the box still lying on the woodpile (for not one of the bees on the surrounding flowers discovered it) and so they came back one after another, loaded themselves and departed—but now they went off with very little preliminary circling, as if assured of their course.

We were furnished with little boxes of red—blue—green—yellow—and white paint in dry powder, and with a stick we sprinkled a little of the red powder on the back of one while he was feeding—gave him a little dab—and it settled down amid the fuzz of his back and gave him a distinct red jacket. He went off like most of them toward some hives about three quarters of a mile distant, and we observed by the watch the time of his departure. In just twenty-two minutes red jacket came back, with enough of the powder still on his back to mark him plainly. He may have gone more than three quarters of a mile. At any rate he had a head wind to contend with while laden. They fly swiftly and surely to their nests never resting by the way—and I was surprised, though I had been informed of it, at the distance to which the village bees go for flowers....

We also caught and sent forth a bumblebee who maneuvered like the others—though we thought he took time to eat some before he loaded himself and then he was so overloaded and bedaubed that he had to alight after he had started and it took him several minutes to clean himself.

It is not in vain that the flowers bloom and bloom late too in favored spots. To us they are a culture and a luxury, but to bees meat and drink. The tiny bee which we thought lived far away there in a flower bell in that remote vale—he is a great voyager and anon he rises up over the top of the wood and sets sail with his sweet cargo straight for his distant haven. How well they know the woods and fields and the haunt of every flower! The flowers perchance are widely dispersed because the sweet which they collect from the atmosphere is rare but also widely dispersed—and the bees are enabled to travel far to find it. A precious burthen like their color and fragrance—a crop which the heavens bear and deposit on the earth.

OCTOBER 1, 1858
Let a full grown but young cock stand near you. How full of life he is, from the tip of his bill through his trembling wattles and comb and his bright eye to the extremity of his clean toes! How alert and restless—listening to every sound and watching every motion. How various his notes from the finest and shrillest alarum as a hawk sails over—surpassing the most accomplished violinist on the short strings—to a hoarse and terrene voice or cluck. He has a word for every occasion—for the dog that rushes past and the partlet cackling in the barn. And then how elevating himself and flapping his wings he gathers impetus and air and launches forth that world-renowned ear-piercing strain. Not a vulgar note of defiance—but the mere effervescence of life like the bursting of a bubble in a wine cup. Is any gem so bright as his eye?

OCTOBER 3, 1858
One brings me this morning a Carolina rail [sora] alive—this year's bird evidently from its marks. He saved it from a cat in the road near the Battle Ground. On being taken up it pecked a little at first—but was soon quiet. It staggers about as if weak on my windowsill and pecks at the glass—or stands with its eyes shut half

asleep and its back feathers hunched up. Possibly it is wounded. I suspect it may have been hatched here!

Its feet are large and spreading—qualifying it to run on mud or pads. Its crown is black but chin white and its back feathers are distinctly edged with white in streaks.

OCTOBER 4, 1859

The birds seem to delight in these first fine days of the fall in the warm hazy light. Robins, bluebirds (in families on the almost bare elms), phoebes—and probably purple finches. I hear half strains from many of them as the song sparrow, bluebird, etc. and the sweet *phe-be* of the chickadee.

Now the year itself *begins* to be ripe—ripened by the frost like a persimmon.

OCTOBER 6, 1860

The crow methinks is our only large bird that hovers and circles about in flocks in an irregular and straggling manner—filling the air over your head and sporting in it as if at home here. They often burst up above the woods where they were perching, like the black fragments of a powder mill just exploded.

OCTOBER 7, 1842

A little girl has just brought me a purple finch or American linnet. These birds are now moving south. It reminds me of the pine and spruce, and the juniper and cedar on whose berries it feeds. It has the crimson hues of the October evenings and its plumage still shines as if it had caught and preserved some of their tints (beams?). We know it chiefly as a traveler. It reminds me of many things I had forgotten. Many a serene evening lies snugly packed under its wing.

OCTOBER 8, 1851

This warm day is a godsend to the wasps. I see them buzzing about the broken windows of deserted buildings as Jennie Dugan's—the yellow-knotted.

OCTOBER 8, 1852

As I was paddling along the north shore, after having looked in vain over the pond for a loon—suddenly a loon sailing toward the middle a few rods in front set up his wild laugh, and betrayed himself.... I could commonly hear the plash of the water when he came up and so also detected him. It was commonly a demoniac laughter yet somewhat like a water bird—but occasionally when he had balked me most successfully and come up a long way off, he uttered a long-drawn unearthly howl probably more like a wolf than any other bird. This was his looning. As when a beast puts his muzzle to the ground and deliberately howls—perhaps the wildest sound I ever heard, making the woods ring. And I concluded that he laughed in derision of my effort—confident of his own resources. Though the sky was overcast the pond was so smooth that I could see where he broke the surface if I did not hear him. His white breast—the stillness of the air—the smoothness of the water were all against. At length having come up fifty rods off he uttered one of those prolonged unearthly howls—as if calling on the god of loons to aid him—and immediately there came a wind from the east and rippled the surface, and filled the whole air with misty rain. I was impressed as if it were the prayer of the loon and his god was angry with me.

OCTOBER 8, 1857

Walking through the Lee farm swamp a dozen or more rods from the river I found a large box trap closed. I opened it and found in it the remains of a gray rabbit, skin, bones, and mold closely fitting the right-angled corner of one side. It was wholly inoffensive, as so much vegetable mold, and must have been dead some years. None of the furniture of the trap remained but the box itself with a lid which just moved on two rusty nails—the stick which held the bait, the string, etc., etc. were all gone. The box had the appearance of having been floated off in an upright position by a freshet. It had been a rabbit's living tomb—he had gradually starved to death in it. What a tragedy to have occurred within a box in one of our quiet swamps. The trapper lost his box, the rabbit its life. The box had not been gnawed. After days and nights of moaning and struggle heard for a few rods through the swamp, increasing weakness and emaciation—and delirium—the rabbit breathed its last. They tell you of opening the tomb and finding by the contortions of the body that it was buried alive. This was such a case. Let the trapping boy dream of the dead rabbit in its ark as it sailed like a small meeting house with its rude spire—slowly with a grand and solemn motion, far amid the alders.

OCTOBER 9, 1860
I wonder that the very cows and the dogs in the street do not manifest a recognition of the bright tints about and above them.

I saw a terrier dog glance up and down the painted street before he turned in at his master's gate—and I wondered what he thought of those lit trees, if they did not touch his philosophy or spirits—but I fear he had only his common doggish thoughts after all.

He trotted down the yard as if it were a matter of course after all—or else as if he deserved it all.

OCTOBER 10, 1851
The air this morning is full of bluebirds—and again it is spring.

OCTOBER 10, 1856
While moving the fence today dug up a large reddish, mummy-like chrysalid or nymph (i.e. of the sphinx moth).

OCTOBER 10, 1858

I find the undersides of the election cake fungi there [Abel Hosmer's wood turtle path] covered with *pink* colored fleas—apparently poduras [springtails]—skipping about when it is turned up to the light.

OCTOBER 11, 1856

In the path as I go up the hill beyond the springs—on the edge of Stow's sproutland—I find a little snake which somebody has killed with his heel. It is apparently *Coluber amoenus,* the red snake [northern redbelly snake].[24] Brown above, light red beneath—about eight inches long, but the end of its tail is gone (only ¾ of an inch of it left). I count some one hundred and twenty-seven *plates.* It is a conspicuous light red beneath—then a bluish gray line along the sides, and above this brown—with a line of lighter or yellowish brown down the middle of the back.

OCTOBER 13, 1851

The alert and energetic man leads a more intellectual life in winter than in summer. In summer the animal and vegetable in him are perfected as in a torrid zone—he lives in his senses mainly. In winter cold reason and not warm passion has her sway—he lives in thought and reflection. He lives a more spiritual and less sensual life.

If he has passed a merely sensual summer, he passes his winter in a torpid state like some reptiles and other animals.

OCTOBER 15, 1855

Saw a striped squirrel on a rail fence with some kind of weed in his mouth. Was it milkweed seed? At length he scud swiftly along the middle rail past me and instead of running over or around the posts, he glided through the little hole in the post left above the rails—as swiftly as if there had been no post in the way. Thus he sped through five posts in succession in a straight line—incredibly quick, only stooping and straightening himself at the holes.

OCTOBER 16, 1857

I saw some blackbirds, apparently grackles [rusty blackbirds], singing, after their fashion, on a tree by the river. Most had those grayish brown heads and necks—some at least much ferruginous or reddish brown reflected. They were pruning themselves and splitting their throats in vain trying to sing as the other day. All the melody flew off in splinters.

OCTOBER 16, 1859

When I get to Willow Bay I see the new musquash houses erected—conspicuous on the now nearly leafless shores. To me this is an important and suggestive sight—as, perchance, in some countries new haystacks in the yards. As to the Esquimaux the erection of winter houses.

I remember the phenomenon annually for thirty years. A more constant phenomenon here than the new haystacks in the yard—for they were erected here probably before man dwelt here and may still be erected here when man has departed. For thirty years I have annually observed about this time or earlier, the freshly erected winter lodges of the musquash along the riverside reminding us that if we have no gypsies we have a more indigenous race of furry quadrupedal men maintaining their ground in our midst still. This may not be an annual phenomenon to you. It may not be in the Greenwich almanac—or ephemeris—but it has an important place in my Kalendar. So surely as the sun appears to be in Libra or Scorpio, I see the conical winter lodges of the musquash rising above the withered pontederia and flags. There will be some reference to it, by way of parable or otherwise in *my* New Testament. Surely, it is

muskrat

a defect in our *Bible* that it is not truly *ours,* but a Hebrew Bible. The most pertinent illustrations for us are to be drawn, not from Egypt or Babylonia, but from New England. . . .

Men attach a false importance to celestial phenomena as compared with *terrestrial*—as if it were more respectable and elevating to watch your neighbors than to mind your own affairs. The nodes of the stars are not the knots we have to untie. The phenomena of our year are one *thing*—those of the almanac *another!* For October, for instance, instead of making the sun enter the sign of the scorpion I would much sooner make him enter a musquash house. Astronomy is a fashionable study, patronized by princes, but not fungi. "Royal Astronomer."

The snapping turtle too must find a place among the constellations—though it may have to supplant some doubtful characters already there. If there is no place for him overhead, he can serve us bravely underneath supporting the earth.

OCTOBER 16, 1859

Returning, the river is perfectly still and smooth. The broad, shallow water on each side bathing the withered grass looks as if it were ready to put on its veil of ice at any moment.... So near are we to winter.

Then nearer home I hear two or three song sparrows on the buttonbushes sing as in spring—that memorable tinkle—as if it would be last as it was first.

OCTOBER 18, 1855

I find the white fragments of a tortoise shell in the meadow—thirty or forty pieces, straight-sided polygons—which apparently a hay cart passed over. They look like broken crockery. I brought it home and amused myself with putting it together. It is a painted tortoise. The variously formed sections or component parts of the shell are not broken but only separated. To restore them to their places is like the game which children play with pieces of wood completing a picture. It is surprising to observe how these different parts are knitted together by countless minute teeth on their edges. Then the scales which are not nearly so numerous and therefore larger commonly are so placed over the former as to break joints always, as appears by the indented lines at their edges and the serrations of the shell. These scales too *slightly* overlap each other, i.e. the foremost over the next behind—so that they may not be rubbed off. Thus the whole case is bound together like a very stout bandbox. The bared shell is really a very interesting study. The sternum in its natural position looks like a well contrived drag—turned up at the sides in one solid piece....

To rebuild the tortoise shell is a far finer game than any geographical or other puzzle, for the pieces do not merely make part of a plane surface—but you have got to build a roof and a floor and the connecting walls. These are not only thus dovetailed and braced and knitted and bound together—but also held together by the skin and muscles within. It is a *band*box.

OCTOBER 18, 1857

As I was returning over Hubbard's stump fence pasture, I heard some of the common black field crickets (¾ of an inch long) two or three rods before me make as I thought a peculiar shrilling, like a clear and sharp twittering of birds—that I looked up for some time to see a flock of small birds going over, but they did not arrive. These fellows were, one or two, at the mouth of their burrows— and as I stood over one I saw how he produced the sound, by very slightly lifting his wing cases (if that is the name of them) and shuf-fling them (transversely of course) over each other about ⅛ of an inch, perhaps three or four times, and then stopping.

Thus they stand at the mouths of their burrows, in the warm pastures, near the close of the year, shuffling their wing cases over each other (the males only) and produce this sharp but pleasant creaking sound—helping to fetch the year about. Thus the sounds of human industry and activity—the roar of cannon, blasting of rocks, whistling of locomotives, rattling of carts, tinkering of arti-

field cricket

sans, and voices of men—may sound to some distant ear like an earth song and the creaking of crickets. The crickets keep about the mouths of their burrows as if apprehending cold.

OCTOBER 20, 1859
Saw a tree toad on the ground in a sandy wood path—it did not offer to hop away—may have been chilled by the rain (?). It is marked on the back with black—somewhat in the form of the hylodes.

OCTOBER 20, 1857
Melvin tells me that Skinner says he thinks he heard a wildcat [bobcat] scream in E. Hubbard's Wood—by the Close. It is worth the while to have a Skinner in the town else we should not know that we had wildcats. They had better look out or he will skin them—for that seems to have been the trade of his ancestors. How long Nature has maneuvered to bring our Skinner within earshot of that wildcat's scream!

OCTOBER 22, 1852
When I approached the pond over Heywood's Peak, I disturbed a hawk (a fish hawk?) on a white pine by the water watching for his prey—with long narrow sharp wings and a white belly. He flew slowly across the pond somewhat like a gull. He is the more picturesque object against the woods or water—for being white beneath.

OCTOBER 23, 1853
Many phenomena remind me that now is to some extent a second spring,—not only the new-springing and blossoming of flowers, but the peeping of the hylodes for some time, and the faint warbling of their spring notes by many birds.

OCTOBER 23, 1857

I find one of those small hard dark brown millipede worms partly crawled into a hole in a chestnut.

OCTOBER 24, 1858

That large hornets' nest which I saw on the 4th is now deserted and I bring it home. But in the evening warmed by my fire two or three come forth and crawl over it—and I make haste to throw it out the window.

OCTOBER 25, 1860

Saw in E. Hubbard's clintonia swamp a large [wolf] spider with a great golden colored abdomen as big as a hazelnut on the wet leaves. There was a figure in brown lines on the back in the form of a pagoda—with its stories successively smaller. The legs were pale or whitish with dark or brown bars.

OCTOBER 26, 1853

I well remember the time this year when I first heard the dream of the toads. I was laying out house-lots on Little River in Haverhill. We had had some raw, cold and wet weather. But this day was remarkably warm and pleasant and I had thrown off my outside coat. I was going home to dinner—past a shallow pool which was green with springing grass and where a new house was about being erected—when it occurred to me that I heard the dream of the toad. It rang through and filled all the air—though I had not heard it once. And I turned my companion's attention to it—but he did not appear to perceive it as a new sound in the air. Loud and prevailing as it is, most men do not notice it at all. It is to them perchance a sort of simmering or seething of all nature. That afternoon the dream of the toads rang through the elms by Little River and affected the thoughts of men though they were not conscious that they heard it.

OCTOBER 26, 1857

I see two great fish hawks (*possibly* blue herons)[25] slowly beating northeast against the storm—by what a curious tie circling ever near each other and in the same direction, as if you might expect to find the very motes in the air to be paired. Two long undulating wings conveying a feathered body through the misty atmosphere—and thus inseparably associated with another planet of the same species. I can just glimpse their undulating lines. Damon and Pythias they must be....

Where is my mate—beating against the storm with me?

OCTOBER 26, 1857

These regular phenomena of the seasons get at last to be (they were *at first* of course) simply and plainly phenomena or phases of my life. The seasons and all their changes are in me. I see not a dead eel or floating snake—or a gull—but it rounds my life, and is like a line or accent in its poem. Almost I believe the Concord would not rise and overflow its banks again were I not here. After a while I learn what my moods and seasons are. I would have nothing subtracted—I can imagine nothing added. My moods are thus *periodical*, not two days in my year alike. The perfect correspondence of Nature to man, so that he is at home in her! ...

Those sparrows too are thoughts I have. They come and go—they flit by quickly on their migrations, uttering only a faint *chip*. I know not whither or why exactly—one will not rest upon its twig for me to scrutinize it. The whole copse will be alive with my rambling thoughts—bewildering me by their very multitude but they will all be gone directly without leaving me a feather.

My loftiest thought is somewhat like an eagle that suddenly comes into the field of view—suggesting great things and thrilling the beholder, as if it were bound hitherward with a message for me—but it comes no nearer but circles and soars away, growing dimmer. Disappointing me till it is lost behind a cliff or a cloud.

OCTOBER 27, 1851

Saw a woodcock feeding, probing the mud with its long bill under the railroad bridge within two feet of me for a long time. Could not scare it far away. What a disproportionate length of bill. It is a sort of badge they wear as a punishment for greediness in a former state.

OCTOBER 28, 1852

As I was eating my dinner of rice today with an open window a small species of wild bee with many yellow rings about the abdomen came in and alighted on the molasses pitcher. It took up the molasses quite fast and soon made quite bare and white a considerable space on the nose of the pitcher which was smeared with molasses — then having loaded itself it circled round the pitcher a few times while I was helping myself to some molasses and flew against a closed window, but ere long finding the open one by which it had entered it winged its way to its nest. Probably if I had been willing to leave the window open and wait awhile it would have returned.

OCTOBER 28, 1855

As I paddle under the hemlock bank this cloudy afternoon — about 3 o'clock — I see a screech owl sitting on the edge of a hollow hemlock stump about three feet high, at the base of a large hemlock. It sits with its head drawn in, eying me with its eyes partly open — about twenty feet off. When it hears me move, it turns its head toward me — perhaps one eye only open, with its great glaring golden iris. You see two whitish triangular lines above the eyes meeting at the bill — with a sharp reddish brown triangle between and a narrow curved line of black under each eye. At this distance and in this light you see only a black spot where the eye is and the question is whether the eyes are open or not. It sits on the lee side of the tree this raw and windy day. You would say that this was a bird without a neck. Its short bill which rests upon its breast scarcely projects at all — but in a state of rest the whole upper part of the

eastern screech owl

bird from the wings is rounded off smoothly excepting the horns, which stand up conspicuously or are slanted back. After watching it ten minutes from the boat I landed two rods above and stealing quietly up behind the hemlock, though from the windward, I looked carefully around it and to my surprise saw the owl still sitting there—so I sprang round quickly with my arm outstretched and caught it in my hand. It was so surprised that it offered no resistance at first—only glared at me in mute astonishment with eyes as big as saucers. But ere long it began to snap its bill—making quite a noise—and as I rolled it up in my handkerchief and put it in my pocket, it bit my finger slightly.

I soon took it out of my pocket and tying the handkerchief left it on the bottom of the boat.

So I carried it home and made a small cage in which to keep it for a night. When I took it up it clung so tightly to my hand as to sink its claws into my fingers and bring blood.

When alarmed or provoked most it snaps its bill and hisses. It puffs up its feathers to nearly twice its usual size, stretches out its neck, and with wide open eyes stares this way and that, moving its head slowly and undulatingly from side to side — with a curious motion. While I write this evening I see that there is ground for much superstition in it. It looks out on me from a dusky corner of its box with its great solemn eyes — so perfectly still itself. I was surprised to find that I could imitate its note as I remember it -- by a *guttural* whinnering.

OCTOBER 29, 1855

Carried my owl to the hill again. Had to shake him out of the box — for he did not go out of his own accord. (He had learned to alight on his perch — and it was surprising how lightly and noise-lessly he would hop upon it.) There he stood on the grass at first bewildered — with his horns pricked up and looking toward me. In this strong light the pupils of his eyes suddenly contracted and the iris expanded till they were two great brazen orbs with a center spot merely. His attitude expressed astonishment more than anything. I was obliged to toss him up a little that he might feel his wings and then he flapped away low and heavily to a hickory on the hillside twenty rods off. (I had let him out in the plain just east of the hill.)

OCTOBER 29, 1857

I see evidently what Storer calls the little brown snake, *Coluber ordinatus* — driven out of the grass of the meadow by the flood. Its head is raised to the surface for air — and it appears sluggish and enfeebled by the water. Putting out my paddle it immediately coils about it and is raised into the boat. It has a distinct pale pink abdomen — slightly bluish forward. Above it is pale brown — with a still lighter brown stripe running down the middle of the back, on each side of which is a line of dark brown spots about ⅛ of an inch apart, as the two lines are also ⅛ of an inch apart. This snake is about one foot long. I hold it in my hand and it is quite inoffensive.

OCTOBER 31, 1850

As once he was riding past Jennie Dugan's was invited by her boys to look into their mother's spring house. He looked in. It *was* a delectable place to keep butter and milk cool and sweet in dog days — but there was a leopard frog swimming in the milk, and another sitting on the edge of the pan.

OCTOBER 31, 1853

I slowly discover that this is a gossamer day. I first see the fine lines stretching from one weed or grass stem or rush to another sometimes seven or eight feet distant — horizontally and only four or five inches above the water. When I look further I find that they are everywhere and on everything — sometimes forming conspicuous fine white gossamer webs on the heads of grasses, or suggesting an Indian bat. They are so abundant that they seem to have been suddenly produced in the atmosphere by some chemistry — spun out of air — I know not for what purpose. I remember that in Kirby and Spence it is not allowed that the spider can walk on the water to carry his web across from rush to rush — but here I see myriads of spiders on the water making some kind of progress and one at least with a line attached to him. True they do not appear to walk well — but they stand up high and dry on the tips of their toes and are blown along quite fast. They are of various sizes and colors though mostly a greenish brown or else black. Some very small. These gossamer lines are not visible unless between you and the sun. We pass some black willows now of course quite leafless — and when they are between us and the sun they are so completely covered with these fine cobwebs or lines, mainly parallel to one another, that they make one solid woof, a misty woof, against the sun. They are not drawn taut but curved downward in the middle like the rigging of a vessel—the ropes which stretch from mast to mast. As if the fleets of a thousand Lilliputian nations were collected one behind another under bare poles. But when we have floated a few feet further—and thrown the willow out of the sun's range—not a thread can be seen on it.

NOVEMBER 1, 1853
Now that the sun is fairly risen I see and hear a flock of larks in Wheeler's meadow on left of the Corner road, singing exactly as in spring and twittering also, but rather faintly—or suppressedly—as if their throats had grown up or their courage were less.

NOVEMBER 3, 1858
The jay is the bird of October. I have seen it repeatedly flitting amid the bright leaves of a different color from them all—and equally bright and taking its flight from grove to grove. It too, with its bright color, stands for some ripeness in the bird harvest. And its scream, it is as if it blowed on the edge of an October leaf.

NOVEMBER 4, 1858
Why, it takes a sharpshooter to bring down even such trivial game as snipes and woodcocks—he must take very particular aim, and know what he is aiming at. He would stand a very small chance if he fired at random into the sky, being told that snipes were flying there, and so it is with him that shoots at beauty. Not till the sky falls will he catch larks unless he is a trained sportsman. He will not bag any if he does not already know its seasons and haunts and the color of its wing—if he has not dreamed of it so that he can *antici-pate* it—then indeed he flushes it at every step, shoots double and on the wing—with both barrels—even in cornfields. The sportsman trains himself—dresses, and watches unweariedly—and loads

blue jay

and primes for his particular game. He prays for it—and so he gets it. After due and long preparation, schooling his eye and hand, dreaming awake and asleep, with gun and paddle and boat, he goes out after meadow-hens—which most of his townsmen never saw nor *dreamed* of—paddles for miles against a head wind, and *therefore* he gets them. He had them halfway into his bag when he started and has only to shove them down. The fisherman too dreams of fish—till he can almost catch them in his sink-spout. The hen scratches and finds her food right under where she stands but such is not the way with the hawk.

The true sportsman can shoot you almost any of his game from his windows. It comes and perches at last on the barrel of his gun—but the rest of the world never see it, with the feathers on. He will keep himself supplied by firing up his chimney. The geese fly exactly under his zenith and honk when they get there. Twenty musquashes have the refusal of each one of his traps—before it is empty.

NOVEMBER 6, 1857

Turning over the wet chestnut leaves in the hollows—looking for nuts—I found a red-backed salamander between three and four inches long, bluish gray beneath (*Salamandra erythronota*). It jerked itself about in a lively manner trying to hide itself under the leaves, and would quickly slip out of my fingers. Its motions appeared to partake of those of a snake and a frog—between a squirm and a hop. It was not particularly swift—yet from the character of the motion and its glossiness, it was *glancing*. A dozen rods further I turned [up] another, very similar—but without a red back, but rather slightly clay-colored. I did not observe any transverse bands—else it might be the *S. fasciata* [marbled salamander].

NOVEMBER 7, 1855

A gray squirrel (as day before yesterday) runs down a limb of an oak and hides behind the trunk—and I lose him. A red one runs along the trees to scold at me boldly or carelessly—with a chuckling, bird-like note—and that other peculiar sound at intervals between a purr and a grunt. He is more familiar than the gray—and more noisy. What sound does the gray make?

NOVEMBER 7, 1857

Stedman Buttrick speaking of R.W.E.'s cow that was killed by lightning and not found for some days, said that they heard a "bellering" of the cows some days before they found her—and they found the ground much trampled about the dead cow. That that was the way with cows in such cases—if such an accident happened to one of their number, they would have spells of gathering around her and "bellering."

NOVEMBER 7, 1858
The fields are bleak—and they are, as it were, vacated. The very earth is like a house shut up for the winter, and I go knocking about it in vain. But just then I heard a chickadee on a hemlock—and was inexpressibly cheered to find that an old acquaintance was yet stirring about the premises and was then assured to be there all winter. All that is evergreen in me revived at once.

NOVEMBER 7, 1858
I hear one faint cricket's chirp this afternoon.

Going up the lane beyond Farmer's—I was surprised to see fly up from the white stony road two snow buntings, which alighted again close by—one on a large rock, the other on the stony ground. … Their soft rippling notes as they went off reminded me [of] the northeast snowstorms to which ere long they are to be an accompaniment.

NOVEMBER 8, 1850
The stillness of the woods and fields is remarkable at this season of the year.… As you walk however the partridge still bursts away. The silent dry almost leafless, certainly fruitless, woods. You wonder what cheer that bird can find in them. The partridge bursts away from the foot of a shrub oak like its own dry fruit, immortal bird! This sound still startles us.

NOVEMBER 8, 1850
I saw a squash bug go slowly behind a clapboard to avoid winter. As some of these melon seeds come up in the garden again in the spring—so some of these squash bugs come forth. The flies are for a long time in a somnambulic state. They have too little energy or

vis vitae to clean their wings or heads which are covered with dust. They buzz and bump their heads against the windows two or three times a day or lie on their backs and that is all—two or three short spurts.

NOVEMBER 8, 1853

Birds generally wear the russet dress of nature at this season. They have their fall no less than the plants—the bright tints depart from their foliage or feathers—and they flit past like withered leaves in rustling flocks. The sparrow is a withered leaf.

NOVEMBER 8, 1858

I wandered over bare fields where the cattle lately turned out roamed restless and unsatisfied with the feed—I dived into a rustling young oak wood where not a green leaf was to be seen. I climbed to the geological axis of elevation—and clambered over curly-pated rocks whose strata are on their edges, amid the rising woods—and again I thought, They are all gone surely, and left me alone—not even a man Friday remains. What nutriment can I extract from these bare twigs? Starvation stares me in the face. "*Nay nay!*" said a nuthatch, making its way head-downward about a bare hickory close by. "The nearer the bone the sweeter the meat. Only the superfluous has been swept away. Now we behold the naked truth. If at any time the weather is too bleak and cold for you—keep the sunny side of the trunk, for there is a wholesome and inspiring warmth such as the summer never afforded. There are the winter mornings—with the sun on the oak-wood tops. While buds sleep, thoughts wake." ("Hear! hear!" screamed the jay from a neighboring copse, where I had heard a tittering for some time.) "Winter has a concentrated and nutty kernel if you know where to look for it." And then the speaker shifted to another tree—further off—and reiterated his assertions, and his mate at a distance confirmed them—and I heard a suppressed chuckle from a red squirrel that heard the last remark but had kept silent and invisible all the while. Is that you? "Yes sir," said he. Then running down a slanting bough he called out—rather impudently—"Look here! just get a snug-fitting fur coat and a pair of fur gloves like mine and you may laugh at a northeast storm," and then he wound up with a slang phrase in his own lingo—accompanied by a flourish of his tail— just as a newsboy twirls his fingers with his thumb on his nose and inquires, "Does your mother know you are out?"

NOVEMBER 9, 1851
I hear a cricket singing the requiem of the year under the Clam-shell Bank. Soon all will be frozen up and I shall hear no cricket chirp in the land.

NOVEMBER 9, 1855
Saw in the pool at the Hemlocks what I at first thought was a brighter leaf moved by the zephyr on the surface of the smooth dark water—but it was a splendid male summer duck which allowed us to approach within seven or eight rods, sailing up close to the shore, and then rose and flew up the curving stream.... What an ornament to a river to see that glowing gem floating in contact with its waters—as if the hummingbird should recline its ruby throat and its breast on the water—like dipping a glowing coal in water. It so affected me....

That duck was all jewels combined showing different lusters as it turned on the unrippled element in various lights. Now brilliant glossy green—now dusky violet—now a rich bronze—now the reflections that sleep in the ruby's grain.

NOVEMBER 9, 1857
Mr. Farmer tells me that one Sunday he went to his barn having nothing to do and thought he would watch the swallows— republican swallows. The old bird was feeding her young—and he

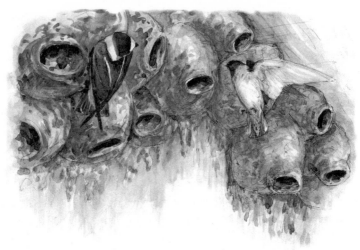

cliff swallow

sat within fifteen feet overlooking them.[26] There were five young and he was curious to know how each received its share, and as often as the bird came with a fly the one at the door (or opening) took it and then they all hitched round one notch—so that a new one was presented at the door who received the next fly—and this was the invariable order. The same one never receiving two flies in succession. At last the old bird brought a very small fly—and the young one that swallowed it did not desert his ground but waited to receive the next, but when the bird came with another, of the usual size, she commenced a loud and long scolding at the little one, till it resigned its place, and the next in succession received the fly.

NOVEMBER 10, 1858
Hearing in the oak and nearby a sound as if someone had broken a twig—I looked up and saw a jay pecking at an acorn. There were several jays busily gathering acorns on a scarlet oak. I could hear them break them off. They then flew to a suitable limb and placing the acorn under one foot, hammered away at it busily—looking

round from time to time to see if any foe was approaching—and soon reached the meat, and nibbled at it, holding up their heads to swallow, while they held it very firmly with their claws. (Their hammering made a sound like the woodpeckers.) Nevertheless it sometimes dropped to the ground before they had done with it.

NOVEMBER 11, 1850
Some circumstantial evidence is very strong, as when you find a trout in the milk.

NOVEMBER 12, 1851
Methinks the hawk that soars so loftily and circles so steadily and apparently without effort has earned this power by faithfully creeping on the ground as a reptile in a former state of existence. You must creep before you can run—you must run before you can fly.

NOVEMBER 12, 1853
I hear one cricket singing still, faintly deep in the bank, now after one whitening of snow. [*Penciled addition:* Was it not a frog?] His theme is life immortal. The last cricket, full of cheer and faith, piping to himself, as the last man might.

NOVEMBER 13, 1851
A cold and dark afternoon, the sun being behind clouds in the west. The landscape is barren of objects—the trees being leafless—and so little light in the sky for variety. Such a day as will almost oblige a man to eat his own heart. A day in which you must hold on to life by your teeth. You can hardly ruck up any skin on nature's bones. The sap is down—she won't peel....

Truly a hard day, hard times these. Not a mosquito left. Not an insect to hum. Crickets gone into winter quarters. Friends long since gone there—and you left to walk on frozen ground, with your hands in your pockets....

Now is there nothing—not even the cold beauty of ice crystals, and snowy architecture. Nothing but the echo of your steps over the frozen ground, no voice of birds or frogs. You are as dry as a farrow cow. . . .

The walker now fares like cows in the pastures, where is no grass but hay—he gets nothing but an appetite. If we must return to hay, pray let us have that which has been stored in barns—which has not lost its sweetness. The poet needs to have more stomachs than the cow—for for him no fodder is stored in barns. He relies upon his instinct which teaches him to paw away the snow to come at the withered grass.

Methinks man came very near being made a dormant creature. Just as some of these animals. The ground squirrel for instance which lays up vast stores—is yet found to be half dormant, if you dig him out. Now for the oily nuts of thought which you have stored up.

NOVEMBER 13, 1855

Going over Swamp Bridge Brook at 3 P.M. I saw in the pond by the roadside a few rods before me, the sun shining bright, a mink swimming—the whole length of his back out. It was a rich brown fur glowing internally as the sun fell on it like some ladies' boas—not black as it sometimes appears especially on ice. It landed within three rods, showing its long, somewhat cat-like neck and I observed was carrying something by its mouth—dragging it over land. At first I thought it a fish—maybe an eel—and when it had got half a dozen feet, I ran forward and it dropped its prey and went into the wall. It was a muskrat, the head and part of the fore legs torn off and gone—but the rest still fresh and quite heavy including hind legs and tail. It had probably killed this muskrat in the brook—eaten so much and was dragging the remainder to its retreat in the wall.

NOVEMBER 13, 1858

I see some feathers of a blue jay scattered along a wood path—and at length came to the body of the bird. What a neat and delicately ornamented creature—finer than any work of art in a lady's boudoir, with its soft light *purplish blue* crest and its dark blue or purplish secondaries (the narrow half) finely barred with dusky.

It is the more glorious to live in Concord because the jay is so splendidly painted.

NOVEMBER 14, 1858

Take a citizen out into an oak sproutland when there is a sugaring of dry snow—and a cold cutting northwest wind rustles the leaves. ... Every resounding step on the frozen earth is a vain knocking at the door of what was lately genial Nature—his bountiful mother, now turned stepmother. He is left outside to starve. The rustling leaves sound like the fierce breathing of wolves—an endless pack half famished from the north—impelled by hunger to seize him. Of birds only the chickadees seem really at home. Where they are is a hearth and a bright fire constantly burning....

Now while the frosty air begins to nip your fingers and your nose the frozen ground rapidly wears away the soles of your shoes—as sandpaper might. The old she wolf is nibbling at your very extremities. The frozen ground eating away the soles of your shoes is only typical of the vulture that gnaws your heart this month....

Snow and cold drive the doves to your door and so your thoughts make new alliances.

NOVEMBER 15, 1850

You can tell when a cat has seen a dog by the size of her tail.

NOVEMBER 15, 1857

Going by my owl-nest oak, I saw that it had broken off at the hole and the top fallen—but seeing in the cavity some leaves I climbed up to see what kind of nest it was, and what traces of the owls were left. Having shinnied up with some difficulty to the top of this great stump some fifteen or eighteen feet high I took out the leaves slowly—watching to see what spoils had been left with them. Some were pretty green—and all had evidently been placed there this fall. When I had taken all out with my left hand, holding on to the top of the stump with my right, I looked round into the cleft—and there I saw sitting nearly erect at the bottom in one corner a little *Mus leucopus* [white-footed mouse], panting with fear, and with its large black eyes upon me. I held my face thus within seven or eight inches of it as long as I cared to hold on there—and it showed no sign of retreating. When I put in my hand it merely withdrew downward into a snug little nest of hypnum [moss] and apparently the dirty white wool-like pappus of some plant as big as a batting ball. Wishing to see its tail I stirred it up again when it suddenly rushed up the side of the cleft, out over my shoulder and right arm and leaped off, falling down through a thin hemlock spray some fifteen or eighteen feet to the ground—on the hillside, where I lost sight of it, but heard it strike. It will thus make its nest at least sixteen feet up a tree, improving some cleft or hollow, or probably bird's nest, for this purpose. These nests *I suppose* are made when the trees are losing their leaves, as those of the squirrels are.

NOVEMBER 18, 1851

Now at sundown I hear the hooting of an owl,—*hōo hoó hóo—hoorer—hóo*. It sounds like the hooting of an idiot or a maniac broke loose. This is faintly answered in a different strain apparently from a greater distance—almost as if it were the echo, i.e. so far as the *succession* is concerned.

This is my music each evening. I heard it last evening. The men who help me call it the "hooting owl" and think it is the cat owl [great horned owl]. It is a sound admirably suited [to] the swamp and to the twilight woods—suggesting a vast undeveloped nature which men have not recognized nor satisfied. I rejoice that there are owls. They represent the stark twilight unsatisfied thoughts I have.

NOVEMBER 18, 1857
Crows will often come flying much out of their way to caw at me.

NOVEMBER 19, 1853
Got 1½ bushels of cranberries, mixed with chaff.

Brought home one of those little shells found in the shore wreck which look like a bugle-horn.

NOVEMBER 19, 1855
Minott had two cats on his knee—one given away without his knowledge a fortnight before had just found its way back. He says he would not kill a cat for twenty dollars—no, not for fifty. Finally he told his women folks that he would not do it for five hundred or any sum. He thought they loved life as well as we.

NOVEMBER 21, 1850
I saw Fair Haven Pond with its island and meadow between the island and the shore—and a strip of perfectly still and smooth water in the lee of the island—and two hawks, fish hawks perhaps, sailing over it. I did not see how it could be improved. Yet I do not see what these things can be. I begin to see such an object when I cease to *understand* it—and see that I did not realize or appreciate it before—but I get no further than this. How adapted these forms and colors to my eye—a meadow and an island; what are these things? Yet the hawks and the ducks keep so aloof! and nature is so reserved! I am made to love the pond and the meadow as the wind is made to ripple the water.

NOVEMBER 22, 1858

About the first of November a wild pig from the West—said to weigh three hundred pounds—jumped out of a car at the depot and made for the woods. The owner had to give up the chase at once not to lose his passage, while some railroad employees pursued the pig even into the woods 1½ miles off—but then the pig turned and pursued them so resolutely that they ran for their lives and one climbed a tree. The next day being Sunday they turned out in force with a gun and a large mastiff, but still the pig had the best of it—fairly frightened the men by his fierce charges—and the dog was so wearied and injured by the pig that the men were obliged to carry him in their arms. The pig stood it better than the dog. Ran between the gun man's legs, threw him over and hurt his shoulder, though pierced in many places by a pitchfork. At the last accounts, he had been driven or baited into a barn in Lincoln—but no one durst enter—and they were preparing to shoot him. Such pork might be called venison. [*Penciled addition:* Caught him at last in a snare—and so conveyed him to Brighton.]

NOVEMBER 25, 1850

I saw a muskrat come out of a hole in the ice. He is a man wilder than Ray or Melvin. While I am looking at him I am thinking what he is thinking of me. He is a different sort of man, that is all. He would dive when I went nearer then reappear again, and had kept open a place five or six feet square so that it had not frozen, by swimming about in it. Then he would sit on the edge of the ice and busy himself about something. I could not see whether it was a clam or not. What a cold-blooded fellow—thoughts at a low temperature, sitting perfectly still so long on ice covered with water, mumbling a cold wet clam in its shell. What safe low moderate thoughts it must have. It does not get onto stilts. The generations of muskrats do not fail. They are not preserved by the legislature of Massachusetts.

NOVEMBER 25, 1857

Returning I see a fox run across the road in the twilight from Potter's into Richardson's woods. He is on a canter—but I see the whitish tip of his tail. I feel a certain respect for him—because though so large he still maintains himself free and wild in our midst, and is so original so far as any resemblance to our race is concerned. Perhaps I like him better than his tame cousin the dog for it.

NOVEMBER 26, 1858

The Pouts' Nest was frozen just enough to bear—with two or three breathing-places left.... Looking more attentively, I detected also a great many minnows about one inch long either floating dead there or frozen into the ice—at least fifty of them. They were shaped like bream, but had the transverse bars of perch.... They have about seven transverse dusky bars like a perch! Yet from their form and single dorsal fin I think they are breams—are they not a new species?

NOVEMBER 26, 1859

I see here today one *brown creeper* busily inspecting the pitch pines. It begins at the base and creeps rapidly upward by starts—adhering close to the bark and shifting a little from side to side often till near the top—then suddenly darts off downward to the base of another tree where it repeats the same course. This has no black cockade, like the nuthatch.

NOVEMBER 27, 1858

I get seventeen more of these little breams of yesterday....

   They appear to be the young of the *Pomotis obesus* [banded sunfish] described by Charles Girard to the Natural History Society in April '54—obtained by [Spencer Fullerton] Baird in fresh water about Hingham and Charles River in Holliston.

I got more perfect specimens than the bream drawn above. They are exceedingly pretty seen floating dead on their sides in a bowl of water with all their fins spread out.

From their size and form and position—they cannot fail to remind you of coins in the basin....

How much more remote the newly discovered species seems to dwell than the old and familiar ones—though both inhabit the same pond. Where the *Pomotis obesus* swims must be a new country—unexplored by science. The seashore may be settled, but aborigines dwell unseen only thus far inland. This country is so new that species of fishes and birds and quadrupeds inhabit it which science has not yet detected. The water which such a fish swims in must still have a primitive forest decaying in it.

NOVEMBER 28, 1857
Spoke to Skinner about that wildcat which he says he heard a month ago in Ebby Hubbard's woods. He was going down to Walden in the evening to see if geese had not settled in it (with a companion) when they heard this sound which his companion at first thought made by a coon—but S. said no, it was a wildcat. He says he has heard them often in the Adirondack region where he has purchased furs. He told him he would hear it again soon and he did—somewhat like the domestic cat, a low sort of growling and then a sudden quick repeated caterwaul or *yow yow yow* or *yang yang yang*. He says they utter this from time to time when on the track of some prey.

NOVEMBER 28, 1858
And all the years that I have known Walden these striped breams have skulked in it without my knowledge! How many new thoughts then may I have?

NOVEMBER 29, 1853

Some years ago a boy in Lincoln was bitten by a raccoon and died of hydrophobia.

NOVEMBER 30, 1858

I cannot but see still in my mind's eye those little striped breams [banded sunfish] poised in Walden's glaucous water. They balance all the rest of the world in my estimation at present, for this is the bream that I have just found, and for the time I neglect all its brethren and am ready to kill the fatted calf on its account. For more than two centuries have men fished here and have not distinguished this permanent settler of the township. It is not like a new bird, a transient visitor that may not be seen again for years—but there it dwells and has dwelt permanently. Who can tell how long? When my eyes first rested on Walden the striped bream was poised in it, though I did not see it, and when Tahatawan²⁷ paddled his canoe there. How wild it makes the pond and the township to find a new fish in it. America renews her youth here. But in my account of this bream I cannot go a hair's breadth beyond the mere statement that it exists—the miracle of its existence, my contemporary and neighbor, yet so different from me! I can only poise my thoughts there by its side—and try to think *like* a bream for a moment. I can only think of precious jewels—of sunrise—poetry—beauty—and the mystery of life. I only see the bream in its orbit as I see a star, but I care not to measure its distance or weight. The bream *appreciated* floats in the pond as the center of the system—another image of God. Its life no man can explain more than he can his own. I want you to perceive the mystery of the bream. I have a contemporary in Walden. It has fins where I have legs and arms. I have a friend among the fishes—at least a new acquaintance. Its character will interest me, I trust, not its clothes and anatomy. I do not want it to eat. Acquaintance with it is to make my life more rich and eventful. It is as if a poet or an anchorite had moved into the town—whom

I can see from time to time and think of yet oftener. Perhaps there are a thousand of these striped bream which no one had thought of in that pond—not their mere impressions in stone, but in the full tide of the bream life.

DECEMBER 1, 1856
I see men like frogs, their peeping I partially understand.

DECEMBER 1, 1857
Walking in Ebby Hubbard's woods I hear a red squirrel barking at me amid the pine and oak tops—and now I see him coursing from tree to tree. How securely he travels there fifty feet from the ground—leaping from the slender bending twig of one tree across an interval of three or four feet and catching at the nearest twig of the next, which so bends under him that it is at first hard to get up it. His traveling a succession of leaps in the air at that height without wings! And yet he gets along about as rapidly as on the ground.

DECEMBER 3, 1853
Some of the clamshells, freshly opened by the muskrats and left lying on their half sunken cabins where they are kept wet by the waves show very handsome rainbow tints.... It is a somewhat saddening reflection that the beautiful colors of this shell for want of light do not exist—until its inhabitant has fallen a prey to the spoiler, and it is thus left a wreck upon the strand. Its beauty then beams forth and it remains a splendid cenotaph to its departed tenant—symbolical of those radiant realms of light to which the latter has risen, suggesting what glory he has gone to.

DECEMBER 4, 1856
Sophia says that just before I came home *Min* caught a mouse and was playing with it in the yard. It had got away from her once or twice and she had caught it again—and now it was steal-

ing off again as she lay complacently watching it with her paws tucked under her, when her friend Riordan's stout but solitary cock stepped up inquisitively, looked down at it with one eye turning his head, then picked it up by the tail and gave it two or three whacks on the ground and giving it a dexterous toss into the air, caught it in its open mouth and it went head foremost and alive down his capacious throat in the twinkling of an eye—never again to be seen in this world. *Min* all the while with paws comfortably tucked under her, looking on unconcerned. What matters it one mouse more or less to her?

DECEMBER 5, 1858

How singularly ornamented is that salamander [eastern newt].

Its brightest side—its yellow belly—sprinkled with fine dark spots is turned downward. Its back is indeed ornamented with two rows of bright vermilion spots—but these can only be detected on the very closest inspection, and poor eyes fail to discover them even then, as I have found.

eastern newt

DECEMBER 6, 1857

Flannery tells me he is cutting in Holbrook's Swamp in the Great Meadows—a lonely place. He sees a fox repeatedly there—and also a white weasel[28] once with a mouse in its mouth in the swamp.

DECEMBER 8, 1853

At midday (3 P.M.) saw an owl fly from toward the river and alight on Mrs. Richardson's front yard fence. Got quite near it and followed it to a rock on the heap of dirt at Collier's cellar. A rather dark brown owl above—with a decided owl head (and eyes) though not very broad—with longitudinal tawny streaks (or the reverse) none transverse, growing lighter down the breast and at length clear rusty yellowish or cream color beneath and about feathered feet. Wings large and long with a distinct large black spot beneath—bill and claws I think black. Saw no ears. Kept turning its head and great black eyes this way and that when it heard me—but appeared not to see me. Saw my shadow better, for I approached on the sunny side. I am inclined to think it the short-eared owl though I could see no ears—though it reminded me of what I had read of the hawk owl. It was a foot or more long and spread about three feet. Flew somewhat flappingly and yet hawk-like. Went within two or three rods of it.

DECEMBER 10, 1840

I discover a strange track in the snow, and learn that some migrating [northern river] otter has made across from the river to the wood, by my yard and the smith's shop, in the silence of the night. I cannot but smile at my own wealth, when I am thus reminded that every chink and cranny of nature is full to overflowing. That each instant is crowded full of great events. Such an incident as this startles me with the assurance that the primeval nature is still working and makes tracks in the snow.

It is my own fault that he must thus skulk across my premises by night. Now I yearn toward him—and heaven to me consists in a complete communion with the otter nature.

Standing there though in this *bare* November landscape, I am reminded of the incredible phenomenon—of small birds in winter. That ere long amid the cold powdery snow, as it were a fruit of the season will come twittering a flock of delicate crimson-tinged birds (lesser redpolls) [common redpolls] to sport and feed on the seeds and buds now just ripe for them on the sunny side of a wood—shaking down the powdery snow there in their cheerful social feeding, as if it were high midsummer to them. These crimson aerial creatures have wings which would bear them quickly to the regions of summer, but here is all the summer they want. What a rich contrast—tropical colors, crimson breasts, on cold white snow. Such etherealness, such delicacy in their forms—such ripeness in their colors in this stern and barren season. It is as surprising as if you were to find a brilliant crimson flower—which flourished amid snows. They greet the chopper and the hunter in their furs. Their maker gave them the last touch and launched them forth the day of the Great Snow.

He made this bitter imprisoning cold before which man quails—but he made at the same time these warm and glowing creatures to twitter and be at home in it.

I wished to ally myself to the powers that rule the universe. I wished to dive into some deep stream of thoughtful and devoted life—which meandered through retired and fertile meadows far from towns. I wished to do again, or for once, things quite congenial to my highest thought and most sacred nature. To lurk in crystalline thought like the trout under verdurous banks—where stray mankind should only see my bubble come to the surface.

DECEMBER 12, 1856

Wonderful—wonderful is our life and that of our companions! That there should be such a thing as a brute animal—not human! And that it should attain to a sort of society with our race!! Think of cats, for instance; they are neither Chinese nor Tartars; they do not go to school, nor read the Testament. Yet how near they come to doing so—how much they are like us who do so! What sort of philosophers are we who know absolutely nothing of the origin and destiny of cats? At length, without having solved any of these problems, we fatten and kill and eat some of our cousins!!

DECEMBER 14, 1855

Suddenly I heard the screwing mew and then the whir of a partridge on or beneath an old decaying apple tree which the pines had surrounded. There were several such—and another partridge burst away from one. They shoot off swift and steady showing their dark-edged tails—almost like a cannonball.

DECEMBER 14, 1855

Further over toward the river I see the tracks of a deer mouse on a rock which suddenly come to an end where apparently it had ascended a small pine by a twig which hung over it. Sometimes the mark of its tail was very distinct. Afterwards I saw in the pasture westward where many had run about in the night. In one place many had crossed the cowpath in which I was walking—in one trail—or the same one had come and gone many times.

DECEMBER 14, 1858

I see at Derby's shop a barred owl, *Strix nebulosa* [*S. varia*], taken in the woods west of the factory on the 11th—found (with its wing broke) by a woodchopper. It measures about 3½ feet in alar extent by eighteen to twenty inches long—or *nearly* the same as the cat owl, but is small and without horns. It is very mild and quiet—

bears handling perfectly well—and only snaps its bill with a loud sound at the sight of a cat or dog. It is apparently a female since it is large and has white spots on the wings. The claws are quite dark, rather than dark horn-color. It hopped into the basin of the scales—and I was surprised to find that it weighed only one pound and one ounce. It may be thin fleshed on account of its broken wing—but how light-bodied these flyers are! It has no yellow iris like the cat owl, and has thin bristles about its yellow bill, which the other has not. It has a very smooth and handsome round head—a brownish gray.

Solemnity is what they express—fit representatives of the night.

DECEMBER 15, 1856

The hooting of the owl! That is a sound which my red predecessors heard here more than a thousand years ago. It rings far and wide occupying the spaces rightfully—grand, primeval, aboriginal sound. There is no whisper in it of the Buckleys, the Flints, the Hosmers who recently squatted here—nor of the first parish nor of Concord Fight—nor of the last town meeting.

DECEMBER 16, 1840

The motion of quadrupeds is the most constrained and unnatural; it is angular and abrupt, except in those of the cat tribe, where undulation begins. That of birds and fishes is more graceful and independent—they move on a more inward pivot. The former move by their weight or opposition to nature, the latter by their buoyancy or yielding to nature. Awkwardness is a resisting motion, gracefulness is a yielding motion. The line which would express the motion of the former would be a tangent to the sphere, of the latter a radius. But the subtlest and most ideal and spiritual motion is undulation. It is produced by the most subtle element falling on the next subtlest—and the latter impelling itself. Rippling is a more graceful flight. If you consider it from the hilltop you will detect in it the wings of birds endlessly repeated. The two waving lines which express their flight seem copied from the ripple. There is something analogous to this in our most inward experiences. In enthusiasm we undulate to the divine spiritus—as the lake to the wind.

DECEMBER 16, 1850

The snow everywhere was covered with snow fleas like pepper. When you hold a mass in your hand, they skip and are gone before you know it. They are so small that they go through and through the new snow. Sometimes when collected they look like some powder which the hunter has spilled in the path.

DECEMBER 17, 1856

It is pretty poor picking out of doors today—there's but little comfort to be found. You go stumping over bare frozen ground, sometimes clothed with curly yellowish withered grass like the back of half-starved cattle late in the fall—now beating this ear now that to keep them warm.

DECEMBER 19, 1854

Off Clamshell I heard and saw a large flock of *Fringilla linaria* [common redpoll] over the meadow.... Suddenly they turn aside in their flight and dash across the river to a large white birch fifteen rods off, which plainly they had distinguished so far.

I afterward saw many more in the Potter swamp up the river. They were commonly brown or dusky above streaked with yellowish white or ash and more or less white or ash beneath. Most had a crimson crown or frontlet and a few a crimson neck and breast, very handsome. Some with a bright-crimson crown had clean white breasts. I suspect that these were young males. They keep up an incessant twittering, varied from time to time with some mewing notes, and occasionally for some unknown reason they will all suddenly dash away with that universal loud note (twitter) like a bag of nuts. They are busily clustered in the tops of the birches picking the seeds out of the catkins—and sustain themselves in all kinds of attitudes, sometimes head downwards while about this. Common as they are now—and were winter before last—I saw none last winter.

DECEMBER 19, 1856

As I stand here, I hear the hooting of my old acquaintance the [great horned] owl in Wheeler's Wood. Do I not oftenest hear it just before sundown? This sound heard near at hand is more simply animal and guttural—without resonance or reverberation—but heard here from out the depths of the wood, it sounds peculiarly hollow and drum-like, as if it struck on a tense skin drawn around, the tympanum of the wood, through which all we denizens of nature hear. Thus it comes to us an accredited and universal or melodious sound—is more than the voice of the owl, the voice of the wood as well. The owl only touches the stops, or rather wakes the reverberations. For all nature is a musical instrument on which her creatures play—celebrating their joy or grief unconsciously often. It sounds now *hoo | hoo hoo* (very fast) *| hoorer | hoo*.

DECEMBER 20, 1851

Saw a large hawk circling over a pine wood below me—and screaming apparently that he might discover his prey by their flight. Traveling ever by wider circles. What a symbol of the thoughts, now soaring now descending—taking larger and larger circles or smaller and smaller! ... As if that hawk were made to be the symbol of my thought, how bravely he came round over those parts of the wood which he had not surveyed—taking in a new segment. Annexing new territories.

DECEMBER 24, 1850

Saw a [northern] shrike pecking to pieces a small bird, apparently a snow bird. At length he took him up in his bill, almost half as big as himself and flew slowly off with his prey dangling from his beak. I find that I had not associated such actions with my idea of birds. It was not birdlike.

DECEMBER 24, 1851

Saw also some pine grosbeaks—magnificent winter birds—among the weeds and on the apple trees. Like large catbirds at a distance—but nearer at hand some of them when they flit by are seen to have gorgeous heads, breasts, and rumps (?) with red or crimson reflections—more beautiful than a steady bright red would be. The note I heard a rather faint and innocent whistle of two bars.

DECEMBER 25, 1857

Heywood says that some who have gone into Ebby Hubbard's barn to find him have seen the [brown] rats run over his shoulders—they are so familiar with him.

DECEMBER 26, 1851

I observed this afternoon that when Edmund Hosmer came home from sledding wood and unyoked his oxen, they made a business of stretching and scratching themselves with their horns and rubbing against the posts—and licking themselves in those parts which the yoke had prevented their reaching all day. The human way in which they behaved affected me even pathetically. They were too serious to be glad that their day's work was done—they had not spirits enough left for that. They behaved as a tired woodchopper might. This was to me a new phase in the life of the laboring ox. It is painful to think how they may sometimes be overworked. I saw that even the ox could be weary with toil.

DECEMBER 26, 1859

I see a brute with a gun in his hand standing motionless over a musquash house which he has destroyed. I find that he has visited every

ox

one in the neighborhood of Fair Haven Pond above and below—
and broken them all down laying open the interior to the water—
and then stood watchful close by for the poor creature to show its
head there for a breath of air. There lies the red carcass of one whose
pelt he has taken on the spot, flat on the bloody ice, and for his
afternoon's cruelty that fellow will be rewarded with a ninepence
perchance. When I consider what are the opportunities of the civilized man for getting ninepences and getting light—this seems to
me more savage than savages are. Depend on it that whoever thus
treats the musquash's house—his refuge when the water is frozen
thick—he and his family will not come to a good end.

DECEMBER 27, 1857
Do not despair of life. You have no doubt force enough to overcome your obstacles. Think of the fox prowling through wood and

field in a winter night for something to satisfy his hunger. Notwith-standing cold and the hounds and traps his race survives. I do not believe any of them ever committed suicide.

DECEMBER 28, 1852

Unless the humming of a gnat is as the music of the spheres—and the music of the spheres is as the humming of a gnat—they are naught to me.

DECEMBER 29, 1851

Yesterday nobody dreamed of today—nobody dreams of tomor-row. Hence the weather is ever the news. What a fine and measure-less joy the gods grant us thus—letting us know nothing about the day that is to dawn. This day yesterday was as incredible as any other miracle. Now all creatures feel it, even the cattle chewing stalks in the barnyards. And perchance it has penetrated even to the lurking places of the crickets under the rocks.

DECEMBER 30, 1851

When the fish hawk in the spring revisits the banks of the Musketa-quid, he will circle in vain to find his accustomed perch. And the hen hawk will mourn for the pines lofty enough to protect her brood. A plant which it has taken two centuries to perfect—rising by slow stages into the heavens—has this afternoon ceased to exist. Its sapling top had expanded to this January thaw as the forerunner of summers to come. Why does not the village bell sound a knell. I hear no knell tolled—I see no procession of mourners in the streets—or the woodland aisles. The squirrel has leaped to another tree. The hawk has circled further off—and has now settled upon a new eyrie but the woodman is preparing [to] lay his axe at the root of that also.

DECEMBER 31, 1851

I observed this afternoon the old Irish woman at the shanty in the woods—sitting out on the hillside bare-headed in the rain and on the icy though thawing ground, knitting. She comes out like the ground squirrel at the least intimation of warmer weather.

DECEMBER 31, 1853

There are a few sounds still which never fail to affect me—the notes of the wood thrush[29] and the sound of a vibrating chord. These affect me as many sounds once did often and as almost all should. The strains of the Aeolian harp and of the wood thrush are the truest and loftiest preachers that I know now left on this earth. I know of no missionaries to us heathen comparable to them. They as it were lift us up in spite of ourselves. They intoxicate, they charm us.

JANUARY 1, 1854

The white-in-tails or grass finches linger pretty late flitting in flocks—before—but they come so near winter only as the white in their tails indicates. They let it come near enough to whiten their tails perchance and they are off. The snow buntings and the tree sparrows are the true spirits of the snowstorm—they are the animated beings that ride upon it and have their life in it.

The snow is the great betrayer. It not only shows the tracks of mice, otters, etc., etc. which else we should rarely if ever see—but the tree sparrows are more plainly seen against its white ground, and they in turn are attracted by the dark weeds which it reveals. It also drives the crows and other birds out of the woods to the villages for food. We might expect to find in the snow the footprint of a life superior to our own of which no zoology takes cognizance. Is there no trace of a nobler life than that of an otter or an escaped convict to be looked for in the snow. Shall we suppose that that is the only life that has been abroad in the night. . . . Did this great snow come to reveal the track merely of some timorous hare—or of the Great Hare, whose track no hunter has seen?

JANUARY 6, 1859

Miles had hanging in his barn a little owl (*Strix Acadica*) [saw-whet owl] which he caught alive with his hands about a week ago. He had forced it to eat—but it died. It was a funny little brown bird—spotted with white, 7½ inches long to the end of the tail, or eight to the end of the claws, by nineteen in alar extent—not so long by considerable as a robin though much stouter. This one had three (not two) *white* bars on its tail—but no noticeable white at the tip. Its curving feet were feathered quite to the extremity of the toes—looking like whitish (or tawny white) mice, or as when one pulls stockings over his boots. As usual the white spots on the upper sides of the wings are smaller and a more distinct white—while those beneath are much larger but a subdued satiny white. Even a bird's wing has an upper and under side—and the last admits only of more subdued and tender colors.

JANUARY 7, 1857

There, in that Well Meadow field perhaps—I feel in my element again, as when a fish is put back into the water. I wash off all my chagrins—all things go smoothly as the axle of the universe.

JANUARY 8, 1854

Stood within a rod of a downy woodpecker on an apple tree. How curious and exciting the blood-red spot on its hindhead! I ask why it is there—but no answer is rendered by these snow-clad fields. It is so close to the bark I do not see its feet. It looks behind as if it had on a black cassock open behind and showing a white undergarment between the shoulders and down the back. It is briskly and incessantly tapping all round the dead limbs—but rarely twice in a place—as if to sound the tree and so see if it has any worm in it or perchance to start them. How much he deals with the bark of trees — all his life long tapping and inspecting it. He it is that scatters those fragments of bark and lichens about on the snow at the base of trees. What a lichenist he must be — or rather perhaps it is fungi makes his favorite study for he deals most with dead limbs. How briskly he glides up or drops himself down a limb — creeping round and round and hopping from limb to limb — and now flitting with a rippling sound of his wings to another tree.

JANUARY 8, 1857
I picked up on the bare ice of the river opposite the oak in Shattuck's land — on a small space blown bare of snow — a fuzzy caterpillar, black at the two ends and red-brown in the middle rolled into a ball or close ring — like a woodchuck.[30] I pressed it hard between my fingers and found it frozen. I put it into my hat — and when I took it out in the evening, it soon began to stir and at length crawled about, but a portion of it was not quite flexible. It took some time for it to thaw. This is the fifth cold day, and it must have been frozen so long. It was more than an inch long.

JANUARY 10, 1854
I cannot thaw out to life the snow fleas which yesterday covered the snow like pepper, in a frozen state.

JANUARY 10, 1854
I mistook the creaking of a tree in the woods the other day for the scream of a hawk. How numerous the resemblances of the animate to the inanimate!

JANUARY 12, 1855
The cold is merely superficial — it is summer still at the core, far far within. It is in the cawing of the crow — the crowing of the cock — the warmth of the sun on our backs. I hear faintly the cawing of

a crow far far away—echoing from some unseen woodside—as if deadened by the springlike vapor which the sun is drawing from the ground. It mingles with the slight murmur of the village—the sound of children at play—as one stream empties gently into another, and the wild and tame are one. What a delicious sound. It is not merely crow calling to crow—for it speaks to me too. I am part of one great creature with him—if he has voice I have ears. I can hear when he calls—and have engaged not to shoot nor stone him, if he will caw to me each spring.

JANUARY 14, 1855
Skated to Baker Farm with a rapidity which astonished myself— before the wind, feeling the rise and fall (the water having settled in the suddenly cold night) which I had not time to see.... A man feels like a new creature, a deer perhaps, moving at this rate. He takes new possession of nature in the name of his own majesty.

JANUARY 14, 1857
These numerous cocoons attached to the twigs overhanging the stream in the still and biting winter day suggest a certain fertility in the river borders—impart a kind of life to them—and so are company to me.

There is so much more life than is suspected in the most solitary and dreariest scene. They are as much as the lisping of a chickadee.

JANUARY 15, 1852
It is good to see Minott's hens pecking and scratching the ground. What never failing health they suggest! Even the sick hen is so naturally sick—like a green leaf turning to brown. No wonder men love to have hens about them and hear their creaking note. They are even laying eggs from time to time still—the undespairing race!

JANUARY 15, 1857

The tracks of the mice near the head of Well Meadow were particularly interesting.... How snug they are somewhere under the snow now, not to be thought of—if it were not for these pretty tracks—and for a week or fortnight even of pretty still weather the tracks will remain to tell of the nocturnal adventures of a tiny mouse who was not beneath the notice of the Lord. So it was so many thousands of years before Gutenberg invented printing with *his* types—and so it will be so many thousands of years after his types are forgotten—perchance. The deer mouse will be printing on the snow of Well Meadow to be read by a new race of men.

JANUARY 21, 1852

One day when I went out to my woodpile or rather my pile of stumps—I observed two large ants on the chips—the one red, the other much larger and black, fiercely contending with one another, and rolling over on the chips.[31] It was evidently a struggle for life and death which had grown out of a serious feud. Having once got hold, they never let go of each other—but struggled and wrestled and rolled on the chips, each retaining his hold with mastiff-like pertinacity. Looking further I found to my astonishment that the chips were covered with such combatants—that it was not a *duellum* but a *bellum,* a war between two races of ants, the red always pitted against the black, and frequently two red ones to one black. It was the only war I had ever witnessed—the only battlefield I ever trod while the battle was raging. Internecine war. The red republicans and the black despots or imperialists.

JANUARY 21, 1853

Minott says his mother told him she had seen a [white-tailed] deer come down the hill behind her house—where J. Moore's now is— and cross the road and the meadow in front. Thinks it may have been eighty years ago.

As I flounder along the Corner road, against the root fence a very large flock of snow buntings alight with a wheeling flight—amid the weeds rising above the snow in Potter's heater piece [a triangular plot of land], a hundred or two of them. They run restlessly amid the weeds—so that I can hardly get sight of them through my glass—then suddenly all arise and fly only two or three rods alighting within three rods of me. (They keep up a constant twittering.) It was as if they were any instant ready for a longer flight, but their leader had not so ordered it. Suddenly away they sweep again and I see them alight in a distant field where the weeds rise above the snow—but in a few minutes they have left that also and gone further north. Beside their *rippling* note, they have a vibratory twitter—and from the loiterers you hear quite a tender peep as they fly after the vanishing flock.

What independent creatures! They go seeking their food from north to south. If New Hampshire and Maine are covered deeply with snow, they scale down to Massachusetts for their breakfasts. Not liking the grain in this field, away they dash to another distant one, attracted by the weeds rising above the snow. Who can guess in what field, by what river or mountain they breakfasted this morning. They did not seem to regard me so near—but as they went off their wave actually broke over me as a rock. They have the pleasure of society at their feasts—a hundred dining at once, busily talking while eating, remembering what occurred at Grinnell Land.

As they flew past me they presented a pretty appearance— somewhat like broad bars of white alternating with bars of black.

JANUARY 22, 1852

Having occasion to get up and light a lamp in the middle of a sultry night I observed a stream of large black ants passing up and down one of the bare corner posts—those descending having their large white larvae in their mouths, the others making haste up for another load. I supposed that they had found the heat so great just under the roof as to compel them to remove their offspring to a cooler place by night. They had evidently taken and communicated the resolution to improve the coolness of the night to remove their young to a cooler and safer locality. One stream running up another down with great industry.

JANUARY 22, 1859

The energy and excitement of the musquash hunter even, not despairing of life but keeping the same rank and savage hold on it that his predecessors have for so many generations, while so many are sick and despairing—even this is inspiriting to me. Even these deeds of death are interesting as evidences of life—for life will still prevail in spite of all accidents. I have a certain faith that even musquash are immortal and not born to be killed by Melvin's double B (?) shot.

JANUARY 23, 1858

At Ditch Pond I hear what I suppose to be a fox barking—an exceedingly husky hoarse and ragged note, prolonged perhaps by the echo, like a feeble puppy—or even a child endeavoring to scream, but choked with fear, yet it is on a high key. It sounds so through the wood—while I am in the hollow—that I cannot tell from which side it comes. I hear it bark forty or fifty times at least. It is a peculiar sound—quite unlike any other woodland sound that I know....

The dog is to the fox as the white man to the red. The former has attained to more clearness in his bark—it is more ringing and musical, more developed, he explodes the vowels of his alphabet better—and beside he has made his place so good in the world that he can run without skulking in the open field. What a smothered—ragged—feeble and unmusical sound is the bark of the fox! It seems as if he scarcely dared raise his voice lest it should catch the ear of his tame cousin and inveterate foe.

JANUARY 23, 1860

He [Minott] has stood on the steep hill southwest side of Moore's Swamp and seen two foxes chase a white rabbit [snowshoe hare] all about in it. The rabbit would dodge them in the thicket—and now and then utter a loud cry of distress. The foxes would hunt one into the meadow and then dash into the thicket again. This was where the wood had been cut and he could see plainly.

He says that the white rabbit loves to sit concealed under the overarching cinnamon ferns (which he calls "buck horns") on the sunny side of a swamp—or under a tuft of brakes which are partly fallen over.

That a hound in its headlong course will frequently run over the fox—which quickly turns and gets off three or four rods before the former can stop himself.

JANUARY 24, 1858

At Nut Meadow Drive the small-sized water bugs are as abundant and active as in summer. I see forty or fifty circling together in the smooth and sunny bays all along the brook. This is something new to me. What must they think of this winter? It is like a child waked up and set to playing at midnight. Methinks they are more ready to dive to the bottom when disturbed than usual. At night, of course, they dive to the bottom and bury themselves—and if in the morning they perceive no curtain of ice drawn over their sky, and the pleasant weather continues, they gladly rise again and resume their gyrations in some sunny bay among the alders and the stubble. I think that I never noticed them more numerous—but the fact is I never looked for them so particularly. But I fear for their nervous systems, lest this be too much activity—too much excitement.

The sun falling thus warmly for so long on the open surface of the brook tempts them upward gradually—till there is a little group gyrating there as in summer. What a funny way they have of going to bed. They do not take a light and retire upstairs—they go below.

Suddenly it is heels up and heads down and they go down to their muddy bed—and let the unresting stream flow over them in their dreams. They go to bed in another element. What a deep slumber must be theirs and what dreams down in the mud there!

JANUARY 24, 1859

I also see [on the ice of the meadow] a great many of those little brown grasshoppers and one perfectly green one, some of them frozen in but generally on the surface—showing no signs of life— yet when I brought them home to experiment on I found them all alive and kicking in my pocket.

JANUARY 25, 1841

Today I feel the migratory instinct strong in me, and all my members and humors anticipate the breaking up of winter. If I yielded to this impulse it would surely guide me to summer haunts. This ill-defined restlessness and fluttering on the perch do, no doubt, prophesy the final migration of souls out of nature to a serener summer, in long harrows and waving lines in the spring weather, over what fair uplands and fertile pastures winging their way at evening—and seeking a resting place with loud cackling and uproar!

JANUARY 25, 1853

The pickerel of Walden. When I see them lying on the ice or in the well which the fisherman cuts in the ice, I am always surprised by their rare beauty—as if they were a fabulous fish. They are so foreign to the streets or even the woods, handsome as flowers and gems, golden and emerald—a transcendent and dazzling beauty which separates by a wide interval from the cadaverous cod and haddock at least a day old which we see. They are as foreign as Arabia to our Concord life as if the two ends of the earth had come together. These are not green like the pines—or gray like the stones—or blue like the sky; but they have if possible to my eye

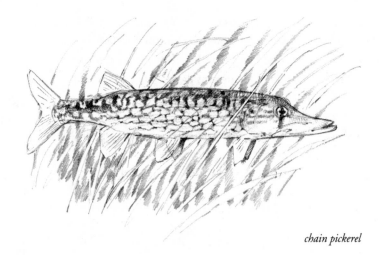

chain pickerel

yet rarer colors like precious stones. It is surprising that these fishes are caught here. They are something tropical. They are true topazes inasmuch as you can only conjecture what place they came from. The pearls of Walden. Some animalized Walden water. That in this deep and capacious spring far beneath the rattling teams and chaises and tinkling sleighs that travel the Walden road this great gold and emerald fish swims!! I never chanced to see this kind of fish in any market. With a few convulsive quirks they give up their diluted ghosts.

JANUARY 25, 1856
If you would be convinced how differently armed the squirrel is naturally for dealing with pitch pine cones—just try to get one off with your teeth. He who extracts the seeds from a single closed cone with the aid of a knife will be constrained to confess that the squirrel earns his dinner. It is a rugged customer and will make your fingers bleed. But the squirrel has the key to this conical and spiny chest of many apartments. He sits on a post vibrating his tail and twirls it as a plaything.

But so is a man commonly a locked up chest to us—to open whom, unless we have the key of sympathy, will make our hearts bleed.

JANUARY 27, 1855
Started a [snowshoe] hare among shrub oaks—it had been squatting in a slight hollow, rather concealed than sheltered. They always look poverty stricken.

JANUARY 27, 1859
I see some of those little cells perhaps of a wasp or bee—made of clay or clayey mud. It suggests that these insects were the first potters. They look somewhat like small stone jugs.

JANUARY 30, 1841
I tread in the tracks of the fox which has gone before me by some hours, or which perhaps I have started, with such a tiptoe of expectation, as if I were on the trail of the Spirit itself which resides in these woods, and expected soon to catch it in its lair.…

Here is the distinct trail of a fox stretching quarter of a mile across the pond. Now I am curious to know what has determined its graceful curvatures, its greater or less spaces and distinctness, and how surely they were coincident with the fluctuations of some mind. Why they now lead me two steps to the right, and then three to the left. If these things are not to be called up and accounted for in the Lamb's Book of Life, I shall set them down for careless accountants. Here was one expression of the divine mind this morning.

The pond was his journal, and last night's snow made a *tabula rasa* for him. I know which way a mind wended this morning, what horizon it faced, by the setting of these tracks—whether it moved slowly or rapidly; by the greater or less intervals and distinctness—for the swiftest step leaves yet a lasting trace.…

Fair Haven Pond is *scored* with the trails of foxes, and you may see where they have gamboled and gone through a hundred evolutions, which testify to a singular listlessness, and leisure in nature.

Suddenly looking down the river I saw a fox some sixty rods off, making across the hills on my left. As the snow lay five inches deep, he made but slow progress, but it was no impediment to me. So yielding to the instinct of the chase, I tossed my head aloft, and bounded away, snuffing the air like a fox hound; and spurning the world and the humane society at each bound. It seemed the woods rang with the hunter's horn, and Diana and all the satyrs joined in the chase, and cheered me on. Olympian and Elean youths were waving palms on the hills.

JANUARY 30, 1854
The winter, cold and bound out as it is, is thrown to us like a bone to a famishing dog, and we are expected to get the marrow out of it. While the milkmen in the outskirts are milking so many scores of cows before sunrise these winter mornings—it is our task to milk the winter itself. It is true it is like a cow that is dry and our fingers are numb—and there is none to wake us up.

JANUARY 30, 1855
Said the raccoon made a track very much like a young child's foot. He [Minott] had often seen it in the mud of a ditch.

JANUARY 30, 1860
There are certain sounds invariably heard in warm and thawing days in winter—such as the crowing of cocks, the cawing of crows, and sometimes the gobbling of turkeys. The crow flying high touches the tympanum of the sky for us and reveals the tone of it. What does it avail to look at a thermometer or barometer—compared with listening to his note! He informs me that nature is in the tenderest mood possible—and I hear the very flutterings of her heart.

JANUARY 30, 1860

The snow flea seems to be a creature whose summer or prime of life is a thaw in the winter. It seems not merely to enjoy this interval like other animals — but then chiefly to exist. It is the creature of the thaw. *Moist snow* is its element. That thaw which merely excites the cock to sound his clarion as it were *calls to life* the snow flea.

JANUARY 31, 1854

Our thoughts hide unexpressed like the buds under their downy or resinous scales. They would hardly keep a partridge from starving. If you would know what are my winter thoughts look for them in the partridge's crop.

FEBRUARY 1, 1856

Our kitten Min, two thirds grown, was playing with Sophia's broom this morning, as she was sweeping the parlor, when she suddenly went into a fit, dashed round the room — and the door being opened, rushed up two flights of stairs and leaped from the attic window to the ice and snow by the side of the door-step — a descent of a little more than twenty feet — passed round the house and was lost. But she made her appearance again about noon at the window quite well and sound in every joint — even playful and frisky.

FEBRUARY 2, 1860

We walked, as usual, on the fresh track of a fox peculiarly pointed — and sometimes the mark of two toenails in front separate from the track of the foot in very thin snow. ⌒   ⌒ And as we were kindling a fire on the pond by the side of the island we saw the fox himself at the inlet of the river. He was busily examining along the sides of the pond by the buttonbushes and willows — smelling in the snow. Not appearing to regard us much he slowly explored along the shore of the pond then halfway round it. At Pleasant Meadow evidently looking for mice (or moles?) in the grass of the bank—smelling in the shallow snow there amid the stubble, often retracing his steps and pausing at particular spots. He was eagerly searching for food—intent on finding some mouse to help fill his empty stomach. He had a blackish tail and blackish feet. Looked lean and stood high. The tail peculiarly large for any creature to carry round. He stepped daintily about—softly—and is more to the manor born than a dog. It was a very arctic scene this *cold* day—and I suppose he would hardly have ventured out in a warm one.

FEBRUARY 3, 1855
Some little boys ten years old are as handsome skaters as I know. They sweep along with a graceful floating motion leaning now to this side then to that (like a marsh hawk beating the bush).

FEBRUARY 5, 1854
Shall we not have sympathy with the muskrat which gnaws its third leg off—not as pitying its sufferings but through our kindred mortality appreciating its majestic pains and its heroic virtue. Are we not made its brothers by fate. For whom are psalms sung and mass said—if not for such worthies as these. When I hear the church organ peal—or feel the trembling tones of the bass viol—I see in imagination the musquash gnawing off his leg. I offer a note that his affliction may be sanctified to each and all of us.

FEBRUARY 5, 1859
When we have experienced many disappointments, such as the loss of friends, the notes of birds cease to affect us as they did.[32]

FEBRUARY 6, 1854
I see the track of a [New England cottontail] rabbit about the Cliff—there are hollows in the snow on the tops of the rock, shaped like a milk pan and as large where he has squatted or whirled round.

FEBRUARY 7, 1855

The coldest night for a long long time was last. Sheets froze stiff about the faces. Cat mewed to have the door opened—but was at first disinclined to go out. When she came in at nine she smelt of meadow hay. We all took her up and smelled of her it was so fragrant. Had cuddled in some barn. People dreaded to go to bed. The ground cracked in the night as if a powder mill had blown up and the timbers of the house also. My pail of water was frozen in the morning so that I could not break it.

FEBRUARY 7, 1857

Hayden the elder tells me that the quails have come to his yard every day for almost a month—and are just as tame as chickens. They come about his woodshed—he supposes to pick up the worms that have dropped out of the wood—and when it storms hard gather together in the corner of the shed. He walks within say three or four feet of them without disturbing them. They come out of the woods by the graveyard, and sometimes they go down toward the river.

FEBRUARY 8, 1839

When the poetic frenzy seizes us, we run and scratch with our pen, delighting, like the cock, in the dust we make, but do not detect where the jewel lies, which perhaps we have in the meantime cast to a distance, or quite covered up again.

FEBRUARY 8, 1857

In the society of many men, or in the midst of what is called success I find my life of no account—and my spirits rapidly fall. I would rather be the barrenest pasture lying fallow than cursed with the compliments of kings—than be the sulfurous and accursed desert where Babylon once stood. But when I have only a rustling oak leaf or the faint metallic cheep of a tree sparrow for variety in my winter walk—my life becomes continent and sweet as the kernel of a nut....

You think that I am impoverishing myself by withdrawing from men—but in my solitude I have woven for myself a silken web or *chrysalis* and nymph-like shall ere long burst forth a more perfect creature, fitted for a higher society.

FEBRUARY 9, 1851

The last half of January was warm and thawy. The swift streams were open and the muskrats were seen swimming and diving and bringing up clams, leaving their shells on the ice. We had now forgotten summer and autumn, but had already begun to anticipate spring.

FEBRUARY 11, 1854

Snow fleas lie in black patches like some of those dark rough lichens on rocks or like ink spots three or four inches in diameter—about the grass stems or willows, on the ice which froze last night. When I breathe on them I find them all alive and ready to skip. Also the water, when I break the ice, arouses them.

FEBRUARY 12, 1851

A beautiful day with but little snow or ice on the ground. Though the air is sharp, as the earth is half bare the hens have strayed to some distance from the barns. The hens standing around their lord and pluming themselves and still fretting a little strive to fetch the year about.

FEBRUARY 12, 1854

To make a perfect winter day—like this—you must have a clear sparkling air. With a sheen from the snow—sufficient cold—little or no wind and the warmth must come directly from the sun. It must not be a thawing warmth. The tension of nature must not be relaxed. The earth must be resonant if bare—and you hear the lisping tinkle of chickadees from time to time and the unrelenting steel-cold scream of a jay—unmelted—that never flows into a song. A sort of wintry trumpet—screaming cold. Hard tense frozen music—like the winter sky itself. In the blue livery of winter's band. It is like a flourish of trumpets to the winter sky. There is no hint of incubation in the jay's scream. Like the creak of a cart-wheel. There is no cushion for sounds now. They tear our ears.

FEBRUARY 12, 1858

Those small holes in the ground—musquash, mice, etc.—thickly beset with crystals of frost, remind me of the invisible vapor rising thence which may be called Earth's breath—though you might think it were the breath of a mouse. In cold weather you see not only men's beards and the hair about the muzzles of oxen whitened with their frozen breath, but countless holes in the banks—which are the nostrils of the earth, white with the frozen earth's breath.

FEBRUARY 12, 1860

In winter not only some creatures, but the very earth is partially dormant—vegetation ceases, and rivers to some extent cease to flow. Therefore when I see the water exposed in midwinter it is as if I saw a skunk or even a striped squirrel out. It is as if the woodchuck unrolled himself and snuffed the air to see if it were warm enough to be trusted.

FEBRUARY 14, 1840

A very meager natural history suffices to make me a child—only their names and genealogy make me love fishes. I would know even the number of their fin rays—and how many scales compose the lateral line. I fancy I am amphibious and swim in all the brooks and pools in the neighborhood, with the perch and bream, or doze under the pads of our river amid the winding aisles and corridors formed by their stems, with the stately pickerel.

I am the wiser in respect to all knowledges, and the better qualified for all fortunes, for knowing that there is a minnow in the brook. Methinks I have need even of his sympathy—and to be his fellow in a degree. I do like him sometimes when he balances himself for an hour over the yellow floor of his basin.

FEBRUARY 16, 1859

The hen hawk and pine are friends. The same thing which keeps the hen hawk in the woods—away from the cities—keeps me here. That bird settles with confidence on a white pine top—and not upon your weathercock. That bird will not be poultry of yours— lays no eggs for you—forever hides its nest. Though willed—or *wild,* it is not willful in its wildness. The unsympathizing man regards the wildness of some animals, their strangeness to him, as a sin. As if all their virtue consisted in their tamableness. He has always a charge in his gun ready for their extermination. What we call wildness is a civilization other than our own. The hen hawk shuns the farmer but it seeks the friendly shelter and support of the pine. It will not consent to walk in the barnyard but it loves to soar above the clouds. It has its own way and is beautiful, when we would fain subject it to our will. So any surpassing work of art is strange and wild to the mass of men—as is genius itself.

FEBRUARY 18, 1857

I am excited by this wonderful air—and go listening for the note of the bluebird or other comer. The very grain of the air seems to have undergone a change—and is ready to split into the form of the bluebird's warble. Methinks if it were visible or I could cast up some fine dust which would betray it, it would take a corresponding shape. The bluebird does not come till the air consents—and his wedge will enter easily. The air over these fields is a foundry full of molds for casting bluebirds' warbles. Any sound uttered now would take that form—not of the harsh vibrating rending scream of the jay, but a softer flowing curling warble, like a purling stream, or the lobes of flowing sand and clay. Here is the soft air and the moist expectant apple trees—but not yet the bluebird. They do not quite attain to song.

FEBRUARY 18, 1860

I think that the most important requisite in describing an animal, is to be sure and give its character and spirit—for in that you have, without error, the sum and effect of all its parts, known and unknown. You must tell what it is to man. Surely the most important part of an animal is its *anima,* its vital spirit—on which is based its character, and all the peculiarities by which it most concerns us. Yet most scientific books which treat of animals leave this out altogether, and what they describe are as it were phenomena of dead matter. What is most interesting in a dog e.g. is his attachment to his master—his intelligence, courage, and the like—and not his anatomical structure or even many habits which affect us less.

FEBRUARY 19, 1852

The strains from my muse are as rare nowadays, or of late years, as the notes of birds in the winter—the faintest occasional tinkling sound, and mostly of the woodpecker kind, or the harsh jay or crow. It never melts into a song. Only the *day-day-day* of an inquisitive titmouse.[33]

FEBRUARY 19, 1854

I saw a buttonbush with what at first sight looked like the open pods of the locust or of the water asclepias attached. They were the light ash-colored cocoons of the *A. promethea,* four or five—with the completely withered and faded leaves wrapped around them, and so artfully and admirably secured to the twigs by fine silk wound round the leaf-stalk and the twig—which last add nothing to its strength, being deciduous, but aid its deception. They are taken at a little distance for a few curled and withered leaves left on. . . .

Each and all such disguises and other resources remind us that not some poor worm's instinct merely, as we call it, but the mind of the universe rather which we share has been intended upon each particular object.

FEBRUARY 20, 1857

What is the relation between a bird and the ear that appreciates its melody? To whom perchance it is more charming and significant than to any else? Certainly they are intimately related—and the one was made for the other. It is a natural fact. If I were to discover that a certain kind of stone by the pond shore was affected—say partially disintegrated by a particular natural sound as of a bird or insect—I see that one could not be completely described without describing the other. I am that rock by the pond side.

FEBRUARY 20, 1860

J. Farmer tells me that his grandfather once when moving some rocks in the winter found a striped squirrel frozen stiff. He put him in his pocket and when he got home laid him on the hearth—and after a while he was surprised to see him running about the room as lively as ever he was.

FEBRUARY 21, 1855

When the leaves on the forest floor are dried and begin to rustle under such a sun and wind as these—the news is told to how many myriads of grubs that underlie them! When I perceive this dryness under my feet I feel as if I had got a new sense, or rather I realize what was incredible to me before—that there is a new life in Nature beginning to awake, that her halls are being swept and prepared for a new occupant. It is whispered through all the aisles of the forest that another spring is approaching. The wood mouse listens at the mouth of his burrow—and the chickadee passes the news along.

FEBRUARY 23, 1857

What mean these turtles, these coins of the muddy mint issued in early spring! The bright spots on their backs are vain unless I behold them. The spots *seem* brighter than ever when first beheld in the spring, as does the bark of the willow.

I have seen signs of the spring. I have seen a frog swiftly sinking in a pool—or where he dimpled the surface as he leapt in. I have seen the brilliant spotted tortoises stirring at the bottom of ditches. I have seen the clear sap trickling from the red maple.

FEBRUARY 24, 1857

I am surprised to hear the strain of a song sparrow from the riverside. And as I cross from the causeway to the hill—thinking of the bluebird—I that instant hear one's note from deep in the softened air. It is already 40°, and by noon is between 50° and 60°. As the day advances I hear more bluebirds—and see their azure flakes settling on the fence posts. Their short rich crispy warble curls through the air. Its grain now lies parallel to the curve of the bluebird's warble—like boards of the same lot. It *seems* to be one of those early springs of which we have heard, but have never experienced. Perhaps they are fabulous.

FEBRUARY 28, 1856

Our young Maltese cat Min, which has been absent five cold nights, the ground covered deep with crusted snow—her first absence—and given up for dead, has at length returned at daylight, awakening the whole house with her mewing and afraid of the strange girl we have got in the meanwhile. She is a mere wrack of skin and bones—with a sharp nose and wiry tail. She is as one returned from the dead. There is as much rejoicing as at the return of the prodigal son—and if we had a fatted calf we should kill it.

Various are the conjectures as to her adventures—whether she has had a fit, been shut up somewhere or lost, torn in pieces by a certain terrier or frozen to death. In the meanwhile she is fed with the best that the house affords—minced meats and saucers of warmed milk—and with the aid of unstinted sleep in all laps in succession is fast picking up her crumbs. She has already found her old place under the stove—and is preparing to make a stew of her brains there.

NOTES

I am indebted to Peter Alden for many of the zoological details below.

1. The call given year round by the black-capped chickadee is the long *chick-a-dee-dee-dee*. The territorial song, a sweet *phe-bee,* is given only from February to June, when the chickadee is staking out a territory.

2. The mourning cloak is the only local butterfly that overwinters as an adult, and is therefore usually the first butterfly seen on warm days in early spring.

3. Probably the southern flying squirrel. The northern flying squirrel has a more restricted range and prefers hilly terrain. When held in the hand, its belly fur appears gray at the base rather than all white.

4. Probably an amber snail (family *Succineidae*).

5. The Wilson's snipe is now a very rare and local breeder in Massachusetts. Thoreau is describing the bird's territorial sound.

6. Thoreau may have been observing the American black duck, or possibly a flock of ring-necked ducks. Ring-necked ducks may appear mainly black and assemble in Concord's rivers in early spring.

7. The Concord River had been dammed since the 1700s, preventing migratory fish from swimming upstream.

8. The vesper sparrow, common in the open landscapes of the 1800s, now breeds in fewer than a dozen places in Massachusetts.

9. "Texas" was a western section of Concord where the Thoreau family lived from 1844 to 1850.

10. Dozens of great blue herons nest in Concord today. Newly created beaver ponds with dead trees rising from the water provide nesting sites secure from the predation of raccoons.

11. A hermit thrush, based on the date. The wood thrush does not return to Concord until the second week of May.

12. Thoreau first wrote "golden-crested wren," then corrected himself in pencil.

13. Torrey and Allen write, "Though here, where the 'seringo-bird' makes its first appearance in the Journal, its identity with the savanna sparrow seems to have been unquestioned by Thoreau, it proved afterwards … to be almost as puzzling to him as the ever elusive 'night-warbler.' The probability is that the 'seringo' in this and most other cases was the savanna sparrow, but it may sometimes have been the yellow-winged, or grasshopper, sparrow, or even, as Thoreau once suspected, the grass finch, or vesper sparrow. It is quite likely that at times the bird he saw was not the bird he heard."

14. Thoreau apparently means to write *C. ordinatus*, DeKay's brown snake (now *Storeria dekayi*).

15. Thoreau presumably began writing on May 12 but didn't finish until later.

16. In *Thoreau on Birds*, Francis H. Allen identifies the red-bird as the scarlet tanager, writing, "'Old election day' in Massachusetts came on the last Wednesday in May.… The last of these May 'elections' was held in 1831, but 'old election day' was observed as a sort of holiday for years after, and it was the custom to conduct shooting-matches on that day, when birds of all kinds were shot indiscriminately." No cardinals were present in the Northeast in the 1800s except as caged birds.

17. "Let us sing of greater things": Virgil's fourth Eclogue.

18. Probably the ebony jewelwing, a species of damselfly.

19. Probably the bald-faced hornet.

20. Torrey and Allen write, "The situation of the nest and Thoreau's description of the notes indicate a long-eared owl rather than a screech owl." The owl's plumage also supports this identification.

21. Probably the Karner blue, an endangered race of the melissa blue butterfly, now gone from Massachusetts.

22. David Spooner identifies Thoreau's alder cricket as the snowy tree cricket.

23. The northern mockingbird was perhaps the rarest bird Thoreau sighted in Concord. Although a few mockingbirds nested in the state, they were known from only five towns in the mid-1800s, the closest being Groton and Marshfield. Mockingbirds are now common residents over most of Massachusetts, especially in areas with thickets of invasive multiflora roses.

24. Thoreau caught another of these snakes on September 9, 1857, writing, "It is apparently *Coluber amoenus*, and perhaps this is the same with Storer's

occipito-maculatus." *Coluber amoenus* is the eastern worm snake, and although it has a pinkish belly, Thoreau was probably observing the northern redbelly snake, *Storeria occipitomaculata*.

25. Probably great blue herons, given the description.

26. Farmer was apparently describing an incident from earlier in the year. The eggs of cliff swallows hatch before July 20, and the last young fledge by mid-August at the latest.

27. In *The Cambridge Companion to Henry David Thoreau*, Robert D. Richardson writes, "Before the white man came to Musketaquid and renamed the place and the river, it was a principal village of the Mattacusets tribe, ruled over by Nanepashemet, a 'great king or sachem' who lived in what is now Medford. The local chief of Musketaquid was Tahatawan, who, together with Nanepashemet's widow, called by the English 'Squaw Sachem,' consented to the sale of Concord to the newcomers."

28. Either an ermine or a long-tailed weasel, both of which appear white in winter.

29. Probably a hermit thrush.

30. The banded woolly bear caterpillar, whose adult form is the Isabella tiger moth.

31. David Spooner thinks it likely that these are the red wood ant (*Formica rufa*) and the black ant *F. fusca*.

32. Written two days after the death of his father.

33. A black-capped chickadee. The tufted titmouse did not reach Massachusetts from the South until around the 1960s.

Key to Place-Names

Acton D1

Annursnack Hill D2

Assabet River E3

Assabet Spring E4

Baker, James J6

Ball's Hill D7

Bare Hill J7

Beck Stow's Swamp E7

Bedford C8

Brister's Spring G6

Britton's Camp G7

Carlisle A4

Charles Miles's Swamp H3

Clematis Brook K5

Conantum J4

Concord River D6

Damon Meadows Swamp G1

Mrs. Dennis's F3

Emerson's lot H6

Fair Haven Hill H5

Fair Haven Bay (Pond) J5

Flint's Pond H8

Goose Pond H7

Gowing's Swamp F7

Great Fields F6

Great Meadows D7

Hubbard's Grove G4

Hunt House E5

Lee's Bridge K4

Lee's Cliff K4

Lee's Hill F4

Lincoln K7

Marlborough Road H1

Martial Miles's Swamp H2

Melvin's Preserve C4

Miles, Martial H3

Mill Dam F5

Minott, Abel K5

Mount Misery K6

Sassafras Island, in Flint's Pond J8

Shattuck, H. L. D5

Sleepy Hollow Cemetery F6

Smith's Hill G8

Sudbury L2

Sudbury River L4

Tarbell, D. G2

Thoreau's house, at Walden Pond H6

Thoreau's house, in Concord F5

Walden Pond H6

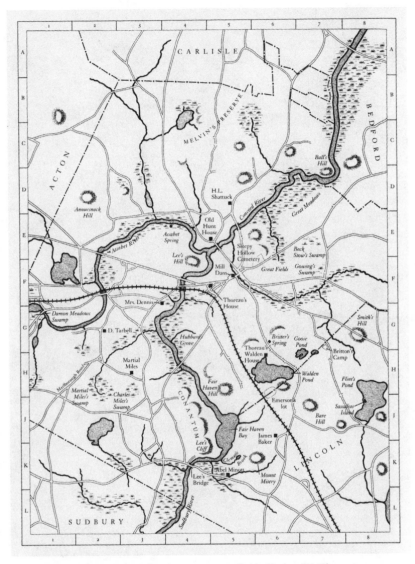

Concord, Massachusetts, based on a map compiled by Herbert W. Gleason in 1906. (From Faith in a Seed, *by Henry D. Thoreau. Copyright © 1993 by Island Press. Reproduced by permission of Island Press, Washington, DC.)*

BIBLIOGRAPHY

Alden, Peter. *Walden Biodiversity Day II*. Concord, MA: privately published, 2009. Record of 2,692 species of animals, plants, and fungi found on two days near Walden Pond by hundreds of biologists under the leadership of Edward O. Wilson. Contact peteralden@aol.com.

Alden, Peter, and Brian Cassie. *National Audubon Society Field Guide to New England*. New York: Knopf, 1998.

Anderson, Charles R. *Thoreau's World: Miniatures from His Journal*. Englewood Cliffs, NJ: Prentice-Hall, 1971.

Arnett, Ross H., Jr. *American Insects: A Handbook of the Insects of America North of Mexico*. Boca Raton, FL: CRC Press, 1993, 1997.

Bosco, Ronald A., ed. *Nature's Panorama: Thoreau on the Seasons*. Amherst: University of Massachusetts Press, 2005.

DeGraaf, Richard M., and Deborah D. Rudis. *Amphibians and Reptiles of New England: Habits and Natural History*. Amherst: University of Massachusetts Press, 1983.

DeKay, James E. *Zoology of New York or the New-York Fauna*. 5 vols. Albany: W. and A. White and J. Visscher, 1842–1844.

Eaton, Richard Jefferson. *A Flora of Concord*. Cambridge: Harvard University Museum of Comparative Zoology, 1974.

Foster, David R. *Thoreau's Country: Journey through a Transformed Landscape*. Cambridge: Harvard University Press, 1999.

Godin, Alfred J. *Wild Mammals of New England*. Baltimore: Johns Hopkins University Press, 1977.

Grant, Steve, ed. *Daily Observations: Thoreau on the Days of the Year*. Amherst: University of Massachusetts Press, 2005.

Griscom, Ludlow. *The Birds of Concord: A Study in Population Trends*. Cambridge: Harvard University Press, 1949.

Harding, Walter, ed. *In the Woods and Fields of Concord*. Salt Lake City: Gibbs Smith, 1982.

———, ed. *Thoreau as Seen by His Contemporaries*. New York: Dover, 1989.

Harding, Walter, and Michael Meyer. *The New Thoreau Handbook*. New York: New York University Press, 1980.

Hartel, Karsten E., David B. Halliwell, and Alan E. Launer. *Inland Fishes of Massachusetts*. Lincoln: Massachusetts Audubon Society, 2002.

Howarth, William. *The Book of Concord: Thoreau's Life as a Writer*. New York: Penguin, 1983.

Kaufman, Kenn, and Kimberly Kaufman. *Kaufman Field Guide to Nature of New England*. Boston: Houghton Mifflin, 2012.

Maynard, W. Barksdale. *Walden Pond: A History*. New York: Oxford University Press, 2004.

McGregor, Robert Kuhn. *A Wider View of the Universe: Henry Thoreau's Study of Nature*. Urbana: University of Illinois Press, 1997.

Miller, Perry. *Consciousness in Concord: The Text of Thoreau's Hitherto Lost Journal (1840–1841) Together with Notes and a Commentary*. Boston: Houghton Mifflin, 1958.

Mott, Wesley T., ed. *Bonds of Affection: Thoreau on Dogs and Cats*. Amherst: University of Massachusetts Press, 2005.

Myerson, Joel, ed. *The Cambridge Companion to Henry David Thoreau*. Cambridge: Cambridge University Press, 1995.

Primack, Richard B. *Walden Warming: Climate Change Comes to Thoreau's Woods*. Chicago: University of Chicago Press, 2014.

Richardson Jr., Robert D. *Henry Thoreau: A Life of the Mind*. Oakland: University of California Press, 1986.

Sorrie, Bruce A., and Paul Somers. *The Vascular Plants of Massachusetts: A County Checklist*. Westborough: Massachusetts Division of Fisheries and Wildlife, 1999.

Spooner, David. *Thoreau's Vision of Insects and the Origins of American Entomology*. Bloomington, IN: Xlibris, 2002.

Thoreau, Henry David. *The Journal of Henry D. Thoreau*. Ed. Bradford Torrey and Francis H. Allen. 1906; New York: Dover, 1962.

———. *Of Woodland Pools, Spring-Holes, and Ditches*. Berkeley, CA: Counterpoint, 2010.

———. *Thoreau on Birds*. Ed. Francis H. Allen. Boston: Beacon, 1993.

———. *The Writings of Henry D. Thoreau*. Online Journal Transcripts, vols.

18–33. Santa Barbara: University of California, Santa Barbara. Online at http://thoreau.library.ucsb.edu/writings_journals.html.

———. *The Writings of Henry David Thoreau: Journal*, vols. 1–8, various eds. Princeton: Princeton University Press, 1981–2002.

Veit, Richard R., and Wayne R. Petersen. *Birds of Massachusetts*. Lincoln: Massachusetts Audubon Society, 1993.

Walton, Richard K. *Birds of the Sudbury River Valley: An Historical Perspective*. Lincoln: Massachusetts Audubon Society, 1984.

Zwinger, Ann, and Edwin Way Teale. *A Conscious Stillness: Two Naturalists on Thoreau's Rivers*. Amherst: University of Massachusetts Press, 1984.

INDEX

Abercrombie, James (1706–1781), 71
adder, checkered (milk snake), 90
adder, water (northern water snake),
  77–78
Adirondacks, 200
Agassiz, Louis (1807–1873), xiv–xv,
  17–18, 79, 83, 96
Alcott, Bronson (1799–1888), 72
alewife, 43
Andromeda calyculata (leatherleaf),
  82–83
Andromeda Ponds, 27
Annursnack Hill, 130
ant, 104–105, 135; black, xiii, 217–
  219, 237; red, xiii, 217, 237
Arctomys (woodchuck, *Marmota
  monax*), 50
*Arvicola hirsutus=Microtus pennsyl-
  vanicus* (meadow vole), 143
Asclepias cornuti=A. syriaca (milk-
  weed), 130
Assabet River, 26, 44, 131, 154
Assabet Spring, 39
Association for the Advancement of
  Science, xv
Attacus: cecropia=Hyalophora cecropia
  (cecropia moth), 95–96; *luna*

(luna moth), 125, 131; *promethea*
  (promethea moth), 125, 231–232
Audubon, John James (1785–1851),
  20

Babylon, 227
Bachman, Rev. John (1790–1874),
  20
Baird, Spencer Fullerton (1823–
  1887), 199
Baker Farm, 56, 216
Barrett, Sam (1812–1872), 78
Bartlett, Edward, 142
bat: hoary, 142; New York (red bat),
  105–106
Battle Ground, 170
bay-wing (vesper sparrow), 47, 77
bear, black, xviii, 23
beaver, American, xviii, 23, 235
Beaver Pond, 16
Beck Stow's, 76, 85, 95
Bedford Road, 95
bee, 52, 63, 75, 82–83, 121, 135, 182,
  223; bumblebee, 66, 69, 136,
  155–156, 167, 169; honeybee, xxii,
  37–39, 66, 74, 167–170; mining
  (common sand wasp), 73–74

beetle, 59, 62–63; dogbane leaf, 157; ribbed pine borer, 3; scarab, 67, 87–88, 90, 111, 114–115; tiger, 24; water scavenger, 149; whirligig, 9, 123–124, 220

bird of paradise, 108

bittern: American, 110; green (green heron), 106, 134–135

blackbird, 4, 15, 31, 54, 85, 99, 113, 119: cow (brown-headed cowbird), 44, 107; crow (common grackle), 15, 75–76; red-winged, 10, 16, 71, 76, 78, 84–85, 94–95; rusty, 76, 175

bluebird, eastern, ix, 4, 8–9, 11, 36, 52, 131, 171, 173, 230–231, 233

bluegill, 106, 142, 153, 229

blue jay, 10, 186–187, 190, 192–193, 195, 228–231

bobcat, 179, 200

bobolink, 95, 121–122, 143–145

bobwhite, 111, 130, 227

Bosphorus, 93

Boston, Massachusetts, 72, 131, 136

bream (bluegill), 106, 142, 153, 229

bream, striped (banded sunfish), 199–202

Brewer, Thomas Mayo (1814–1880), xiv, 92

Brighton, Massachusetts, 138, 198

Brooks, Abel, 68

Brown, James P., 27, 167

Brown, John (merchant), 52

Brown, Simon, 73

Buckley family, 207

Bufo the First, 66

bug: huckleberry-bug (shield bug), 135; squash, 189; water (whirligig beetle), 123–124

bullfrog, American, 73, 102, 112, 116, 122, 134

bullhead, brown, xiv, 47, 102–103, 199

bumblebee, 66, 69, 136, 155–156, 167, 169

bunting, indigo, 103–104; snow, xxii, 3, 189, 213, 218

Burying Ground Hill, 66

butterfly, ii, 54, 67, 149, 155, 167; American copper, 130, 132; black swallowtail, 97; clouded sulphur, 127, 130; eastern comma, 41; eastern tailed blue, 68; eastern tiger swallowtail, 97, 128; Karner blue or melissa blue, 124, 236; monarch, 130; mourning cloak, 16, 30, 235; red admiral, 165; spring azure, 62–63, 67

Buttrick, Stedman (1796–1874), 188

Cabot, James Elliot (1821–1903), xiv

caddisfly, 8, 129

Cambridge, Massachusetts, xiv, 131

Cape Cod, x, 81–82

cardinal, 236

Cardinal Shore, 164

cat, house, xv, xxii, 63, 85–88, 96, 116, 158, 170, 195, 197, 200, 202–203, 206–207, 225, 227, 233–234

catbird, gray, 85, 98–99, 147, 210

caterpillar, 17, 78, 149, 151; eastern tiger swallowtail, 128; tent, 88; woolly bear, xvi, 215, 237

Catostomus bostoniensis=C. commersonii (white sucker), 88

cattle, xvi–xvii, xxiii, 16, 73, 77, 93, 110, 126, 142, 146, 150, 173, 188–190, 194, 208, 212, 224

Chalmers, Rev. Thomas (1780–1847), 29

Champollion, Jean-François (1790–1832), 94

Channing, William Ellery (1818–1901), 4, 62, 109–111, 164–165

chanticleer, 95

Charles River, 199

cherry bird (cedar waxwing), 117

chewink (eastern towhee), 109, 142, 149

chickadee, black-capped, 4, 7–8, 10, 60, 75, 97, 159, 171, 189, 195, 216, 228, 233, 235, 237

chicken, domestic, xix, 15–16, 64, 95, 112, 126, 170, 187, 203, 215–216, 224–225, 227–228

chip-bird (chipping sparrow), 69, 131, 181

chipmunk, eastern, xxiv, 7, 13–14, 26, 174, 194, 213, 229, 232

chrysalis, 3, 16, 228

chub, 46

cicindela (tiger beetle), 24

Cistuda blandingii=Emydoidea blandingii (Blanding's turtle), xiv, 146–147

clam, freshwater, 59, 79, 84, 123, 198, 202, 228

Clamshell Hill, 3, 37, 112, 129, 143, 191, 208

Clark's wood, 91

Clemmys guttata (spotted turtle), 146

Cliff or Cliffs, 27, 36, 40, 109, 226

cocoon, 95–96, 105, 124–125, 216, 231

cod, 221

Cold Heart Leaf Pond, 167

Collier's cellar, 204

Coluber amoenus=Storeria occipito-maculata (northern redbelly snake), 174, 236–237; *Coluber eximius=Lampropeltis triangulum* (milk snake), 90; *Coluber ordinatus=Storeria dekayi* (brown snake), 184–185, 236; *Coluber punctatus=Diadophis punctatus* (ring-necked snake), 76–77

Common, 65

Conantum, 43, 69, 142, 159

Concord Fight, 207

Concord River, xvi–xvii, xix, 43, 181, 235

Condylura macroura=C. cristata (star-nosed mole), 100

Coombs, 163

Corner Road, 8, 186, 218

cougar, xviii, 23

cowbird, brown-headed, 44, 107

creeper, black and white (black and white warbler), 92–93; brown, 199

cricket: alder (snowy tree cricket), 136, 236; field, xviii, 56, 65, 69, 97, 108, 113, 115, 135, 143, 146, 148–149, 178–179, 189, 191, 193, 212; mole, xvii, 143, 145; snowy tree, 136, 152, 236

crossbill, red, 44–45

crow, American, xxiii, 4, 15, 32, 40, 99, 133, 165, 171, 197, 213, 215–216, 224, 231 cuckoo, St. Domingo (black-billed cuckoo), 78

Dakin's land, 88
damselfly, 73, 105, 114, 124, 236
deer, white-tailed, xvii–xviii, 23, 129, 216–217
Demerara, Guyana, 83
Dennis's field, 150
Depot, 64–65, 67, 114, 148, 163, 198
Derby's shop, 206
devil's needle (damselfly), 73, 105, 114, 124, 236
dipper, little (horned grebe), 166–167
Ditch Pond, 219
Dodd, Jonathan M., 52
dog, xvi, xxiii, 7, 36, 63, 80, 110, 115, 119–120, 131, 136, 140, 146, 157–158, 170, 195, 198–199, 207, 219, 224, 226, 231; bulldog, 143; hound, 53, 212, 220, 224; mastiff, 217; terrier, 173, 234
dorbug (scarab beetle), 67, 87–88, 90, 111, 115
dove, 163, 195; mourning, 51, 113, 126
dragonfly, 91
dream frog (American toad), xviii, 64, 67–68, 70–71, 180
duck, 34, 40, 42, 63, 163, 197; American black, 42, 46, 235; bufflehead, 56; common golden-eye, 51; domestic, 166; ring-necked, 235; wood, 145, 191
Dugan, Jennie, 172, 185

eagle, 27, 32, 181; white-headed (bald), 40, 59

earthworm, xvii, 9, 37, 145
earwig, 3
eel, American, xix, 181, 194
Emerson, Ralph Waldo (1803–1882), xv, 17, 83, 115, 142, 188
Emmons, Ebenezer (1799–1863), 100
Emydidae, family of pond turtles, 79
Emys guttata=Clemmys guttata (spotted turtle), 146
Emys insculpta=Glyptemys insculpta (wood turtle), 79; *picta= Chrysemys picta* (painted turtle), 79
ermine, 96, 204, 237
Esquimaux, 175
Everett's orchard, 160

Fair Haven, xvii, 18–19, 28, 40, 59, 167, 197, 211, 224
Falco fuscus=Accipiter velox (sharp-shinned hawk), 68
Farmer, Jacob (1801–1872), 77, 91, 111, 119, 189, 191, 232, 237
finch, grass (vesper sparrow), 47, 213, 236; purple, 44, 46, 171
firefly, 112, 114–115, 118, 134
fish, ix, xiv, 1–18, 43, 53, 72, 80, 83, 112, 124, 187, 207, 214, 229, 235
Flannery, Michael (1800–1900), 140, 204
flea, snow, xvi, 208, 215, 225, 228
flicker, northern, xix, 12–13, 24, 35, 109, 118
Flint family, 207
Flint's Pond (Sandy Pond, Lincoln), 51, 76, 115, 133, 165
fly, 80, 192; crane, 14, 52–53; house-

fly, 189–190; mayfly, 91; spotted (deer fly), 129
flycatcher, olive-sided, 101
Flying Childers, 150
flying squirrel, southern, ix, 20–22, 115, 235
fox, red, xiv, xvi, 53, 116, 120, 157–158, 199, 204, 211–212, 219–220, 223–226
Fringilla: hyemalis=Junco hyemalis (dark-eyed junco), 29–30, 45; *linaria=Acanthis flammea* (redpoll), 208; *savanna=Passerculus sandwichensis* (Savannah sparrow), 65; *socialis=Spizella passerina* (chipping sparrow), 64–65
frog, xvi–xvii, 28–29, 52, 57, 77, 82, 130, 188, 193–194, 202, 233; American bullfrog, 73, 102, 112, 116, 122, 134; dream (American toad), xviii, 64, 67, 70–71, 79, 180; gray tree, 79, 122, 149, 179; green, 54; northern leopard, 27–28, 69, 122, 185; pickerel, 27–28, 39, 69, 71–72, 122; shad (northern leopard), 122; spring peeper, 27, 34, 64, 67; wood, 24–25, 34, 92, 122, 161

gazelle, 157
ghost horse (northern walkingstick), 150, 167
Girard, Charles Frédéric (1822–1895), 199
glow-worm, 118, 159
gnat, 16, 18, 25, 53, 212
goldeneye, common, 51
goldfinch, American, 142

Goodwin, John (1803–1860), 145
goose, Canada, 16–17, 23, 26, 46, 188; domestic, 42
Goose Pond, 60
Gourgas lot, 165
grackle, common, 15, 75–76; rusty (rusty blackbird), 76, 175
grasshopper, 143, 149, 151, 158, 163, 221
Great Fields, 11
Great Meadows, 11, 31, 42, 45–47, 123, 204
grebe, horned, 166–167
Green Bay, 163
Greenwich almanac, 175
Grinnell Land (Ellesmere Island, Canada), 218
grosbeak, pine, 210; rose-breasted, 109
grouse, ruffed, 7, 10, 50, 60–61, 74–75, 111, 119, 149, 189, 206, 225
grub, 3, 19, 40, 121, 134, 232
gryphon, 101
gull, xix, 40, 46, 179, 181; herring, 15
Gutenberg, Johannes (c. 1398–1468), 217

haddock, xv, 221
Hadley place, 64
hare, snowshoe, 53, 214, 220, 223
harrier, northern, 57, 92, 123, 226
Harris, Thaddeus William (1795–1856), 97, 131
Hastings, Jonas (1805–1873), 167
Haverhill, Massachusetts, 180
hawk, 33, 51–52, 115, 187, 193, 209, 215; Cooper's, 91–92; fish (osprey), 45–47, 136, 179, 181,

hawk (continued)
197, 212; hen (red-tailed hawk),
26–27, 32, 59, 64, 170, 212, 230;
marsh (northern harrier), 57,
92, 123, 226; rough-legged, 32;
sharp-shinned, 68
Hayden, 47, 227
Helix albolabris=Cepaea hortensis
(white-lipped snail), 36
Hemlock Brook, 35
hen, meadow or mud (Virginia
rail), 113, 187
heron; great blue, xxii, 55–56, 181,
235, 237; green, 106, 134–135
Heywood, Abel, 142
Heywood, George (1826–1897),
160, 210
Heywood's Peak, 56, 179
Hingham, Massachusetts, 199
Hoar, Samuel (1778–1856), 134
hog, 100, 104, 111
Holbrook's Swamp, 204
Holden Wood, 83
Holliston, Massachusetts, 199
honeybee, xxii, 37–39, 66, 74,
167–170
hornet, bald-faced, 114, 120, 165–
166, 180, 236
horse, xvi, 32, 67, 114, 150, 157, 159
Hosmer, Abel (1747–1832), 174
Hosmer, Edmund (1798–1881), 210
Hosmer, J., 62
Hosmer family, 207
Hosmer's orchard, 72
Hosmer Spring, 129
housefly, 189–190
Hubbard, Cyrus (1792–1865), 112
Hubbard, Ebby, 200, 202, 210

Hubbard property, 11, 15, 43, 48, 70,
74, 80, 109–110, 123, 126, 130,
160–161, 165, 178–180
huckleberry-bug (shield bug), 135
humblebee (bumblebee), 66
hummingbird, ruby-throated, 80,
82–83, 191
hyla (spring peeper), 19, 41
*Hylodes pickeringii=Pseudacris cru-
cifer* (spring peeper), 24, 27, 34,
68, 79, 122, 179

Indians, American, 4, 15, 23, 50,
57–58, 163, 166, 185, 207
Indies, 79
indigo-bird (indigo bunting),
103–104
Irish people, 39–40, 87, 104, 140, 213
Isis, 136

jewelwing, ebony, 114
Jones, Joshua, 134
junco, dark-eyed (*Junco hyemalis*),
29–30, 45

Kalendar, 175
killdeer, 126
kingbird, eastern, 90, 99, 109
kingfisher, belted, 60, 73
kinglet, ruby-crowned, 60, 66
Kirby, William (1759–1850), xiv, 185

Lamb's Book of Life, 223
lark (eastern meadowlark), 10, 28,
45, 186
Laurel Glen, 24, 122
Ledum Swamp, 109
leech, 47, 80, 126

Lee's Cliff, 24, 30, 70, 101
Lewis, 114
Lincoln, Massachusetts, 198, 201
Lind, Jenny (1820–1887), 40
linnet, American, 171
Little River, 180
locust, xxii, 135, 145, 158; alder, 152
loon, common, xiii, 42, 56, 172
Loring's Pond, 97
Lynn, Massachusetts, 25
lynx, Canadian, 23

Mackay, 44
Maracaibo, Venezuela, 83
Marlborough road, 62, 104
marmot, 53
martin, purple, 51–52
mayfly, 91
meadowlark, eastern, 10, 28, 45, 186
Meeting House, 65–66
Melvin, George (b. 1813), xvi, 179,
    198, 219
merganser, common, 28–29, 44, 51
Merriam, Joe, 62
Middle Conantum Cliff, 69
Miles, Jimmy, 214
Mill Brook, 65, 76
millipede, 180
Min (Thoreau's cat), 202–203, 225,
    233–234
mink, American, 25, 72, 85, 194
minnow, 8, 29, 39, 129, 199, 230
Minott, George (1783–1861), 4, 197,
    216–217, 220, 224
Mississippi, 93
mockingbird, northern, 147–148,
    236
Mohawks, 166

mole, star-nosed (*Condylura ma-
    croura*), xvii, xxiii, 99–101, 225
Monroe, 76, 166
Moore, J., 217
Moore's Swamp, 220
moose, x, xviii, 23
mosquito, 104–105, 115, 128, 155, 193
moth, cecropia, 95–96; emperor
    (imperial), 105, 131; Isabella tiger,
    215; luna, 125–126, 131; pro-
    methea, 124–125, 231; sphinx, 70,
    99, 173
mouse, xv, 20, 56, 96, 101, 166,
    202–204, 213–214, 225–226, 229;
    meadow (meadow vole), 143,
    151; meadow jumping, 93–94;
    North American deer, 128–129,
    206, 217; white-footed, 196;
    wood, 233
Musketaquid or Musketicook (Con-
    cord River), 134–135, 212, 237
muskrat or musquash (common
    muskrat), ix, xvi, xvii–xviii, 15,
    25, 34, 79, 85, 102, 175–176, 188,
    194, 198, 202, 210–211, 219, 226,
    228–229
Mus leucopus (white-footed deer
    mouse, *Peromyscus leucopus*), 196
myrtle-bird (yellow-rumped war-
    bler), 74

Nanepashemet, 237
Natural History Society, 199
Nawshawtuct, 95
newt, eastern, 203
nighthawk, common, 94, 101–102,
    114, 158
North River, 6

nuthatch, white-breasted, 4–6, 190, 199

Nut Meadow, 8, 220

Nuttall, Thomas (1786–1859), xiv, 89, 94, 142

oriole, 44, 60, 72, 88, 109

osprey, xvii, 45–47, 136, 179, 181, 197, 212

otter, northern river, xviii, 204–205, 213

ovenbird, 101, 116, 122–123

owl, 195–196, 207; barred, 206–207; cat (great horned), 196–197, 206–207, 209; eastern screech, ix, 119–120, 182–184; long-eared, 119–120; saw-whet, 214; short-eared, 204

ox, 210–211, 229

Painted Cup Meadow, 105

Pallas, Peter Simon (1741–1811), 18

panther, 23

Papilio asterias=P. polyxenes (black swallowtail), 97

parrot, 45, 51

partridge (ruffed grouse), 7, 10, 50, 60–61, 74–75, 111, 119, 149, 189, 206, 225

parula, northern, 69

Pedrick, 147

peeper, spring, 19, 24, 27, 34, 41, 68, 79, 122, 179

peetweet (spotted sandpiper), 109, 111

perch, yellow, xiii, 89, 142, 199, 229

petrel, 66

pewee (eastern phoebe), 42, 70

phoebe, eastern, 42, 53, 70, 101, 151, 171

phoenix, 101

pickerel, chain, xvi, 39–40, 80, 106, 130, 142, 221–222, 229

pig, ix, xvi, xxii, 117, 137–141, 198

pigeon, wild (passenger pigeon), xxiii, 52, 88, 112, 136, 154, 157, 160, 163–164

pike, northern, 18, 40

pine borer, ribbed, 3

Pine Hill, 32

Pleasant Meadow, 225

plover, upland (upland sandpiper), 112

podura (springtail), 174

Pokelogan, 155

Pomotis obesus=Enneacanthus obesus (banded sunfish), 199–200

Ponkawtasset (Punkatasset Hill), 57, 91

Potter's, 199, 208, 218

pout (brown bullhead), xiv, 47, 102–103, 199

Pratt, Minot (1805–1878), 132, 167

Prichard, 85

Punk Oak, 48

quail (bobwhite), 111, 130, 227

rabbit, 97, 117, 127, 172–173; New England cottontail, 226; white (snowshoe hare), 220

raccoon, northern, 200–201, 224, 235

racer, North American, 69, 76

rail, Carolina (sora), 170–171; Virginia, 113

railroad, xvii, 15, 41–42, 45, 57, 73, 92–94, 99, 136, 151, 182, 198

Rallus virginianus=R. limicola (Virginia rail), 113

Rana: fontinalis (green frog, *Lithobates clamitans*), 54; *halecina= R. pipiens* (northern leopard frog), 69, 122; *palustris* (pickerel frog), 28, 39, 69, 71–72; *pipiens*, 28

Ranunculus (buttercup), 112

rat, black, 43–44

rat, brown, 43–44, 210

Ray, Heman (1783–1868), xvi, 198

redpoll, common (*Fringilla linaria= Acanthis flammea*), 205, 208–209

redpoll, yellow (palm warbler), 60

reptile, 174, 193

Rice, Israel, 36, 164

Rice, Reuben (1790–1888), 167

Richardson's woods, 199

Riordan, Patrick, 203

robin, American, 4, 7, 9, 13, 43, 45, 51, 57–58, 60, 78, 99, 113, 171, 214; golden (oriole), 60, 88

Rock, 13

Rupert's Land, Hudson Bay, 33

R.W.E. (Ralph Waldo Emerson), xv, 17, 83, 142, 188

salamander, 203 (eastern newt); marbled (*Salamandra fasciata*), 188; red-backed (*Salamandra erythronata=Plethodon cinereus*), 188

Salix: nigra var. *falcata* (black willow), 125; *sericea* (silky willow), 66

salmon, 43

sandpiper: solitary (*Totanus solitarius=Tringa solitaria*), 164; spotted, 109, 111, 127; upland, 112

Sardanapalus, 63

Saw Mill, 63, 157

Second Division Brook, 124

Sericocarpus conyzoides (probably white wood aster, *Eurybia divaricata*), 132

shad, 43

shad-fly (mayfly), 91

shark, 151

Shattuck's land, 215

sheldrake (merganser), 28–29, 44

shiner, golden, 129

shrike, northern, 209–210

skater insect (water strider), 41, 120, 158

Skinner, 179, 200

skunk, striped, xxii, 8–9, 33–34, 54, 116–117, 229

Sleepy Hollow, 11, 84

slug, xxiii

Smith, Julius, 105

snail: amber, 31, 235; white-lipped (*Helix albolabris=Cepaea hortensis*), 36

snake, xix, 85, 149, 181, 188; black (North American racer), 69, 76, DeKay's brown (*Coluber ordinatus=Storeria dekayi*), 58, 184–185, 236; eastern ribbon, 61; garter, 51, 105; milk (*Coluber eximius=Lampropeltis triangulum*), 90; northern redbelly (*Storeria occipitomaculata*), 174, 236–237; northern water,

snake (continued)
77–78; ring-necked (*Coluber punctatus=Diadophis punctatus*), 76–77; smooth green, 84, 107; striped (garter snake), 51, 105

snipe, Wilson's, 36, 164, 186, 235

snow bird (dark-eyed junco, *Junco hyemalis*), 45, 209–210

Solidago stricta=S. juncea (early goldenrod), 132

Solomon's ring, xiii

sora, 170–171

sparrow, 16, 190: American tree, 16, 213, 227; chipping (*Fringilla socialis=Spizella passerina*), 64–65, 69, 131, 181; field, 58–60, 128, 135; fox-colored (fox sparrow), 33; grasshopper, 236; rush (field sparrow), 58–60, 128, 135; Savannah (*Fringilla savanna=Passerculus sandwichensis*), 65, 236; song, 10, 16, 33, 47, 109–110, 171, 177, 233; vesper, 47, 213, 235–236; white-throated, xviii, 61

spectrum (northern walkingstick), 167

Spence, William (1783–1860), xiv, 185

sphinx, 101–102

spider, 185–186: goldenrod crab, 149; wolf, 180; yellow garden, 161–163

springtail, 174

squirrel, 116–117, 157, 196, 212, 222; eastern gray, 188; ground or striped (chipmunk), xxiv, 7, 13–14, 26, 174–175, 194, 213, 229,

232; red, xvii, 6–7, 92, 113, 117, 164–165, 190–191, 202; southern flying, ix, 20–22, 115, 235

stake driver (American bittern), 110

Sternothaerus odoratus=Sternotherus odoratus (musk turtle), 159

Storer, David Humphreys (1804–1891), xiv, 39, 58, 77, 90, 184, 236–237

Storer, Horatio (1830–1922), xiv

Stow, Beck, 76, 85, 95

Stow, Nathan, 88, 174

Strix acadica=Cryptoglaux acadica (saw-whet owl), 214

Strix nebulosa=S. varia (barred owl), 206

sucker, white (*Catostomus bostoniensis=C. commersonii*), 17, 23, 45–47, 53, 83–84, 88, 155

Sudbury, Massachusetts, 122

Sumner, Charles (1811–1874), 154

sunfish, banded (*Pomotis obesus=Enneacanthus obesus*), 199–202

swallow: bank, 76, 88; barn, 76, 127; chimney (chimney swift), 76, 132–133; Chinese (edible-nest swiftlet), 133; republican (cliff swallow), 76, 191–192, 237; white-bellied (tree swallow), 45, 76, 107–108, 110–111

swallowtail; black (*Papilio asterias=Papilio polyxenes*), 97; eastern tiger, 97, 128

Swamp Bridge Brook, 194

swift, chimney, 76, 132–133

swiftlet, edible-nest, 133

Tahatawan, 201, 237
Tall's Island, 58
tanager, scarlet, 84, 87, 103–104, 236
teal, green-winged, 154
telltale, greater (greater yellowlegs),
    93, 112
Texas, 47, 77, 235
Thoreau, Jane (1784–1864), 29
Thoreau, John (1787–1858), 137, 140
Thoreau, Maria (1794–1881), 29
Thoreau, Sophia (1819–1876), 80, 85,
    96, 109, 163, 202, 225
thrasher, brown, 60, 64, 69, 83, 116,
    148
thrip, 163
thrush: hermit, 58, 62–64, 213, 235,
    237; Wilson's (veery), 115; wood,
    xviii, 53, 57–58, 62–64, 118, 122,
    213, 235
tipulidae (crane flies), 14, 52
titmouse, 231, 237
toad: American, xviii, xxiii, 37,
    52, 61, 64–65, 67–68, 70–72,
    79–80, 122, 149–150, 180; tree
    (gray tree frog), 79, 122, 149, 179
tortoise, 122, 150
Totanus solitarius=Tringa solitaria
    (solitary sandpiper), 164
towhee, eastern, 109, 142, 149
transcendentalism, xv–xvi
Trillium Woods, 75
trout, brook, xvii, 11, 39, 193, 205
turkey, domestic, 149, 224
turkey, wild, xviii, 23
Turnpike, 75, 92
turtle, xv, xix–xx, 11, 28, 37, 83, 150;
    Blanding's (Emydoidea blan-

dingii), xiv, 146–147; eastern
    box, 81–82; mud (snapping
    turtle), 80, 122, 152–153; musk,
    159; painted (Emys picta=
    Chrysemys picta), xiv, 79, 104–
    105, 122, 153–154, 177–178; snap-
    ping, xiv, xvi–xviii, 35, 80, 122,
    151–153, 158, 176–177; spotted
    (Emys guttata=Clemmys guttata),
    xiv, 40, 62, 122, 146, 233; wood
    (Emys insculpta=Glyptemys in-
    sculpta), 131, 174
turtledove (mourning dove), 113,
    126

Vanessa antiopa (mourning cloak
    butterfly), 16, 30, 235
Vanessa atalanta (red admiral), 165
veery, 115
vireo, yellow-throated, 84
Virgil, 95, 142, 236
vole, meadow (Microtus pennsylvani-
    cus), 143
vulture, 131, 195

Walden Pond, ix, xiii, 56, 58, 89, 103,
    115, 127, 167, 200–201, 221–222
walkingstick, northern, 150, 167
warbler: black and white, 92; Black-
    burnian, 89; black-throated
    green, 92; Canada, 97–98; chest-
    nut-sided, 85; night (ovenbird),
    ix, xviii, 72, 84, 107, 154, 236;
    palm, 60; particolored (northern
    parula), 69; pine, 42, 48; yellow,
    74–75; yellow-rumped, 74
Warren's meadow, 68

wasp, 167, 223; common sand, 73–74; paper, 120–121; yellow-knotted, 172

water scorpion, 132

water strider, 41, 120, 158

Watts, Horatio, 143

waxwing, cedar, 117–118

weasel, long-tailed, 204, 237

Well Meadow, 214, 217

Wesson, 132

Wetherbee, 160

Wharf Rock, 115

Wheeler, 62, 186

Wheeler, Abiel (1807–1896), 40, 209

whippoorwill, 106–107, 154, 159

white-in-tail (grass finch), 213

White Oak, 116

White Pond, 59, 163

wildcat (bobcat), 179, 200

Willow Bay, 175

Wilson, Alexander (1766–1813), xiv, 36, 103, 115, 235

wolf, gray, xviii, 23, 115, 172, 195

wolverine, 23

Wood, Elijah, Jr. (1816–1882), 93

woodchuck, x, xiii, xviii, xxii, xxiv, 9–10, 19, 26, 33, 48–49, 69–70, 108, 110, 113, 117, 119, 122, 127, 151, 215, 229

woodcock, American, 182, 186

woodpecker, xxii, 4, 6, 19, 193, 231; downy, 214; hairy, 99; pigeon (northern flicker), xix, 24, 109, 118

Wood's Bridge, 110

woolly bear caterpillar, xvi, 215, 237

worm, 133, 145, 214–215, 227, 232; earthworm, xvii, 9, 37, 145; intestinal, xv, 96

wren, ruby-crested (ruby-crowned kinglet), 60–61, 66

Wrentham, Massachusetts, 39

Wyman, John, 99, 102

yellowbird (yellow warbler), 74–75

yellow-legs, greater, 93, 112

yellowthroat, Maryland (common yellowthroat), 75, 118